THE ISLAND OF THE ANISHNAABEG

"One Who Lives under the Water,"
detail of illustration on p. 102

THE
ISLAND
OF THE
ANISHNAABEG

•

THUNDERERS

AND

WATER MONSTERS

IN THE

TRADITIONAL

OJIBWE

LIFE-WORLD

•

THERESA S. SMITH

University of Idaho Press / Moscow, Idaho
1995

University of Idaho Press, Moscow, Idaho 83844-1107

Printed in the United States of America.

The author and publisher would like to thank the following for their permission to reproduce illustrations: The McMichael Canadian Collection, The Royal Ontario Museum, and The University of Toronto Press. The author and publisher are grateful to the following artists for their permission to reproduce their work: Shirley Cheechoo, Blake Debassige and Mel Madahbee.

Short sections of Chapters I and III appeared in altered form in *Survival and Renewal: Native American Values, Proceedings of the 1991 Native Studies Conference*, Thomas Shirer and Susan Branstner, eds. (Lake Superior State University Press: 1993, and *The American Indian Culture and Research Journal* 15, 3 (1991), respectively.

Design by Caroline Hagen

99 98 97 96 95   5 4 3 2 1

Library of Congress Cataloging-in-Publication Data

Smith, Theresa S., 1956–
    The island of Anishnaabeg : thunderers and water monsters in the traditional Ojibwe life-world / Theresa S. Smith.
      p. cm.
    Thesis (Ph. D.)—Boston University, 1990.
    Includes bibliographical references (p.   ) and index.
    ISBN 0-8390-171-1
    1. Ojibwa Indians—Religion. 2. Ojibwa mythology. 3. Manitoulin Island (Ont.)—Religious life and customs. I. Title.
E99.C6S715 1995
299'.783—dc20

            94-11075
            CIP

To my parents who began my education.
And to Marji who has helped me to continue it.

CONTENTS

ILLUSTRATIONS

ACKNOWLEDGMENTS

This book began as a dissertation and owes its genesis and present form to a number of influences in two contrasting worlds. The first world is found in the Anishnaabe First Nations of Ontario, particularly those of Manitoulin Island. My work depends entirely on the generosity of the Anishnaabe people upon whose authority I rely. I hope that I honor their experience even as I reflect my own. Special gratitude is extended to my Anishnaabe consultants and friends whose words and wisdom animate this study, especially: Raymond and Delores Armstrong, Leland and Kitty Bell, Blake Debassige and Shirley Cheechoo, James Simon Mishibinijima, William Trudeau, and, for his wonderful painting, Mel Madahbee. I also want to thank Alice and Taylor McFarlan and Lois and Reg White for helping me to make a home on the island.

The second world is an academic one: the classrooms and libraries of Boston University, the State University of New York at Buffalo, and Indiana University of Pennsylvania. In this world I wish to express my appreciation to my teachers, colleagues, and friends at Boston University who advised and supported my program of study: Emily Hanawalt, Tracy Pintchman, Daud Rahbar, and Merlin Swartz. I owe special gratitude to Dennis Tedlock, who first suggested I consider field studies with the Ojibwe people and whose insights into and guidance through Native American Indian religions and narratives was invaluable, and to Alan Olson, who introduced me to hermeneutical studies and directed my graduate career from beginning to end. In his own work as a scholar and teacher, Professor Olson has shown me the standards of excellence and responsibility against which I will always judge myself.

At Indiana University of Pennsylvania I wish to acknowledge the support of the Senate Research Committee and of my colleagues in the Department of Philosophy and Religious studies, especially Sherrill Begres, Albert Bouffard, Patricia McDowell, and Joel Mlecko. I owe a larger debt than they know to my students, especially those who have assisted in the preparation of this manuscript: Tamara Elliot, Holly Heinlen, Rebecca Richwine, and Patricia Roessner.

I am also grateful to Peggy Pace, Director of the University of Idaho Press, for her patient attention, and to Jordan Paper of York University who offered valuable suggestions on this manuscript and who has consistently extended his encouragement to a fellow traveler between two worlds.

Finally, my largest debt is owed to Margery Stone who not only lived and journeyed with this book but typed and edited the first draft during that long, gray Buffalo winter.

Chi Migwetch

INTRODUCTION

One always hears the Thunderers coming, and in Ojibwe territory, where the land is relatively flat, one usually sees them coming as well. Near the northern shore of Lake Superior the forests stretch for miles, and from a height the bush resembles a limitless sea of grass. As storms pass over it their winds bend the treetops in a progressive wave. The clouds move above the forest carrying with them a peculiar effect of shadow and light as they simultaneously darken the sky and are lit from within by flashes of lightning. Storms seem to take a definite course here, searching the land as if they were hunting or stalking someone. When they finally reach the lake they appear to attack it, effecting an odd reversal upon its face. It is as if a gigantic wave has crashed backward into the water, which now darkens, rears up and then falls back again, as the storm flashes bolts down into its depths. The storm has reached its destination, the Thunderers have found their prey, and this prey, the Underwater *manitouk*, the monster(s) Mishebeshu, do not fall easily to the onslaught of the Thunder beings. For this is an Anishnaabe lake-storm, the experience of one battle in an ongoing war of wills between powerful persons.

The traditional Ojibwe life-world as experienced and described through religious symbols, beliefs, and practices is alive with the presence of these other-than-human people—the manitouk. Even though the relationship between Thunderers or Thunderbirds and the Underwater manitouk has been long recognized, it has not received attention that could begin to be described as systematic, thorough, or even interpretive. Rather, these beings are merely noted as traditional antagonists whose battles are enacted in Ojibwe mythology. They would appear to be consigned to the familiar dualistic category found throughout the phenomenology of religions that pits sky against water and/or earth. Invariably, just as the eagle catches the serpent in his talons and the sky gods subdue the chthonic deities, so too the Thunderbirds are understood to hunt and destroy Underwater manitouk and ground snakes.

Although such dualism is, of course, present in the complex, it is but one movement in what I would call a complicated dialectical dance. For in the Ojibwe life-world the serpent is neither cast out of the garden nor imprisoned under Delphi. Rather the Underwater manitouk continue to survive the onslaughts of the Thunderbirds and continue to act, even now, in ways that are sometimes detrimental and, more rarely, helpful to human beings. Further, the Thunderers may often, through carelessness or anger, cause harm to people. And *Anishnaabeg* have been known, on occasion, to marry and/or metamorphose into Thunderbirds themselves.

Thus, the relationship between these manitouk must be understood as the enactment of a structural interchange of energy and will between powerful "persons" whose behavior necessarily affects human life. By careful observation and interpretation I hope to illuminate both the richness of this dialectical relation as a symbolic complex and its immediacy as a lived reality. It is my contention that the Thunder and Underwater manitouk are determinative beings and symbols in the Ojibwe world and that their relationship inscribes a dialectic that both reflects the lived reality of that world and helps to determine the position and existence of the human subject therein. In other words, the human person is suspended between heights and depths both literally and figuratively.

It is important to remember, however, that this dynamic exists in a complex, if somewhat fluid, cosmology. This cosmology includes the horizontal plane wherein directions—especially the four cardinal points—are highly meaningful. However, in the case of the Ojibwe, I would contend that the zenith and nadir take precedence and the radical awareness of this vertical dimension reduces the earthly realm to a kind of precarious middle ground. The human subject travels and dwells on this plane—an island at the center of what I envision as a kind of dialectical cosmos—subject to protection and assault from above and below.

PRELIMINARY DEFINITIONS

Ojibwe

1. Roots of the word

The name Ojibwe comes from the Algonquian word *ojib* meaning "puckered up," a term most authorities maintain is derived from their style of moccasin—that is, the shoe is puckered at the seam. But William Warren, a half-Ojibwe writing in 1885, while citing this meaning, stresses the fact that ojib (pucker up) is combined with *ubwe* (to roast). Thus, he contends, Ojibwe may indeed refer to the aboriginal practice of roasting—until puckered-up, one presumes—captives of war (Warren [1885] 1984, 36). Any confusion regarding the origins of the name pales, however, in the face of the variant spellings of the term. A few include *Ojibwa, Ojibway, Ojebway,* and *Ochipwe.* This last spelling led to the label most familiar in the United States—the Chippewa—which became the official designation adopted by the Bureau of American Ethnology.

2. Use of the term

The term Ojibwe generally refers to a large group of Algonquian people (Vecsey 1983, 22, estimates 50,000 people in Canada and

30,000 in the United States) whose territory extends east to west from Lake Ontario to Lake Winnipeg and north to south from the Severn River Basin to Minnesota, Wisconsin, and Michigan. They are commonly divided into four groups: the Southeastern, Southwestern, Northern (or Saulteux), and Plains (or Bungi) Ojibwe. For the purposes of this study, however, I have chosen to include the Ottawa people under the term Ojibwe, and I also draw upon data from the Potawatomi, Menominee, and some Cree peoples in my interpretations of the Thunder and Underwater manitouk. These groups share a similar geographic distribution and many common cultural/religious elements. In fact, both the Ottawa and Potawatomi are considered by some to be factions of an originally larger Proto-Ojibwe group. Also in this group are the Woodland Cree, the northern neighbors of the Ojibwe, who speak a language so highly cognate that there has been some confusion as to who is Cree and who Ojibwe. An example of this sort of confusion is found among the Native peoples near Thunder Bay, Ontario, who call themselves Cree and the linguists who have classified their dialect as Ojibwe. In fact the dialect has long been referred to as Oji-Cree, a misnomer according to linguists but an appropriate description according to Native speakers.

But my rationale for actual *inclusion* of the Ottawa with the Ojibwe requires some further explanation. First, looking to the scholarly sources, one finds agreement regarding the extreme religious similarities between the Ojibwe and the Ottawa. Ake Hultkrantz makes the point that Ojibwe and Ottawa eschatology, for example, are so close as to be nearly identical (1980, 175). In a similar vein, Jordan Paper notes the "imprecision" of the various tribal designations (Ojibwe, Ottawa, Potawatomi, etc.), acknowledging J. V. Wrights's suggestion that the groups would best be subsumed under a linguistic title—that is, the Algonquian language family. Further, he points to the common usage of Ojibwe as definitive in religious studies of these groups (1980, 175).

Problems arise, however, when one adopts a broad tribal designation for the sake of academic convenience or clarity. I do not wish to open the door to an approach that could serve to reduce the recognition of the diversity of Native North American religious phenomena; however, my own field experience on Manitoulin Island has convinced me that the Southeastern Ojibwe share a religious heritage with the Ottawa to at least the same degree as they do with their Northern or Plains Ojibwe relations. While the work of Euro-American scholars is important, it is even more important to remember that the integrity of the tribal peoples of the Americas demands that they must be the ones, finally, to determine their own identities.

Indigenous Americans have shrugged off and will continue to shrug off Euro-American labels in the process of reclaiming their own names. Although the Native peoples of Manitoulin have begun to prefer the use of the word Anishnaabeg, these people of mixed ancestry most often refer to themselves as Ojibwe. In fact, such usage is somewhat institutionalized on the island as evidenced by the name of their education and resource center: The Ojibwe Cultural Foundation, which serves "people of Ojibwe, Odawa and Potawatomie descent."

3. Origins of the group

Regarding the pre-contact history of the Ojibwe peoples, there is much disagreement as to their origins and cultural development. Scholarly sources agree that their ancestors originated in Northern Asia and moved across the Bering Strait; however, just how far these Paleo-Ojibway traveled is questionable. Vecsey places the rise of their culture within their present Great Lakes domain at the late date of CE 1200 (Vecsey 1983, 8). Others, following the lead of the Ojibwe Mide (Medicine Society) Migration Scrolls, hold to the belief that these people moved several times: first from the Bering Strait to the Atlantic Ocean and then, following an epidemic in about CE 1400, they retraced their steps eventually as far as the western shores of Lake Superior. This migration is not to be understood as a wholesale movement but rather as a gradual dissemination of tribal factions, clans, and even family groups throughout the Canadian Shield area. This movement is consonant with the hunting-gathering character of traditional Ojibwe life.

It is worth noting, however, that many Ojibwes maintain that they—and all other North American tribes—are truly autochthonic. I heard, for instance, an announcer at the Wikwemikong Intertribal Powwow state that all the people present would agree that the Bering

Strait migration was a white man's fiction. Angus Pontiac, an elder from Kaboni on Wikwemikong, reiterated this position. As he said: "We believe we were put *here* on this side—North America—by the Creator. We didn't come anyway through Bering Strait or [by] going across from Africa to South America. People think we did. No. We were put here" (Personal communication, 1988). Such an assertion, while conflicting with archeological evidence, bears witness to a rebirth of Ojibwe confidence and authority in matters of tradition. Further it testifies to the strong sense of belonging on this land that I found very marked on Manitoulin.

Anishnaabe, Anishnaabeg *(pl.)*

All the confusion of terminology described above may well have been avoided if Euro-Americans had chosen to call these people by the name by which they know themselves: the Anishnaabeg. This term is applied in a number of ways: Grim uses it to denote both a cultural and temporal period for the Ojibwe people.[1] Both William Warren[2] and Edward Benton-Banai[3] maintain that the Anishnaabeg are the tribal ancestors of the present-day Ojibwe people. But in contemporary common usage, the word Anishnaabeg is applied to all Ojibwe people and usually is understood to include related Algonquian speakers—primarily the Ottawa, Potawatomi, Menominee, and Cree. It is clear, then, that my usage of the term Ojibwe, as outlined above, closely follows the present meaning of Anishnaabeg. In fact, my own decision to use the word Ojibwe in this study is governed by necessity rather than preference. For those outside Native American Studies, and even those outside Ojibwe studies in particular, exclusive use of Anishnaabe(g) would create more confusion than enlightenment. Thus I attempt a compromise, employing Anishnaabe(g) especially at those points when I endeavor to describe the experience of the human existent from *within* the Ojibwe life-world. I hope that the time is fast approaching when such compromises will be unnecessary, when Anishnaabe identity asserts itself to such a degree that Euro-American labels lose their meaning.

Manitou, Manitouk *(pl.)*

Manitou(k) refers to the power beings of the Ojibwe cosmos. These beings, upon whom the traditional Anishnaabeg were dependent for their very existence and with whom contemporary Anishnaabeg still relate, are never experienced as impersonal forces. It was A. Irving Hallowell (1975, 141-78) who effectively laid to rest the misconception first promulgated by William Jones (1905, 183-90) that manitou(k) is descriptive of an impersonal power—a sort of supernatural "charge" which may be accessed by vision, dream, or the performance of ritual acts. Hallowell's work among the Northern Ojibwe has proven to be a landmark in the history of Ojibwe studies. Through careful phenomenological study, he ascertained that the Anishnaabe(g) experience of manitou(k) is always at the level of personal relationship. This relationship is further enforced by the use of *atisokan(ak)* (specialized form of grandfather[s]) as a form of address. Perhaps the best description/definition of manitou(k) is Hallowell's own—i.e., *other-than-human person(s)*. This personal nature of the Thunder and Underwater manitouk will be explored at some length throughout the course of this study.

SOURCES OF THIS STUDY

The sources of this study may be divided into three areas:

Textual Sources

1. Traditional

These sources include the earliest (sixteenth-nineteenth century) accounts of missionaries and explorers. They are understood to reflect the memories of the pre-contact Ojibwe culture. Careful attention must be paid, however, to the interpretation of these myths and beliefs effected by Euro-Americans during the process of transcription. That is to say, misunderstanding of the Native Americans—sometimes intentional, sometimes not—appears frequently in these sources.

2. Post-contact/transitional

These sources include, for the most part, the earliest ethnographies and transcriptions along with systematic studies done in the first half of this century. Such sources are distinguished by the fact that they deal with Ojibwes who retain, to an easily identifiable extent, their traditional life-ways. It is worth noting that in this group informants are

generally recruited from among the oldest (presumably least acculturated) members of a community.

3. Contemporary

These sources again include some ethnographic and linguistic studies
but for the most part include the written accounts of traditional myths
and practices by contemporary Ojibwe people.

Visual Sources

Included here are the traditional Ojibwe rock paintings found along
the shores of the Great Lakes. Also, representations of these manitouk
in *mide* scrolls are frequent. (The mide society or *midewiwin* is the institutionalized medicine or shamanic society of the Ojibwe. The scrolls
of this society consist of rolls of birchbark on which pictographs are
drawn or inscribed. Their content records the origins and history of the
group as well as ritual instructions.) And the works of contemporary
Ojibwe artists—especially those of Manitoulin Island—are worthy of
much attention as they illustrate how the traditional symbols are envi-
sioned and re-figured by/for contemporary Ojibwe.

Oral Sources

Here are found interviews and conversations with contemporary
Ojibwe people. A few of these contacts were made in Thunder Bay,
Ontario, on the northwestern shore of Lake Superior during the summer of 1986, but most conversations were held between May and Sep-
tember of 1988 on Manitoulin Island, Ontario. This island, the largest
freshwater island in the world, stretching 160 km in length and cover-
ing an area of 2,785 square km, is located in northern Lake Huron, just
to the east of Michigan's Upper Peninsula. Surrounded by the waters
of Lake Huron and the Georgian Bay, it contains more than 100 inland
lakes of varying sizes. The Niagara escarpment ends at a high cliff near
the West Bay First Nation, and just to the north Manitoulin's lime-
stone gives way to the Pre-Cambrian Shield of northern Ontario. The
island's main industries are fishing, beef and dairy farming, lumbering,
and tourism, and out of a population of approximately 11,000 people,
3,000 are Native North Americans. These Native peoples, mainly of
Ojibwe, Ottawa, and Potawatomi descent, largely reside on five Re-

serves (recently renamed First Nations): Sheshegwaning, Sucker Creek, Sheguiandah, West Bay, and Wikwemikong. Sucker Lake also comprises a small Reserve, but it is not currently populated.

Archeological digs at Sheguiandah and most recently at Providence Bay indicate that the island has been peopled for perhaps as long as 10,000 years. Of the three tribes, Ottawa, Ojibwe, and Potawatomi—who together comprise a confederation known as the Three Fires—it would appear that the Ottawa were the first inhabitants of Manitoulin. Nicolet first contacted the Ottawa on the island in 1635 and reported the presence of "les cheveux releves" to Father Vimont[4] (Hodge 1974, 375). Jesuit missions to Manitoulin began in 1648, but due to the warfare between the Hurons and Iroquois in the area surrounding the island, the missionaries left within a few years. By 1652 the Iroquois invaded the island and many Ottawa fled or were killed. Late in the seventeenth century a kind of Dark Age descended upon Manitoulin and written sources concerning its inhabitants grow silent. Mary Lou Fox, director of the Ojibwe Cultural Foundation, describes this period:

> Nearly all [Manitoulin's] inhabitants seem to have deserted it. The exact reason for this exodus remains a mystery, but an Indian tradition suggests that evil spirits descended on the Island, causing much sickness and troubles. To drive out these spirits, the people set fire to the woods during the dry season. The fire swept over the whole Island, leaving only desolation behind (Fox 1978, 4).

For approximately 125 years, then, both Native and Euro-American settlers stayed away from the island. In the early eighteenth century both groups began to populate it, and then in the 1830s the British government instituted a program that called for the forced settlement of Canadian Indians on the island. The rationale for such settlement, as outlined by Lieutenant Governor Sir Peregrine Maitland and his successor, Sir John Colborne, was that the more valuable land around the Southern Georgian Bay should be "cleared" of Indian inhabitants so that white settlers could freely cultivate it. The plan to make Manitoulin in essence a huge Reserve proved unsuccessful. This was so in part because the Ojibwe factions, who were not willing to surrender their hunting and trapping culture for an agricultural one, found the area too small and confining for their activities. By 1862 a new treaty was instituted wherein Indians were required to cede their land back to the government, receiving paltry yearly payments. The residents of the Wikwemikong area on the eastern side of the island, however, refused to sign such an agreement. This large (105,300-acre) section of the island became the Manitoulin Unceded Indian Reserve and later Wikwemikong First Nation, and its present-day inhabitants take pride in the fact that it is the only unceded Reserve in Canada. In fact, strictly speaking, Wikwemikong does not belong to Canada. This independence, coupled with its large size, makes Wikwemikong—or Wiky, as it is commonly called—a remarkably self-contained Native community, especially for this area of Canada.

SPIRITUAL RENAISSANCE

During my field studies on Manitoulin I engaged a language tutor, attended traditional ceremonies and powwows, and conducted extensive interviews with fifteen Ojibwe people between the ages of twenty-five and eighty. The cooperation and hospitality of my friends and acquaintances was remarkable and, I understand, not unusual on an island where recent developments in the visual arts have accustomed both artists and elders to the intrusion of Euro-American interviewers. For the last fifteen years Manitoulin has experienced an explosion of creative energy evidenced by the work of a generation of painters and sculptors inspired by Anishnaabe visual and oral traditions. More recently, both Native music and theater have begun to receive attention on the island, thus adding new layers to an already rich spiritual and artistic renaissance. This renaissance is understood by many Anishnaabeg to be a fulfillment of a series of prophecies known as the Seven Fires. Mary Lou Fox put it this way: "I think that we're in the time of one of these prophecies where they say there would be a time when the waterdrum will sound out clear, where young people will search out the wisdom and advice of their elders. And I think that's happening now . . . It's a very exciting time to be an Indian, to be an Anishnaabe" (Personal Communication, 1988).

Thus there is a spirit of hope on Manitoulin which shows itself in part as a pride in Anishnaabe identity, and an openness—even eagerness—to discuss traditional life-ways. While some scholars of Ojibwe culture would maintain that traditional religion has disappeared under the forces of Christian conversion and Euro-American acculturation, the reality of the spiritual ferment on Manitoulin calls such conclusions into question. However, the complicated nature of religion and its various definitions—heuristic and otherwise—require a thorough treatment if we are to understand the relationship of contemporary Ojibwe sources to those outlined above as Traditional and Post-contact/transitional. Thus I will leave further comment regarding the validity of my oral sources to Chapter One of this book. Suffice it to say, for now, that field studies on Manitoulin may be characterized as addressing two types of source material:

1. Interpretations by Native people of traditional myths, symbols, and beliefs concerning the Thunderbirds and Underwater manitouk;
2. First-hand accounts of contemporary Anishnaabe interaction with the Thunderbirds and Underwater manitouk.

METHODOLOGY

Regarding methodology, I wish to steer clear of any use of the word to describe a technique—especially in that shallow sense decried by Bernard Lonergan, i.e., "a set of rules that, even when followed blindly by anyone, none the less yield[s] satisfactory results" (1979, 7). Rather, methodology, as it is used in the context of this study, is descriptive of an inherently creative enterprise that is truly a 'methodos' or 'journey after' understanding. Or, to put it a bit more prosaically, my methodology will follow closely that outlined by Paul Ricoeur in his project of hermeneutic phenomenology (1976). For it is my conviction that entry —however partial or brief—into a foreign life-world is only achieved through the lengthy route of rigorous phenomenological observation.

When I say that my methodology is grounded in hermeneutic phenomenology I do not mean to imply that the thematic material is subordinated to a static system of interpretation. On the contrary, method acts as a *servant* to understanding inasmuch as my aim is not to systematize the Ojibwe experience but rather to systematize my own entry into it. Helmut Wagner, in speaking of phenomenological method generally, has said that the ideal case is one in which method is "inseparable from the ultimate goal that we pursue with its help"

(1983, 40). In this case, phenomenological hermeneutics may, indeed, act as a kind of psychopomp into the realms of the unconscious, of dream, of myth, and ultimately of the multilayered reality of a foreign life-world. And it is the structure and spirit of the hermeneutical 'spiral' that will allow me not only to enter the Ojibwe mythos but to return from it with something more than artifacts to be displayed in prose as folklore motifs.

The myth, more than any other narrative form, taps the world of power and meaning because its language is not merely implicitly, but explicitly, *symbolic*. Within the myth, symbols may be seen, like the water monster Mishebeshu, to raise their heads during the course of the narrative. Or alternatively, like the Thunderers, they may be heard to speak their names. However, as we will discover, neither the face of the monster nor the voice of the Thunderer is entirely clear. We know that we are in the presence of significant, meaningful persons when we meet these symbols, but in order to understand them we must understand the context of their message, we must render them *intelligible*. We have all heard the thunder; we have only to learn how to listen to it in a different way. We have all wondered what lies below the water; we have only to learn how to recognize Mishebeshu. This is the project of interpretation in which method acts, as said above, not as a static set of rules or systematizing dictator within the Ojibwe life-world, but as a servant to understanding, a guide for strangers on the Anishnaabe island. And even as method systematizes our entry into this world, all interpretations which it yields must answer clearly and completely to the authority of the Anishnaabe experience as it is met both in written and visual sources and especially as it is heard in the words of Native consultants.

While this hermeneutic is an implicit factor in many interpretive studies, I think that any claims regarding its appropriateness for myth studies generally and for the understanding of North American Indian religions in particular will be strengthened by an explicit usage. In this study I begin with an exposition of myth and religion in the Ojibwe context. Next, following a description of the traditional Ojibwe life-world (Chapter Two), I take from that whole the constituent parts, which are the Thunderers (Chapter Three) and Mishebeshu (Chapter Four), and examine them in depth. When this analysis proves complete, or, I should say, *sufficiently* exhaustive, I will be ready to re-join these symbols, observing the dialectic which they inscribe and inter-

preting its significance in relation to Anishnaabe existence and identity
(Chapter Five). Finally, through myths of origin, I will expand upon
the way in which the symbols of Thunderers and Mishebeshu determine human existence in the world and examine, briefly, how this
complex might inform the consciousness of Euro-Americans and the
manner in which we dwell upon the North American continent (Chapter Six and Epilogue). This procedure may sound somewhat mechani-
cal but the structure which I have described is, in action, a fluid movement. The steps I outline will be experienced as phases, for they do not
constitute various tasks but a series of shifting attitudes which continually redefine the horizons of our understanding. It is my hope that by
exposing the inner workings of my method throughout I will neither
obscure nor, in fact, lose the flesh of the body of symbol and meaning
which I seek to describe. I do not want to produce a kind of rattling
skeleton, or, as the Anishnaabeg would call it, a *pauguck*, who rattles
through dry treetops on cold winter nights with neither a home nor a
destination. Rather, to follow the Ojibwe analogy further, explicit
methodology may, if I succeed, be closer to a kind of traditional Woodland painting in which the artist produces an image of an animal whose
stylized vital organs, circulatory system, and breath passages show
through its body. This kind of x-ray art gives the hunter not only power
over his prey but a deep and complex understanding of the depicted
creature because it allows him to see through to the inner workings of
its nature.

The hermeneutical circle is not so much a diagram of method as a
spatial metaphor for a long and rigorous journey. This trip begins in
analysis and ends with a conversion of consciousness. For it is not just
the interpretation which travels into the Ojibwe life-world, meeting
the symbols which reflect and determine that world. Indeed, the interpreter herself makes the journey. And if she returns unchanged then
she might just as well not have gone at all.

NOTE ON STYLE

On the Use of Inclusive Language

In order to avoid the impression of gender-specific forms and the clum-
siness of he/she constructions, I use male and female forms alternately.
I will specifically indicate where pronouns apply to one gender only—

otherwise this alternate use is meant to be inclusive. (Of course this problem could be avoided altogether if I were to write in Ojibwe or Cree where gender-specific pronouns do not exist.)

On the Spelling of Ojibwe Words

Because the Algonquian dialects were not written until the time of European and Native contact, many different transcribers left their mark upon the written word. Therefore when textual sources are cited one will find a number of variant spellings for the same term, most of which are, happily, fairly similar. While both Native and non-Native linguists are currently engaged in establishing a standard orthography, large variations in dialect and pronunciation have meant that standardization has only been achieved within limited dialect areas. For the purposes of this study I have chosen to follow Richard Rhodes' (1985) guide to pronunciation because it most accurately reflects the speech patterns of the Manitoulin area. I have included a simplified version of his guide in Appendix 1. The spellings of Ojibwe words in the various textual sources will remain as they are found; however, it is my hope that a pronunciation guide will, nevertheless, facilitate the reader's understanding of foreign words.

I do, however, make a few exceptions to Rhodes' orthography and pronunciation regarding a few key words. Although the Manitoulin dialect is the one in which I have established most competency, it is one of the least carefully articulated forms of Ojibwe. Further, the dialect is complicated due to the inclusion of many Ottawa and a few Potawatomi words. Thus variant spellings of some important terms are not easily recognizable if one is working from out of this dialect. For the sake of clarity, I use the following variant spellings:

Ojibwe	instead of *Jibwe*
manitou(k)	instead of *mnidoo(g)*
animikeek	instead of *nimkeek*
(Thunderers)	
Mishebeshu	instead of *mshibzhii* or
(Underwater manitou;	*mshibzhiw*
The Great Lynx)	
atisokan(ak)	instead of *adsookaan(eg)*
(Tale(s) of the grandfather(s))	

Note that both manitouk, animikeek, and atisokanak have the /k/ rather than the /g/ suffix to indicate a plural. In fact, at the end of words both the /k/ and /g/ are sounded in essentially the same way. While Ojibwa is a fairly standardized form for Ojibwe, the former spelling is, all too often, mispronounced as Ō jib' wă, when Native peoples prefer Ō jib' wā, or, following both Manitoulin and Severn River orthography: *Jibwe*, Ojibwe.

Non-English words, including Ojibwe terms, will appear in italic only at their first appearance in the text.

Finally, while definitions will be offered for each Ojibwe term as it arises, I also include a short glossary (Appendix 2) to facilitate reference.

NOTES

1. "The nomadic tribal ancestors who crossed the Bering Strait and eventually moved toward the Atlantic Ocean are referred to as the *Paleo-Ojibway*. The sedentary stage of Ojibwe village life on the Atlantic Coast is designated by the tribal term *Anishnaubag*. The totemic clan villages of the time of the first European contact are called *Proto-Ojibway*" (1983, 57). Here Grim effects an interesting marriage of archeological speculation and tribal tradition in his categories.

2. Warren is the source for the plural spelling, Anishnaubag: "This expressive word is derived from *An-ish-aw*, meaning without cause or 'spontaneous', and *in-aub-a-we-se*, meaning 'the human body'. The word *Anish-inaubag*, therefore, literally translated, signifies 'spontaneous man' " (Warren 1885, 56).

3. Benton-Banai translates the singular *Anishnaabe* as Ani (from whence) Nishina (lowered) Abe (the male of the species) (n.d., 3).

4. "Les cheveux releves" referred to the distinctive hairstyles of the Ottawa men.

I

MYTH, RELIGION, AND THE SURVIVAL
OF OJIBWE TRADITION

The myth is a true story. The myth is a story about reality.
—Charles Long, Alpha, 1963

That which we refer to in current usage as
religion cannot be conceived as being separable from
any of the multiple aspects of any American Indian culture.
In no American Indian language is there a single word
or term that could translate as religion.
—Joseph Epes Brown,
The Spiritual Legacy of
the American Indian, *1985*

In the course of this study we will turn, through the use of many sources, to several areas of Anishnaabe authority, including the words of elders, accounts of waking experiences, and dreams, mide scrolls, pictographs, and contemporary artwork. Despite the fluidity of the Ojibwe life-world, a world characterized by a hierarchy of power and a landscape inhabited by metamorphosing people—human and otherwise—these sources exhibit both consonance and interdependence. In other words, they present a web of associations and patterns that is distinctively and consistently Anishnaabe. And the knots which hold this web together, which begin and end the pattern, are the traditional narratives, the mythos of the Ojibwe people.

Hallowell has noted that there is, among the Ojibwe, an "extremely close relationship between . . . reputed personal experience and the mythos" (1934, 377), and others have added that Ojibwe myths may "serve as the primary resources for world view analysis" (Overholt and Callicott 1982, 11). However, this is not to say that the myths act as indices for experience in the world. They are guides, to be sure, but a dialectical and dialogical relationship exists not only between the tellers and the audience of myth, but between these persons and the tales that they create, re-create, and hear. Experience, especially that of the shaman and the dreamer, gives birth to the narratives even as the narratives in turn inform experience.

Among oral cultures, like that of the traditional Ojibwe, we must further refine our understanding regarding the authority of a "corpus" of tales. While we may speak of Ojibwe myth as constituting a body, we should remind ourselves that this body, like all forms in the Anishnaabe cosmos, is a highly mutable one. For Ojibwe tradition is not a "religion of a book." It has no canon, just as it has no dogma. No myths exist in either final or pure form and no telling of a story is definitive. Certainly there are written collections of tales and some are more complete than others, some accurately translated, and some paraphrased.[1] However, the manner in which they have been recorded is, in a strange way, consonant with the traditional act of storytelling whereby the narrator chooses how to speak the tale, what to leave in, what to add, and, above all, what to emphasize in the course of the telling. For in performance the storyteller not only communicates what Joseph Epes Brown has called "the immediacy of the mythological message" (1985, 83), but he offers an interpretation as well. The problem with translation and transcription as interpretation, however, resides in the fact that one's own world view, and all too often one's preconceptions, prejudices, and motives, color the interpretation to such a degree that the tale becomes more the property of the transcriber than the gift of the storyteller. This is one reason why myths should always be heard or read in an informed context. In other words, through reference to other sources, especially first- and secondhand field studies, one may check and test not only the tenor of a transcribed tale but the appropriateness of one's own response to it.

I speak of appropriateness here rather than accuracy for two reasons. First, to say there is an accurate response to the myth would seem to indicate that there is a correct apprehension of the meaning of a tale. There is no one *right* way of reading or hearing myths and certainly no clear cut answer to the questions that they posit and discuss. I

say this especially in reference to practitioners of psychological interpretations who, through the identification of symbols, find that the
myths yield universal and often facile guidelines for living one's inner
life.[2] Secondly, when I speak of appropriateness rather than accuracy, I
do so despite, or perhaps because of, the contemporary reliance of
Euro-American culture on history and the daily recordkeeping of current events. In this world, one of legalistic and journalistic "truth," the
testimony of eyewitnesses, be it through the vision of a person or a
camera, is the touchstone of veracity. However, as we will see, the testimony of the Ojibwe eyewitness to a thunderstorm differs not in par-
ticulars but in its fundamental nature from that offered by a scientific
observer. The scientist might accurately describe the facts of the storm
through reference to meteorological observation and theories but she
will not experience it as an Ojibwe storm. Neither mere 'hyletic' data
nor the index supplied by meteorology prepares us for the visits of
Thunderbirds and the baggage of symbolism and meaning which they
convey with them when they move across the Anishnaabe sky. Only
Ojibwe myths and the experiences informed by these myths can lead
us to standards of veracity within the Ojibwe life-world.

Certainly, as Hallowell has indicated, in the case of the Northern
Ojibwe, myth is functionally true. The traditional oral narratives here
do not belong to a category of fiction nor is their primary purpose one
of entertainment—this despite the fact that most are immensely enter-
taining, often either very humorous or, on occasion, downright blood-
chilling. As Hallowell says:

> After all, what people choose to talk about is always important
> for our understanding of them, and the narratives they choose
> to transmit from generation to generation and listen to over
> and over again can hardly be considered unimportant in a fully
> rounded study of their culture. When, in addition, we dis-
> cover that all their narratives, or certain classes of them, may
> be viewed as *true* stories, their significance for actual behavior
> becomes apparent. For people *act* on the basis of what they
> believe to be true, not on what they think is mere fiction. Thus
> one of the generic functions of the "true" story, in any human
> society, is to reinforce the existing system of beliefs about the
> nature of the universe, man and society (1947, 548-49).

Functionalism, however, does not answer questions regarding the nature of the phenomenon, merely the role that it plays. Functional truth is neither the beginning nor end of myth for each myth is, after all, *about* something, or as I should say in the Ojibwe context, about *someone*. Therefore I would suggest a more comprehensive and detailed definition of myth, including its substance as well as the role in which we find it. Myth, I propose, is the inherently meaningful memory of a people spoken in the form of a symbolic narrative. It both defines and reflects reality and possibility in the world.

When I say that myth is inherently meaningful I am, in essence, making a statement of philosophical faith concerning myth itself and the actual experience of the world from which myth is drawn. It is a statement of faith because it arises in the form of a *choice*, from out of a post-critical consciousness wherein nothing, or very little, would seem to be self-evident. Here I make my choice between subjectivism and objectivism and ask myself, is the world meaningful, is it made real, only through my own perceptions and reflection or does it exist out there as a collection of objects to which I respond? I choose a middle point, not because it is a compromise—it isn't—but because it reflects my own experience of reality and meaning in the world. As I experience myself as a subject I am aware not only of the intuition of essential structures of experience but of my own intentionality through which such structures are constituted. And in turn I recognize that my intentionality, my directed consciousness, does not, cannot, *create* reality. In short, the world is not denied. The world is experienced in all its fullness not as scattered perceptions or mental phantasms but as 'unities of meaning'. And with this I realize that the meaning of experience, the reality of it, if you will, lies neither in the subject nor in the object but somewhere in between in the very act of experiencing.[3]

As memory, myth provides for continuity within a life-world. The memories of myth, born in the worlds of waking experience and dream, are true because they are meaningfully real to their owners. Throughout the course of this study we will explore the extremely close relationship between the Ojibwe experience of the natural world and the myths which concern Thunderers and Underwater manitouk. But here we should first clarify the character of myths as reflecting the content of dreams. In the traditional Ojibwe world-view, sleep is not a withdrawal from life but a distinct personal experience that both requires the engagement of the self and is understood as an arena in which important and even formative life events occur. My own conversations with Ojibwe consultants support this understanding, as do the following remarks by Hallowell.

> Self-related experience of the most personal and vital kind includes what is seen, heard, and felt in dreams. Although there is no lack of discrimination between the experiences of the self when awake and when dreaming, both sets of experience are equally self-related. Dream experiences function integrally with other recalled memory images in so far as these, too, enter the field of self-awareness. When we think autobiographically we only include events that happened to us when awake; the Ojibwa include remembered events that have occurred in dreams (1975, 165).

The occurrences remembered are, in fact, often considered to be "of more vital importance than the events of daily waking life" (Hallowell 1975, 165). This is because it is in the realm of dreams that manitouk, other-than-human visitors, most often appear to human beings. And the relationships which the traditional Ojibwe formed with these dream visitors were essential to the maintenance of human life. In dream, however, the Ojibwe interact not only with the manitouk but with human and animal persons as well. They speak together, travel together, and sometimes one or more of them may undergo metamorphosis. And this pattern of interaction is mirrored not only in waking activities but, most profoundly and consistently, in the recurrent themes of myth.

In myth, generally, those spheres which we may understand as constituting discrete realities merge together. For in the memory of oral narrative the transition from one state of consciousness to another is muted to such an extent that it is hardly discernible. In the Ojibwe mythos birds speak to us, men marry beavers, women are impregnated by the wind, and the Thunderers battle water monsters in a constant struggle for balance in the world. It matters little whether these events happened in the waking world, in a trance state, in a dream, or in a fantasy inasmuch as they are remembered as meaningful events right now and right here in myths. For, as Dorothy replied when she at last found herself back in Kansas, only to be told that her great mythic adventure had been "just" a dream: "But it wasn't a dream. It was a *place*. And you and you and you and you were there. No, Aunt Em, this was a really true, live place."

There is another aspect to the character of myths as memories and that is that these stories are the public and shared property of a people. As such they confer a collective identity in much the same way that our individual autobiographies inform our consciousness of self. The myth provides a kind of history, a history of collective consciousness or, as Jung called it, unconsciousness, which is expressed in symbols. Without the plethora of meaning which symbolic memory provides, we have no bedrock upon which to build the present, to say nothing of the future. A forgetful culture, like an amnesiac individual, would be forced to draw its life upon a slate of consciousness that erases itself daily.

Just as myth brings the memory of dream to the level of spoken narrative, it enacts the world of meaning and value in such a way that it at once legitimates and reflects participation in a community of subjects. In the Ojibwe life-world this community consists, as we shall see, of persons, both human and other-than-human, who act with varying degrees of power and beneficence. Without the memory of myth this community might be reduced from a rich and consonant sacred environment to the nonsensical, amoral, and religiously barren life-world into which the Jesuits thought they had wandered.

It was perhaps partly the undifferentiated quality of aboriginal religions that led many early missionaries to conclude that the Algonquians had *no* religion.[4] The Jesuits, coming out of a tradition wherein the doctrinal, ritual, and ethical dimensions of religion were so strong, must have been confused at meeting Algonquians who, while deemphasizing those aspects, stressed the mythic and experiential elements. Religion was certainly there—it just looked a bit different, and, of course, it lacked the central and transcendent revelatory event which gave the Catholics their truth claim. But while the Jesuits may have thought they were filling a spiritual void, what they really did in the process of conversion was to get the sacred out of the world of the Indians and into their own churches.

Among Native North American cultures one finds a continuity rather than a disjunction between the natural and supernatural worlds. This is not to say that Indians do not differentiate among degrees of power or sacrality—they do and, as we will see, the Ojibwe categorize persons according to the power they possess. But Native Americans traditionally experience the natural world as a fundamentally meaningful arena in which the sacred presents itself, i.e., as a hierophany. This apprehension of the sacred as immanent in the natural world has often been characterized as a primitive or primal experience of religion. Such characterizations, while not always meant to be disparaging, are always inaccurate for the failure to discover the sacred in one's environment is less a product of sophistication than of alienation. As Dennis and Barbara Tedlock have said, "It is not that the Indian has an older, simpler view of the world, to which we as Newtonian thinkers have added another dimension but that he has a comprehensive, double view of the world, while we have lost sight of one whole dimension" (1975, xx).

It is worth noting that the Ojibwes with whom I spoke on Manitoulin often gave the impression that they felt white people were the "simple" ones. I remember Angus Pontiac telling me how, whenever he gave the invocation at a powwow, eagles would fly overhead. The eagle, as a messenger of Kitche Manitou, thus acted in response to the plea of the human for a blessing upon his actions. Pontiac saw this occurrence as a willful, consistent, and propitious act on the part of the birds, and it indicated a great deal about the interconnecting relationships between humans, animals, and the Great Spirit. It showed not only that Kitche Manitou looked with favor upon the dance but that the dancers, as they moved under the eyes of the eagles, must perform with care and grace. When he finished his description Pontiac said, in effect, that non-Natives saw this event differently, with a simplicity and narrowness that robbed the occurrence of its meaning. "When I mention these things," he said, "the white people believe they have a word for everything. They say it's coincidence" (Personal Communication, 1988).

In order to understand this double vision—the American Indian experience of religion—we must begin by standing on a heuristic definition of religion that, while describing more than the role of religion in society, steers free of judgments regarding the content of the religious experience. Here I propose to follow the general movement of Ninian Smart's model.[5] Thus I would say that religion is a multidimensional organism which is born out of the human experience of and response to the ultimate conditions of existence. The recognition of dimensions which appear to greater and lesser extent among religions allows us to identify salient characteristics as they are instantiated in particular members of the genus "Religion." To say that religion is an "organism" is to recognize not only its vitality but its tendency toward development, degeneration, mutation, and—in some cases—regeneration. The ultimate conditions of human existence are those phenomena—be they natural or revealed, experienced firsthand or as the subject of testimony—that determine our world and our lives in that world. And when I say our world I mean, of course, not just our physical environment but the structures of meaning and value which describe reality, the cosmos in its classical sense of the existential arena or universe as an essential and ordered whole. Further, these ultimate conditions not only determine the fact of our existence but the manner in which we live, and so our response to the conditions is ideally one in which we strive to *bimaadiziwin*, or live well, as the Ojibwe would say. These conditions of existence are best understood as the foci of religion which are indeed immanent in the visible world as well as transcendent. The extent to which we recognize immanence determines the extent of our "double vision" and so the extent to which religion, as such, is isolated, or even recognized as standing outside of everyday life.

For the Native North American, generally, the foci of religion are so much a part of the fabric of existence that religion here is best understood as a *lifeway*. Joseph Epes Brown has made the point that attempts to isolate American Indian religion from culture are meaningless. In the case of the Ojibwe, Brown's contention that the word "religion" is not even translatable into a Native American language is correct, albeit with some clarification. The Ojibwe do have two words which have been translated as religion. The first, often translated as prayer, is *namhwin* or *anamiewin*. This word is descriptive only of Christian prayer, however, and when used to denote religion means Christianity. Thus a church is a *namhewgamig* or *anamiewigamig* or house (*gamig* suffix) of prayer. The second word, *mnidooked*, is an intransitive verb with animate subject meaning to worship *mnidoog* (manitouk). Yet mnidooked does not describe an object or even a phenomenon religion. Rather it is descriptive of both an action and an attitude—one of relationship to the manitouk. As the manitouk are immanent in the phenomenal world, no part of the world and no act in it could be outside the realm of mnidooked. Further, mnidooked is not used in any contrasting sense with secular or non-religious spheres of existence but only to contrast with the Christian way of doing things. Mary Lou Fox adds her understanding of this contrast, eschewing any specialized term for Ojibwe religion.

> If you ask me to differentiate between organized religions and religion of Indian people, we really don't have a religion per se, but really it's a way of life and we call it anishnaabe bimaadiziwin. It's just the way you live and it's something that's really twenty-four hours a day. It's your way of thinking and it's not like just on Sunday that you go to church or that you pray at a certain time. But really they say that every act should be an act of thanksgiving and praise (Personal Communication, 1988).

It is far too easy, however, to fall into the trap of romanticizing American Indian lifeways and to place them, along with all primal traditions, into a special category of "pure" religious consciousness. Such categorizing repeats the mistake committed by early European students of American Indian myth and religion who, caught up in the idea of the noble savage, rooted through tribal religions in search of their own past. This mistake is, unfortunately, still committed daily by the non-Native people that Blake Debassige describes as "shake and bake shamans" (Personal Communication, 1988). These seekers after enlightenment, all too eager for easy answers, fail to understand the depth and specificity of the Native experience. They miss what Joseph Epes Brown has called the "impelling sacrificial demands" (1985, 111) of American Indian lifeways. And they fail to recognize that, as in all religions, there are dark and unforgiving aspects in Native American traditions. In the Ojibwe world this means one must recognize that the drummers and dancers of the afternoon powwow give way to the bear-walkers of the night, for nightmare beasts also roam this ineffably beautiful landscape of vision and dream.

Vine Deloria, in a particularly scathing and honest indictment of the de-sacralization of North America, offers some important insights regarding what might be called the character of Native American religion. He suggests that in order for a religion to be life-giving—to be a lifeway—it must provide sustenance in three ways: it must be bound to the land, it must exhibit a strong sense of ethnicity, and it must have rites of physical and spiritual healing[6] (1973, 289-301). Traditional Native American lifeways met these criteria and for centuries provided people with a matrix of meaning which both reflected and determined their lives on this continent. While Deloria declares, unconditionally, that "for this land, God is Red" (1973, 301), we must now ask the question that has been lurking in the background throughout this discussion, that is, is it accurate to speak of Native American religion or lifeway in the present tense? *Is* God still Red or has he, like many native culture heroes, wandered—or been driven—off this world?

Among the Ojibwe, the culture hero/trickster Nanabush is said, for example, to have traveled to the West to escape the onslaught of traders and settlers. Some see him in a large rock formation in the harbor at Thunder Bay known as the Sleeping Giant. No one is sure when or if he will awaken. His sleep would appear to be the mythic realization of the sixth prophecy or fire of the Anishnaabeg: "The sixth fire foretold that during this time grandsons and granddaughters would turn against their elders and the spiritual ways of the Ojibwe and Odawa people would almost disappear" (Fox 1978, 27).

The operative phrase here is, however, "almost disappear" and we recognize that Nanabush is not dead—merely asleep for an indeterminate time. Just as we must recognize the difference between sleep and death, so too we must beware of treating religion as if it were an object that either is or is not present. Religion is, as I have said, not a thing, not a static entity, but a multidimensional activity born out of the human experience of and response to the ultimate conditions of existence. A static understanding of religion is further aggravated in this context by a parallel attitude toward Native Americans which treats them as objects of study. There is an unfortunate tendency among non-Natives to freeze Indians in time and to try to force them to conform to Euro-American ideas of what tribal people should be like. When they depart from these fictive norms they are accused of being nontraditional, acculturated, and somehow inauthentic. But peoples and religions grow, change, sicken, die, and sometimes, luckily, are revived. And while changes are not only accepted but *expected* in the world traditions, they are bemoaned when found in Native American traditions.

An example of this tendency to objectify religion and to mourn changes in Native American traditions is found in Christopher Vecsey's book, *Traditional Ojibwa Religion and Its Historical Changes* (1983). In fairness to Vecsey I must note that his subsequent work has, in many ways, ameliorated the judgements he made there, but given the lack of any recent systematic treatments of Ojibwe religion—especially ones based upon field studies—Vecsey's book continues to promote misconceptions regarding the state of Ojibwe tradition. Founded in part on his experiences at Grassy Narrows, Ontario, in 1979, Vecsey reached the conclusion that "traditional" Ojibwe religion was dead because it exhibited the symptoms of historical change. For Vecsey, "traditional" Ojibwe religion is analogous, if not identical, to pre-contact religious patterns (Vecsey 1983, 6-7). Where religious belief or practice departs from these highly speculative pre-contact norms, "traditional" religion no longer exists. While I must agree that Ojibwe religion does not exist as it once did—i.e., as the plausibility structure for a hunting-gathering culture—it has experienced a great revival in terms of belief and practice and provides both meaning and value within a revised context.

My arguments should not be understood as an attack on Vecsey's conclusions but as a correction on the idea of religion as a static entity and as a second opinion on his diagnosis of the condition of Ojibwe religion. It is also a caution, as much to myself as to anyone else, that while objects are more easily observed than activities and the past is more easily mastered than the present, freedom—both religious and intellectual—challenges rigid academic conclusions regarding the lived experience of contemporary human subjects. Nor do these arguments constitute a defense of the Ojibwe people or their religion. Neither is in need of defense. Rather, they constitute an observation and a self-conscious effort by this Euro-American scholar to learn to *listen* to those who speak best for themselves.

In maintaining that traditional Ojibwe religion has been lost in the three centuries following Euro-American contact, Vecsey's analysis is not unlike Peter Berger's assessment of the fate of the Incas following the killing of Atahualpa by Pizzaro.

The religious world of pre-Columbian Peru was objectively and subjectively real as long as its plausibility structure, namely pre-Columbian Inca society, remained intact . . . By his [Pizzaro's] act, he shattered a world, redefined reality and conse-

quently redefined the existence of those who had been "inhabitants" of this world. What previously had been existence in
the nomos of the Inca world now became, first, unspeakable
anomy, then a more or less nomized existence on the fringes of
the Spaniards' world (Berger 1969, 45-46).[7]

This descent into anomy, while more gradual for the Ojibwe, was trig-
gered, says Vecsey, by a challenge which mnidooked could not meet.
For the manitouk lost their power in the face of the destruction of traditional Ojibwe culture.

The agent of destruction was the new white culture whose missionary, business, and governmental policies effectively shut down the
ancient hunting and gathering society. And one may never underesti-
mate the specific effects of the two greatest killers of aboriginal Americans: disease and alcohol. The second continues to exact an incalcu-
lable toll on Ojibwe people and often travels hand in hand with an
alarming incidence of suicide.[8] Certainly Vecsey's conclusions regarding the degeneration of the Ojibwe religion are not entirely un-
founded, and in fact a decline in traditional values and customs was also
observed among the Ojibwe of Minnesota and Ontario by Ruth Landes
in the 1930s. Landes describes the degeneration of the midewiwin into
a secretive group marked by pervasive fear and accusations of sorcery
(1968).[9] Jenness also found the same general attitude toward the
midewiwin on Parry Island in 1929, but his observations should be
qualified inasmuch as the midewiwin was never widely established
there. Rather, the *wabeno* shaman or "man of the dawn" was the popular form on Parry Island and the mide members were always understood as outsiders and frequently as rivals to the wabeno (1935, 61-62).
Nevertheless, the changes in traditional Ojibwe life were extreme and
statements concerning the illness and death of the old lifeways do require serious answers.

Let me begin to formulate such answers, then, by addressing
Christopher Vecsey's definitive eulogy for traditional Ojibwe religion
as he found (or failed to find) it at Grassy Narrows. Vecsey says, in reference to Anishnaabe lifeways generally:

> In the course of the past three centuries, the Ojibwas' tradi-
> tional religion has disintegrated as they have lost their trust in
> their aboriginal manitos and in themselves. They have stopped

telling their myths as true and meaningful accounts of a living universe, and have changed many of their religious rituals. Today they hold very few shaking tent ceremonies. In addition, the Indians have ceased their traditional puberty quests for visions of guardian manitos. The Ojibwas no longer possess the ability to find game and cure diseases through religious means, and their religious leadership has lost status, prestige, and power. In short, their traditional religion no longer exists (Vecsey 1983, 198).

First, while myths are no longer told in the traditional manner, that is, in the shelter of the family wigwam and only during the long winter months, they are being told again in the mide winter lodges and are still related by many Elders and a growing number of younger storytellers. The Ojibwe Cultural Foundation on Manitoulin has embarked upon an ambitious project that speaks directly to the continuing need of a changing society to stay in touch with the collective memory that is their body of myth. Right now Anishnaabeg are systematically recording (on video as well as audio tapes) the words of their Elders. These tapes are not used in the service of Euro-American scholarship but are shared with community members. The coordinator of the oral history project, Celina Buzwah, explained that the tapes are used quite frequently by children whose questions are best answered through that most "traditional" of all teaching methods—storytelling (Personal Communication, 1991).

William Trudeau is one Elder from Wikwemikong who still narrates the old stories. He has recorded tales for the Ojibwe Cultural Foundation, and when I showed up at his door asking about Thunderbird myths he evidenced the generosity that is characteristic of the Ojibwe. Trudeau stopped his work, took me inside, and proceeded to relate stories for two hours, after which his wife invited me to stay for dinner. He prefaced his storytelling with the kind of disclaimer I was to hear often from people accustomed to Euro-American skepticism: "It's kind of hard to believe it although I believe it myself, you know."

The symbols found in the myths *are* understood as meaningful within the Anishnaabe life-world. This is especially the case for the artists of Manitoulin who express their fears and hopes for their people through a style influenced by the mide scrolls, the Great Lakes pictographs, and the oral narratives. Leland Bell recalls listening to an elderly aunt tell the stories when he was young (Personal Communication, 1988). Melanie Madahbee likewise heard tales while growing up on Wiky, especially tales of the cautionary type for young children (Personal Communication, 1988).[10] And Blake Debassige spoke with me of the immediacy of Nanabush in his life. As a painter and director of the native *De-ba-jeh-mu-jig* (storytellers) theater group, Debassige has been deeply involved with the image of Nanabush, especially as it is expressed in a recent De-ba-jeh-mu-jig production, "Nanabush of the Eighties."

> Who can say what Nanabush is? There are so many variations. There are so many communities that have their own stories. So you can't come up and say I'm the expert, I can say what Nanabush did and what he does and what you can't do . . . I see Nanabush; he's sort of very sly and he's got a smirk on his face and you don't know what he's gonna do next. And I see that in a lot of people. I see it in G _____, I see it in R _____, I see it in J _____. That Nanabush character is in him. And it's alive, it's here today with us (Personal Communication, 1988).

Second, while the Anishnaabeg have changed many of their religious rituals, such change is not necessarily an indication of the depth of religion. Ruth Landes, who I described earlier as having delineated the degeneration of the midewiwin, nevertheless maintained that the Anishnaabe people of the 1930s were "profoundly religious" (1968, 57). And although the puberty vision fast is no longer a mandatory practice, some young Anishnaabeg women do, indeed, fast at the onset of their first menstruation. Such was the case with Leland and Kitty Bells' daughter in the summer of 1988. A traditional dancer, and in midewiwin training, she was to refrain from dancing for a period of one year. Like Native women elsewhere in North America, Ojibwe women must also fast from dancing at powwows while they are menstruating.

At Dreamer's Rock on the White Fish Reserve just to the north of Manitoulin, pilgrimages are still being made. Many of my Native consultants told me of their own trips there. And although present-day vision questers do not, routinely, receive a blessing from guardian manitouk, such visitations are not unknown. At the very least, contemporary Anishnaabeg receive inspiration from this sacred place. As Beth Southcott put it:

Dreamer's Rock
Whitefish River First Nation
Photo by the author

Upon the rock, generations of Ojibwe youth have fasted and prayed for a dream to learn their spirit guides. The Ontario Historical Society has placed a plaque there telling of the dream quest of earlier generations of Ojibwe youth *in the past tense*, completely ignoring the contemporary procession of young painters which daily climbs through woodland trails and scales the smooth flanks of the summit for inspiration. The quest is continuous (Southcott 1984, 123).

Shirley Cheechoo, a Cree artist who grew up in the James Bay area, has lived on Manitoulin for many years. She is not only a visual artist but a playwright and actress who shares her memories and her visions through a number of media. In her painting, "The Feast of Life—Fulfillment," Cheechoo depicts the following experience at Dreamer's Rock:

This is an experience I had on August 17, 1987. A couple of my friends and I went to Dreamer's Rock around four in the morning. We wanted to be on the rock for sunrise. We were lying

Feast of Life, Fulfillment
Shirley Cheechoo
Oil on canvas
Used by permission of the artist

on the rock and doing a sweetgrass and tobacco ceremony. As the new day was to begin a hole in the sky appeared and started to form a circle. My heart was neither excited nor scared, but the feeling my body was going through I can't explain. It was a cloudy day and this opening in the sky just formed the circle around the rock where we lay. A light came down on us and I could see the sparkles of light around me. I knew the spirits were there. I knew I had touched another level of existence. It stayed with us for about a half hour. We left the rock and it started to pour rain. It was like a cleansing to me to step into a new path, a new direction. I felt I was letting go of my old self, my past. I felt I was going to be able to live a new life from that moment. I was going to be able to move now into a new light (Smith 1991a).

Finally, on the subject of ritual, I would add that many traditional rituals, especially those involving the use of sweetgrass and tobacco, are practiced most routinely. I have participated in sweetgrass rituals on a number of occasions and not only within the context of a group activity like a powwow. My language tutor, Raymond Armstrong, and I would burn sweetgrass before our lessons, and my cottage on Manitoulin has been smudged to prevent the nocturnal visits of animals who were driving my dog to prolonged fits of barking. Sweetgrass is ubiquitous on Manitoulin, braided around quill boxes, fixed to medicine wheels, hanging from the rearview mirrors of most automobiles. Just as the smell of old incense permeated the Catholic Churches of my own youth, signaling a sacred atmosphere in a sacred space, so too the scent of sweetgrass delineates the sacrality of the Anishnaabe lifeworld—a sacrality not confined to a building, but immanent in the natural world.

Likewise, tobacco is offered and received as an appropriate gift, a sign of respect between humans and between humans and manitouk. It is common practice to offer tobacco—loose or in the form of cigarettes —to Elders. And tobacco is tendered to a number of manitouk, including Kitche Manitou and the Thunderbirds, in supplication and/or as a gift of thanks. Anishnaabeg regularly, for example, burn tobacco during a thunderstorm in order to invite the Thunderbirds to pass over their homes without striking and to thank them not only for their life-giving rain but for the service they provide in hunting and killing malevolent Underwater manitouk.

Encounters at a somewhat lesser power level would appear to be rather frequent. Both the Armstrongs and Angus Pontiac told me of visits which they expected and received from the eagles, common messengers of Kitche Manitou. All agreed that such visits were exceedingly good omens. The Armstrongs claimed that the eagles visited their home by flying over it every summer. During the course of our acquaintance, the eagles did not come when expected and both Armstrongs were troubled by this, taking it as a bad sign. Happily, the eagles did, finally, arrive signaling, it was hoped, an end to the troubles that had been plaguing the family.

It is clear to me that on Manitoulin Elders have "status, prestige, and power." Joseph Cahill suggests that the current cultural/religious renaissance found among various North American tribes is born out of a conflict between "two symbolic systems" (1975, 286). In their effort to resolve this conflict Amerindians have turned toward a source of authority—the tribal Elders, who are understood to be the keepers of wisdom and tradition. Neglected in recent years, these people are now being sought out both individually and under the leadership of various band councils. Elders' conferences are held regularly, usually at the instigation of the younger members of a group. At the conference which I attended in Sheguiandah, Elders from neighboring provinces and the United States spent the day speaking to a group assembled around a traditional firepit. Their speeches were largely concerned with the reclamation of the old values as foundational in a society plagued by modern problems of poverty, alcoholism, and alienation. The goal of such teachings, as Cahill sees it, is "the adoption of symbolic systems so that they may be suitable to represent and transmit original experiences of the sacred through the course of historical change" (1975, 286). In other words, the lesson sought from the Elders is how may one adopt, re-adopt, or simply remember the Anishnaabe tradition so that one may bimaadiziwin (live well) in a changed world? It is the same dilemma, albeit more acute here, found within all religions.

I must assume that Vecsey's observations—if they were once accurate—are irredeemably dated now. This is most clearly evident in his assessment of Ojibwe art. He sees it as having declined, irretrievably, since the early twentieth century. "The works carry no symbolism and exhibit relatively low standards of artistry in comparison to the earlier work. Ojibwa art stands between a moribund past and an incomprehensible present, with little apparent future in sight" (1983, 58). Vecsey has clearly been out of touch with the Woodland school for some time. This school, which bears the stylistic imprint of the mide scrolls and of x-ray art, was first recognized in the work of Norval Morriseau during the 1960s. Thematically, it has tended to revolve around ancient myths and teachings and has served at once to signal and to fuel a resurgence of traditional religion and culture among their people. As the artist Leland Bell put it: "I see myself painting in the spirit of the rebirth movement of the Anishnaabe people, with its foundations in spiritualism, land, language, and culture" (Smith 1991a).

Not only is the relatively new medium of painting thriving, but the traditional forms, especially beadwork and quillwork, are being executed with great skill and creativity. Examples of very high-quality quillwork may be found all over Manitoulin. Of special importance are the traditional porcupine quill boxes fashioned almost exclusively by women. These artists employ not only the traditional floral decorative

Mishebeshu Quillbox
Mamie Migwans
From the author's collection
Photo by Fred Maize

designs of their ancestors but create boxes based upon geometric Micmac designs, animal images, and renderings of manitouk like the Thunderbirds and even Mishebeshu.

The notion that Ojibwes have lost their game and disease medicines is, again, not wholly accurate. As the necessity and opportunity for finding game have declined, so too, and naturally enough, have the concomitant religious techniques. Yet disease curing is still an active enterprise both in the newly revitalized mide group and among traditional medicine men and women. I went to visit one such healer myself and had to wait in line behind someone who had traveled a great distance in search of a cure. This particular healer combined the old herbal remedies with both Anishnaabeg and Christian prayer. Thus he was, as Norman Williamson has put it, "getting the best out of two metaphysical worlds" (1981, 299-302).

It should be noted here that a large number of Ojibwe people do belong to the Catholic churches on the island. In fact there exist three divisions on Manitoulin: those who have little or nothing to do with Christianity, those who appear to be exclusively involved in Christian churches, and those who combine the two ways. The majority of Ojibwe people would seem to belong to the last category. These people do not, for the most part, see a conflict between the two ways, especially inasmuch as they understand Kitche Manitou and God to be one and the same. It was my experience, however, that the traditional Anishnaabe ways are held at a somewhat deeper level than the Christian beliefs. In other words, while an Ojibwe person might profess and practice the Catholic religion at a conscious level, traditional beliefs operate constantly within his subconscious and readily come to the surface.

A good example of this distinction is found in the behavior of my friend and language tutor, Raymond Armstrong, who for a time was studying to be a deacon in the Catholic church. Armstrong, while involved, especially at a social level, with the church, practiced the sweetgrass ceremony, made pilgrimages to Dreamer's Rock, avoided the lake where a manitou was said to dwell, made tobacco offerings during thunderstorms, recounted stories of powerful shamans, and awaited the visits of the eagles. I further found that when confronted with crisis-provoking events, Christian Ojibwe people would both pray and instinctively turn to traditional practices. Once, when Armstrong was confronted with the possible loss of his arm from a gangrenous wound, he went into the bush to pray, and there, in the midst of what can only be described as a mystical experience, he rubbed dirt into the wound to cure it. He explained this unlikely remedy as an invocation of the power of Grandmother Earth. According to both Armstrong and his wife, the cure was immediately effective and the doctor who had advised amputation was amazed. When I asked him to whom he had prayed, he said the Great Spirit (Kitche Manitou), who was the same as God. His term of choice, however, seemed to be the Creator.

Not all Ojibwes combine the two traditions, however, and for some maladies there is only the Anishnaabe cure. This is especially the case when a person feels that someone is bearwalking or bewitching her. One of my consultants, who told me of his great distress over a lingering feeling of ill health, had exhausted white medical cures. Having reason to believe that a particular person wished him ill, he enlisted the aid of a medicine man. Sometimes the symptoms of sorcery are more specific, as in the case of a woman who had contracted severe stomach pains. A medicine person discerned the presence of a hairball which had been shot into her system by a bearwalker and aided her in expelling it. She told me that it did, indeed, make its way out through her skin.

The first consultant also related his own meeting with an evil shaman one night. Often called bearwalkers, these powerful and malevolent people are understood to change the forms of their traveling souls at will. They are most often seen as lights traveling in the night, but their name comes from their purported tendency to take the form of a bear. In this particular case, the shaman changed from a light to a dog to a porcupine as my consultant watched. The dog form—especially a white dog—appears especially popular on Manitoulin. But I was also told that any time one sees a wild animal close to the house during the daylight hours there is a good chance that one is seeing a bearwalking shaman. In such a case one should go into the house immediately and shut the door. Salvation from this metamorphosing entity was only attained when the man placed dirt in his mouth, for soil is believed to carry both the power and protection of Grandmother Earth.[11]

Thus the Anishnaabeg, who are no fools, know that different medicines from different worlds are appropriate at different times. An aspirin may cure a headache but it won't prevent a bearwalker's attack. And the old medicines, while they may have been partly abandoned or gone underground for a time, never disappeared. As Kitty Bell put it:

> It was always there. Now the people are admitting "yes, we gave up a lot." And it was always taught from the pulpit. "Don't go that way, that fire will surely lead you to hell." They used these scare tactics. But it was always there, people always used these medicines (Personal Communication, 1988).

Kitty's husband, the artist and midewewin member, Leland Bell, further describes this process of reclamation among members of the midewiwin:

In the beginning it was more like a revival of the thing and a lot of the time it involves younger people who are searching for their roots. The way I see it—when I am part of the midewiwin right now—is that we have a chance to mend our ancestors' mistakes, if there were any mistakes done in the midewiwin— either that or Ruth Landes was lying, eh? And we shouldn't feel ashamed if there was something that went on that wasn't quite right, if people went off the track. Because it's true for all people in the world, all major religions have gone through so- cial and political turmoil (Personal Communication, 1988).

In conclusion, then, I would reiterate that, no, the religion of the hunting-gathering Ojibwe does not exist in what we assume to have been its pre-contact form. Yet the present-day practices and beliefs of the Anishnaabeg cannot be dismissed as mere vestiges of the earlier system. Native people, even those who call themselves Christian, re- tain a world view that is fundamentally different from our own. The Ojibwes that I know acknowledge the breakdown of their way of life, but they are struggling out of a heritage which buried their memories under the weight of cultural progress. This progress became a regress for them, but they do not feel that it is too late to recover much of what was misplaced. While much of this study will follow a route laid out by the oldest collections of texts, I have left it to my contemporary consul- tants to validate the truth of my entry into their ancestors' life-world. They don't all remember exactly how and where the Thunder and Un- derwater manitouk travel, but they have given me good advice on how I should try to track the paths of these symbolic realities.

This interpretation is fundamentally concerned with the tradi- tional belief system of the Ojibwe and yet it must move continually be- tween past and present. To disregard the words of the contemporary Anishnaabeg would be to fossilize and objectify the lived reality of their religious tradition. It would also be a denial of the truth of the Seventh Prophecy of the Anishnaabeg:

The seventh fire foretold of the emergence of a new people, a people that would retrace their steps to find the sacred ways that had been left behind. The waterdrum would once again sound its voice. There would be a rebirth of the Ojibwe nation and a rekindling of old fires (Fox 1978, 27).

NOTES

1. The degrees of freedom of translation are many. Rarely do we find collections which include actual transcription in Ojibwe. A notable exception is William Jones' large collection in which he places Ojibwe and English on facing pages (1917 and 1919). Yet even with this "faithful" translation, there are areas of confusion due both to the existence of a number of Ojibwe/Odawa dialects and the nonexistence of a standard Ojibwe orthography. When I went through some of Jones' versions with my language tutor, Raymond Armstrong, he commented upon these problems but did compare the Ojibwe and English favorably. It is clear that Jones tried to transfer the tales without editorial comment. This effort is in contrast to the several collections of myths in which compilers not only edit and interpret but *judge* the worth of the tales. A good example is Mabel Burkholder (1923). Most collections by Euro-Americans stand between these poles of "authenticity" and "literary license." For a discussion and comparison of collections, see Rebecca Kugel (1983).

2. This approach has its roots first in Freudian analysis and the turn toward the inner self, and more explicitly in the work of Jung with his identification of the collective unconscious and the delineation of archetypical patterns therein. Unfortunately, these psychic and mythic patterns are often misinterpreted as characters or personality types into whose roles one may step. With the recent rise of New-Age "metaphysics" the internalization of myth (which had retained sound comparative insights in the hands of Jung and later of Joseph Campbell) has deteriorated into a vague and poorly defined hymn to the self.

3. I have been, of course, paraphrasing Edmund Husserl's project of phenomenology, here, the return to 'pure lived experience' in which *Wesen* is understood to be not a hidden core but a characteristic way of being, apprehended in lived experience. Husserl argued for the reality of the phenomenal world or, as he put it, "No Subjective Idealism" (1962, 152). At the same time he maintained that in order for objects to be perceived as *noema*, as meaningful objects, they must be so constituted by human subjectivity in *noesis* or a 'meaning-giving stage'. Kohak notes that

Husserl's phenomenology stands between empiricism (or naturalism) and idealism as a kind of metatheory, "an alternative to both, taking experience in its lived reality—rather than either of the poles in which reflection splits it—as its basic metatheoretical referent." (1978, 171).

4. Michael Pomedli has summarized this early perception among the Jesuits through a study of *The Jesuit Relations*. He sees this attitude of the missionaries as the first step, or misstep, on a road toward a deeper and more realistic appreciation of Native religion. Pomedli summarizes the earliest Jesuit observations: "The first level of interpretation, then, quite unequivocally regards the natives' lifestyle as lacking any belief in a supernatural being. Jesuit observations confirm that natives are mired in the material, the lowest rung of existence; they lack a religious language, and an organized religious structure. As a consequence, they wallow in superstitious practices and immoral acts." (1987, 279).

5. By Smart's model I mean his general description of religion as a six-sided organism which exhibits doctrinal, ritual, ethical, experiential, mythical, and social dimensions. This model is found throughout his work but especially in *Worldviews: Crosscultural Explorations of Human Beliefs* (1983).

6. Deloria maintains that Christianity fails to meet these criteria on this continent. He sees Christianity as a kind of selfish orphan that washed up on these shores, a stranger in a strange land with no hope of ever understanding North America as long as Christians fail to hear its aboriginal voice. This failure of understanding is most clearly evident in the wholesale destruction of large parts of the environment: "Rather than attempt to graft contemporary ecological concern onto basic Christian doctrines and avoid blame for the current planetary disaster, Christians would be well advised to surrender many of their doctrines and come to grips with the lands now occupied" (1973, 295-96).

7. I would note, however, that Dennis Tedlock has made the point that Berger's analysis constitutes a kind of "top-down" view of Peruvian religion. While the state religion of pre-Columbian Incan civilization was irreparably harmed, local and domestic "worlds" and religions continued to thrive, and to this day ancient practices are remembered and enacted in Central America as well as in South America (Personal Communication, 1988).

8. Steve McGraw, a Native schoolteacher at the Pontiac school on Wikwemikong, spoke with me about a recent suicide attempt by one of his ten-year-old students. As his Euro-American wife, Cheryl, also a teacher, put it, "A lot of people feel like they have two options: suicide or alcohol. It's as if they inherit these options from their families because they grow up seeing their relatives do it" (Personal communication, 1988). During the winter of 1975/76 an epidemic of suicides swept Manitoulin. A total of seven teenagers from Wikwemikong took their own lives (Cinader 1978, 14).

9. The midewiwin or mide society is a shamanic group having four to eight levels of initiation. Initiates always paid a fee—in goods and later in currency as well—to join the group wherein they learned both healing techniques and methods for acquiring personal power. The Thunderers and Mishebeshu, along with a number of other manitouk, play important roles in the midewiwin.

10. The stories to which Madahbee referred were those concerning the owl—*gookookhoo*. Mothers would frequently tell children that if they did not behave, gookookhoo would carry them away. However, as in all aspects of life, parents were also cautioned to be temperate in their use of these threats. If they invoked the power of the owl too often, it might indeed take a child away against the wishes of the parents. See Sister Bernard Coleman, Ellen Frogner, and Estelle Eich (1962, 39-40) for examples of owls who seized children.

11. In this section I have not credited my consultants. This is an intentional lapse. While I recorded many conversations and told all consultants that I might quote them in my work, the discussion of sorcery in this community is an extremely touchy and potentially dangerous one. I feel that it would be a violation of my consultants' trust to credit them here, especially inasmuch as personal experiences with bearwalkers were related in what I believe was unstated confidentiality. At the very least, consultants might incur the displeasure of their community.

II

A PEOPLED COSMOS

Things are going wrong when people think of the land
as a pie that can be sliced up in pieces . . . No matter how you
cut a pie, in the end there's nothing holding it together.
It gets eaten up like pop and chips, like raisins. It's better for
people to live as if they're inside a ball. The sky, upstairs
and downstairs, the four directions: these will hold everything
together and not let anything escape because a ball has a
top to cover us and a bottom to hold us, and everything works
together.
—*Ron Geyshick,*
Te Bwe Win (Truth), 1989

The first step in an interpretation of the determinative relationship between Thunderbird and Underwater manitouk involves a kind of "archaeology" of these symbols. In this analytic phase one must dig
deeply through the linguistic and non-linguistic layers of expression
and experience. Here we undo the symbols, pull them from the obscurity of the multivalent structure that grows around them, and hold
them up to the light of phenomenological scrutiny. What we will discover in this work is that these symbols, like all things in the Ojibwe
world, are not encoded, but en-souled. And as in all "archaeological"
enterprises, the project is not to destroy but eventually to rebuild a
world, to place the pottery shards together again into a vessel which is
as seamless as possible.

As we embark upon an analysis of symbol we must first take the
lay of the land in which we intend to dig. In this study the land in question is the Ojibwe world, the arena in which Thunderers and Mishe-

beshu dwell. While an exhaustive study of this world is beyond the bounds of this book, an introduction to certain elements is necessary. The two broad categories which I choose as foundational to understanding are the multileveled nature of the Ojibwe cosmos and the experience of all reality as "personal." Later in this study we will see how the Thunderers and Underwater manitouk both reflect and help to determine the structure of this "peopled cosmos."

multi-leveled cosmos

The notion of a multileveled world is not exclusive to the Ojibwe. Every shamanic society, from Siberia to Oceania, has shared this intuition of a many-storied universe (Eliade 1974b, 259-87). Like players in an intricate game of ladders and chutes, shamans travel routes mapped by myth and vision to power realms both above and below the sensible world. And returning from their travels they add their testimony to a continually growing corpus of descriptions regarding the structure and character of multileveled reality.

Among the archaic traditions of the world—the Mesopotamian, Indian, Greek, and Japanese for instance—a hierarchy of worlds was the norm. Even contemporary non-shamanic world religions retain earlier cosmographies as symbolic expressions of sacrality both in and beyond this earth. As Eliade has said, "History cannot basically modify the structure of an archaic symbolism. History constantly adds new meanings, but they do not destroy the structure of the symbol" (Eliade 1961, 137). This means that contemporary people—including the Ojibwe—informed by a scientific understanding of cosmology, still find the hierarchical universe to be a resonant image. For example, while most contemporary Christians find Dante's vision to be an empirical impossibility, it remains an existential or psychological reality, for the symbols of descent and ascent contained in the *Divine Comedy* retain their fundamental meanings as expressions of Christian fear and hope.

The levels of the Ojibwe cosmos also contain the symbolism of dread and aspiration and for traditional Anishnaabe, and they retained their concrete reality as well. Therefore, the world consisted of a literal series of layers that were governed by various manitouk. In the sketch below, taken from Sister Bernard Coleman's drawing (1947, 12), there is a spherical form depicting the three main divisions of space. Surmounting the field of the sky is the hand of Kitche Manitou, the Great Spirit, traditional ruler or, as the Ojibwes would say, *ogimaa* (boss) of the heavens. Kitche Manitou was most often understood as a

Kitche Manitou

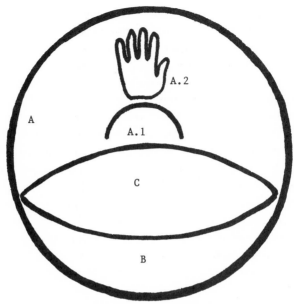

A. Sky Realm A.1 Home of Kitche Manitou A.2 Hand of
Kitche Manitou B. Underworld C. Horizon or Earthly Plane

Diagram of the Cosmos
Rebecca Richwine
From a drawing by Sr. M. Bernard Coleman

Creator, "the master of life" (Brown and Brightman 1988, 107), who, while seemingly inactive in the day-to-day lives of the Anishnaabeg except as a passive presence or principle, could be invoked through solemn rite (Lahontan 1905, 2:448-50; Hilger 1951, 60). Contemporary Ojibwes view Kitche Manitou as largely interchangeable with the Christian god, and invocations and prayers are offered *up* to both.

Sharing the upper realms were the Thunderbirds, who were also said to dwell with the winds at the four corners. Manitouk, like the Anishnaabeg, traveled frequently, but while the humans moved in search of game, the manitouk journeyed according to their own rhythms. Sometimes they moved with the seasons or along prescribed paths, as in the case of the Thunderers or *Ningobianong* (Evening Star). But occasionally their movements were unfathomable. (This was certainly the case with Mishebeshu, as we will see in Chapter 4.) Further, the tendency of manitouk to metamorphose led to a plethora of forms, dwelling places, and names. In fact, even the name Kitche Manitou was not invariably reserved for one Great Spirit. As Kohl relates: "An old Indian with whom I once talked, told me that there were six Kitchi-Manitous. One lived in the heavens, one in the water and the other four, north, south, east and west" (Kohl [1860] 1985, 60).

The underworld in this scheme consisted of several layers including a level in which earthly rhythms were reversed: "In this world it is day when it is night on earth and vice versa, for the sun travels above the earth during the day and under it during the nights" (Hallowell 1942, 6). This mirror world was often understood as the final destination for the dead, who, having followed the path of souls to the West, the South, or along the Milky Way, ended up in this reversed but eminently peaceful and abundant land. Also below was the realm of the Underwater and Underground creatures, sometimes said to lie between the earth and the land of the dead. And at the bottom of it all there seems to have been a place of perpetual darkness.

Like everything in the Anishnaabe world, the hierarchy of layers was somewhat fluid, but the consensus seems to be that a series of levels did exist above the world as well as below it. A Chippewa mide priest described the cosmos to Victor Barnouw.

> The Indians say that this earth has four layers. The bottom layer does not look like the one we are on now. It is night there all the time. That is where the manitou is who is the boss that rules the bottom of the earth. He rules all four layers. There is no special name for him or for the different layers...
>
> The sky has four layers too. In the top layer of the sky there is a manitou who is equal in power to the manitou at the bottom of the earth. It is always day there. It is never night. This manitou has no name, but you can call him Gicimanitou (Great Spirit). There is no name for the top layer. We're right in the middle in between the four earth layers and the four sky layers (Barnouw 1977, 41).

This storied cosmos is not usually discussed in detail by contemporary Ojibwes who tend to speak in terms of apex and nadir, and sometimes, like many other Native Americans, (Grand)Father Sky and (Grand)-

Mother Earth. But there are those who still express knowledge of the various layers.

> Here upon the Earth is a plane, . . . a place marked by time. Nowhere else in the Universe is time necessary . . . Here upon the lap of our Mother the Earth is a place and time that hangs between eight levels of elements. These elements are unseen but are as real and necessary for life as the water you drink. Of these eight elements, four are above the Earth and four are below the earth (Benton-Banai n.d.).

My own consultants did not volunteer detailed descriptions of the various layers, but their attention to the symbolism of the sky and underwater worlds will be explored in depth later in this work. For now let us say that a hierarchy of worlds, while always less then precisely mapped, was and continues to be an important psychological determinant for Anishnaabe consciousness.

The influence of this symbolic reality is most clearly seen in the traditional belief that suspended between these layers lies an island, the earth upon which humans spend their days. Surrounded on all sides by potentially helpful and harmful forces, the island of the Anishnaabeg exists as a discrete world with its own sacred geography. Chiefly this geography is described in terms of the four cardinal directions, which serve as the abodes of the winds and their tutelary spirits, the Thunderbird manitouk. These winds, the brothers of Nanabush (culture hero/trickster), exert their control upon human life by carrying the weather that is sometimes a gift and more often a punishment. Pipe ceremonies here, as among other Native American tribes, always include offerings to the four directions. Like many rituals the rite of the pipe has been reinstituted on Manitoulin as a public and honored practice before meetings, powwows, and even weddings.

Each quarter has its own color: East is yellow for the sunrise, South is red for warmth, West is black for the Thunderheads, and North is invariably snow white. In a world where the ogimaa (boss) manitouk are said to be white, it is not surprising that this color is drawn from the snowfields of the most powerfully pure direction. Winter on the island of the Anishnaabeg is known as a kind of bully, *Bebon*, a powerful old warrior manitou who is said to struggle with the weaker yet persistent *Zeegwun* (Summer) every year. They fight for a maiden

The Four Directions
Melvin Madahbee
Acrylic on canvas
Used by permission of the artist

whose parents, weary of the battle, removed her long ago. She exists
now only as the ephemeral water lily and still her suitors, like their associates *Waubun* (Dawn) and Ningobianong (Evening Star), fight a war
with no discernible object. Their advances and retreats served to mirror and determine the seasonal migrations of traditional Ojibwes from
winter hunting grounds to summer camps (Johnston 1976, 27-31). The
island of this earth was formed by Nanabush and the earth-divers at the
time of re-creation following the great deluge. These foundational actions are related in a series of tales explored at length in Chapter 6.

Clearly, however, while myths form the basis for the origins of
the present world, other activities and experiences legitimize beliefs
regarding its structure. Hallowell observed that among the Saulteux
there existed what he called "empirical" sources of knowledge and authority that substantiated mythic material (1934, 392-93). One was the

observation of the conjurer's performance in his shaking tent as he con- *other ways*
versed with various manitouk.[1] The other sources included: (1) the ob- *of knowing*
servation of natural phenomena, both mundane and extraordinary, (2)
the experience of dream, and (3) the testimony of witnesses regarding
(1) and (2). These three are precisely the sources to which my own consultants referred. And such references were consistently made in the
form of narrations of interactions with personal forces residing on,
above, or below this island. In other words, the Anishnaabe experience
of the world, whether awake or in dream, is an experience of a world
controlled by the actions of persons, human and otherwise. The levels
and directions are not "animated" or "anthropomorphized" by humans
who, in a purely cognitive exercise, posit souls and spirits and ascribe
them to things in the world. Rather, the cosmos is *experienced* as a
place literally crowded with "people."

It was Hallowell who first described the Ojibwe life-world as
"personalistic".[2] Therefore it makes sense to describe Ojibwe personalism by exploring those areas in which he found the category of person
to be made manifest: language, myth, vision/dreams, and behavior.
Given the various connotations of the term 'personalism' in the history
of philosophy and theology, it is important that we be quite clear in our
understanding of what the term entails in this context. Hopefully it will
be clarified as our understanding of the Ojibwe category of 'person' is
elucidated. Suffice it to say, for now, that Ojibwe personalism em-
braces not only the categories of human persons and deities but of
many kinds of other-than-human persons as well: animals, plants,
stones, shells, as well as power beings or manitouk. It is, in short, more
inclusive than any Western form of personalism. Erazim Kohak, in
speaking of an ideal personalism in philosophy, could well be describing the Ojibwe world-view when he calls it a "primordial insight, the
vision of a kosmos, on the other side of skepsis" (1987, 127).

LANGUAGE

Following Hallowell's lead, then, we may first see this "vision of a
kosmos" reflected in the structure of the Ojibwe language. Algonquian
linguists have located two genders in Ojibwe and Cree nouns: the animate and the inanimate. Included in the second classification are non-
living objects and in the first we find all living beings. Also included in

the animate category are nouns that Euro-Americans naturally understand as inanimate—stones and pipes, for instance. Hallowell describes his own experience with animate stones.

> Since stones are grammatically animate, I once asked an old
> man: Are all the stones we see about us alive? He reflected a
> long while and then replied, "No! But some are." This quali-
> fied answer made a lasting impression on me. And it is thor-
> oughly consistent with other data that indicate that the Ojibwa
> are not animists in the sense that they dogmatically attribute
> living souls to inanimate objects such as stones. The hypothe-
> sis which suggests itself to me is that the allocation of stones to
> an animate grammatical category is part of a culturally consti-
> tuted cognitive "set." It does not involve a consciously formu-
> lated theory about the nature of stones. It leaves a door open
> that our orientation on dogmatic grounds keeps shut tight.
> Whereas we should never expect a stone to manifest animate
> properties of any kind under any circumstances, the Ojibwa
> recognize, *a priori*, potentialities for animation in certain
> classes of objects under certain circumstances. The Ojibwa do
> not perceive stones, in general, as animate, any more than we
> do. The crucial test is experience (1975, 147-48).

Hallowell's observation here requires some clarification. In the
Algonquian dialects with which I have some familiarity—Swampy
Cree, Severn Ojibwe, and the Ojibwe-Odawa of Manitoulin—stone
(*asiniy, ahsin* and *sin*) is listed as animate in the first two and inanimate
in the third. Further, asiniy and ahsin, the Cree and Severn forms,
may sometimes be denoted as inanimate.[3] And sin, likewise, is sometimes referred to as animate depending upon the context and the
speaker's attitude toward the stone in question. Thus the genders are
somewhat fluid and so the 'cognitive set' to which Hallowell refers is
even more open than he indicates.

The contemporary Ojibwes with whom I spoke on Manitoulin
generally thought of stones as inanimate with at least two exceptions.
One animate kind of stone was the type which could be found at the
bottom of a tree that had been struck by lightning. Both Raymond
Armstrong and William Trudeau told me that these stones were hurled
by the Thunderers and imbued with their power. Armstrong indicated

that one had to look for the stones immediately after the lightning strike. Once when we were discussing a particularly violent storm that had occurred the night before, he told me that the tree across the road had been struck and he had not, to his regret, looked for thunder stones.

The other stones that were perceived as animate were the Bell Rocks located just to the north of Manitoulin on the La Cloche chain near Dreamer's Rock. Tradition holds that, when struck, the Bell Rocks used to sound across the island, and so they were sometimes used to signal the approach of enemies. Now their voices are somewhat dimmed. However, at least once a year a group of Ojibwe people will travel by boat to these boulders, and after offering sweetgrass they invoke the power of the stones by striking them. The pervasive feeling was that just as the Natives of Manitoulin have reawakened to their ancient ways, so too the sleeping Bell Rocks are called to join the revival. This ceremony should not be understood as a presentational exercise or performance. Rather, the attitude toward the Bell Rocks is one of reverence, and the rocks are treated as if they were persons—in this case, manitouk with the outer form of stones.

The category of animate in Algonquian languages is not fully understood, but it would seem to indicate a *potential* for both movement and for the exercise of volition. In the case of the Bell Rocks there is a potential for sound and one might even say for a kind of speech. This potential should not be understood as the presence in some objects of an impersonal force which pervades the world like the famous Melanesian mana. For dynamism or animatism is a theory that does not reflect the experience that the stone moves or speaks because it has actualized its *own* potential to do so. In short, the stones cannot be *made* to speak by humans. One can only *ask* them if they will do so.

For when one meets the category of 'animate' in the Ojibwe language, one is dealing with two possibilities: here is a person of the human class or of the other-than-human class. In this cognitive set humans do not ex-sist or 'stand out' in the world in any 'Heideggerian' sense. On the contrary, they stand *in* the world as particular types or instantiations of a transcendental personhood characterized, in part, by the potential for animation and by volition. But the world in which they stand is a remarkably fluid one. And one key to understanding the actualization of the potential for personhood reflected in the genders is the Ojibwe notion of *metamorphosis*, especially as it is perceived in myth and in vision or dream.

There are two divisions of tales among the Ojibwe. Those living in the Severn River area distinguish between tipacimowinak (stories) and kanatipacimowinak (sacred stories) (Beardy, Personal Communication, 1986). The latter are said to include the actions of manitouk and traditionally were told only during the winter months when all the waters are frozen. Likewise, among the southeastern groups there is the *dbaajmowin* (story) and the *aadsookaan* (sacred story). Hallowell uses the southeastern form but with the Saulteux dialect pronunciation—atisokan(ak)—and like John Boatman (1992) claims that atisokanak are also the "grandfathers" or manitouk who are the subjects of the tales. It should be noted here that, not surprisingly, dbaajmowin is an inanimate noun and aadsookaan/atisokan is animate.

The seasonal proscriptions regarding sacred narratives were especially stringent whenever the water monster made an appearance in a tale due to the belief that if the lakes were free of ice, then Mishebeshu might visit the storytellers. Since to speak someone's name was to conjure that person, one had to be very careful not to invite an unwanted presence. While this proscription has been relaxed on Manitoulin, consultants often declined to mention Mishebeshu by name during our summer talks. They most often referred to him as "that monster," "the big snake," "the one who is down there," or, most frequently, "that person, that guy."

The atisokanak are full of tales of metamorphosis, presenting a constantly shifting landscape in which characters change appearance according to their needs and wants. Most often humans take the form of animals and vice versa, as in the tale "Clothed-in-Fur." William Jones, who collected nearly 150 narratives, offered the following summary of "Clothed-in-Fur."

> Clothed-in-Fur took leave of his elder sister and went away. He came to a place where some games were going on, and was made to join in the play; but, being annoyed by the Foolish Maidens, he left the place. They followed in pursuit, and a

magic flight ensued. Four times he made his escape. Three of the times were by the help of leaves wafting with the wind,— once by a birch, again by a spruce, and then by a poplar. The fourth escape was by hiding in the knot of a tree which the maidens failed to open. Being free to continue his way, he went on till evening, when he put down his pack and then went out to see what he might kill. On his return, a woman was there and his camp was made. He took the woman to wife, but on the morrow she failed to keep up with her pack. In an attempt to strike her, she turned into a wolf. He had a similar experience with other women, who one after another became a raven, a porcupine, a Canada jay, and a beaver. The Beaver remained with him for a while, and he had two children by her. He lost her by not placing a foot-log over the dry bed of a brook, for the omission caused a river to flow by when she came, and she was carried down stream. He found where she was, but failed to get her to come with him. By another Beaver woman was he followed. On account of her he had to contend with a brown and a white bear who wanted her for a wife. He displayed greater conjuring-power, and so finally overcame them. Then he went back to his former wife, and dwelt with the beaver-kind, living the mystic life peculiar to the animal-folk (W. Jones 1916, 379).[4]

Less often, the land itself is made to change, as in the case of *land △'s* "The Magic Flight," also known as the "Rolling Head" tale. In this tale, the mother has been secretly copulating with snakes and neglecting her children. When her husband discovers her behavior he sends the children away and kills their mother and himself. Sometimes, as in Jones' version, the mother rises as a skeleton, much like a pauguck. More frequently, she becomes a huge rolling, sometimes flaming, head and pursues the children in this form.

The tale is known throughout the Algonquian tribes and is also found among the Iroquois. The version which I am summarizing is taken from W. Jones (1919, 45-102) where it comprises the first section of a much longer story, "The Orphans and Mashos." Here the two young boys fleeing from their evil mother are given common objects (an awl, a comb, flint, and some punk) by "grandmothers" (manitouk) whom they meet on their journey. And when the first grandmother says, "Oh, dear me! My grandchildren, both of you are to be pitied," she declares her intention to help the boys. This pity is precisely the emotion which a vision seeker hopes to elicit from a manitou and is a requisite first step in the formation of a relationship between human and guardian.

The seemingly mundane objects hold the power of metamorphosis. When the boys throw the objects behind them, huge mountains and a great fire spring up to delay their mother's progress. Finally a Grebe who has carried the children across a river offers similar transport to the hideous mother. The Grebe is also a "grandparent" to the children, and he exacts a toll from the mother in the form of a promise: she is to refrain from stepping over him when she alights on the far bank. Naturally the mother, who is disrespectful as well as bloodthirsty, does step over the Grebe and is drowned. The mother is also called a manitou, and so she refers to the Grebe as little brother; however, it appears that this form of address is overly familiar and disrespectful. It is most likely that he should be addressed as an *older* brother, as one who is more powerful.

Further, in stepping over the Grebe she violates a taboo that is well known to the Anishnaabe. Women are traditionally instructed not to step over animals, especially ones which have been killed and are being prepared as food. This proscription is especially strong when a woman is menstruating for at this time she is exhibiting a power that is uncontrollable and so, potentially, dangerous (Smith, 1992-93). The practice is still enforced among older Ojibwes, and I was told of one young woman's humiliation when she stepped over a deer that was being cleaned. The old women who were present took her to task, severely, and insisted that she apologize to the deer and to everyone present.

In this tale, then, we witness not only the experience of metamorphosis, but the guardianship role of the manitou, the obligation of respect on the part of the humans, and the models for human behavior that are to be discovered in myth. We also must recognize that power is relative and one must be careful when dealing with other persons who may possess greater power. This power is most often evidenced—by human and other-than-human persons—in the ability to transform the self and/or the environment.

The most frequent employer of transformation is Nanabush, who appears in a multitude of guises. Most often he is a man or a rabbit, but he has been known to take on the forms of various animals, trees, birds, and rocks. As culture hero and transformer, he is also responsible for changing the appearance of others. It was Nanabush who rewarded the kingfisher with colorful plumage because he aided him in his battle against Mishebeshu. And likewise he punished the buzzard's extreme pride by stripping him of his head feathers. Nanabush is both the paradigmatic changer and the changed. His talent for transformation is sometimes considered extreme even within the context of Ojibwe narrative and is often explained through reference to his own great power or his ability to enlist the aid of powerful manitouk. Hallowell calls metamorphosis "one of the generic properties manifested by beings of the person class," and he continues:

> Within the category of persons there is a gradation of power. Other-than-human persons occupy the top rank in the power hierarchy of animate beings. Human beings do not differ from them in kind, but in power. Hence, it is taken for granted that all the atiso'kanak [manitouk] can assume a variety of forms. In the case of human beings, while the potentiality for metamorphosis exists and may even be experienced, any outward manifestation is inextricably associated with unusual power, for good or evil (1975, 163).

Thus all traditional shamans—the members of the wabeno and mide society and the practitioners of sucking cures and conjuring—undergo change in order to effect cures or prophecies. And bearwalking shamans, as we have seen, change their forms in order to attack their victims. For these sorcerers, metamorphosis is both an exhibition of power and the means whereby that power is directed.

VISION AND DREAM

While the ordinary Anishnaabeg did not have the power to metamorphose under most circumstances, they did transform themselves through altered states of consciousness, in vision, or in dream. Young people began their vision quests with fasting and in isolation sought the attention of manitouk who would become guardians to them. Without *vision quest*

relsh w/ personal
manitolik is
key to be'g
complete person

this personal relationship, which was most often formed at puberty, the individual was considered to be a less than complete person.[5] By throwing himself upon the mercy of a peopled yet capricious environment, the vision quester sought to attract the sympathy of a particular manitou person. Hopefully this person would visit him, usually in animal form, in order to soothe his suffering, thus signaling the beginning of a mutually fruitful relationship. The manitou would guide and protect a man or woman for life and in turn the human was obligated to offer the manitou respect, loyalty, and gift offerings such as tobacco.

In his study of the Round Lake Ojibwa, Edward Rogers describes the reciprocal relationship between human grandparents and grandchildren. He could be describing the human/manitou relationship.

> Between a grandparent and grandchild there is a strong bond of affection and a continual interest in the welfare of each other. It is shown in the kind behavior and indulgence a grandparent bestows on a young grandchild... Grandchildren look to their grandparents for aid and comfort. A man assailed by the *wintiko* asked for his grandmother or other elders saying they could help him when others couldn't. He said he would be willing to listen to his grandmother's words.
>
> Grandchildren reciprocate. One informant told me how he would wait near the camp for his grandfather to return from tending his hare snares... Giving gifts to ones grandparents is instilled early in life. A father instructs his son when, for instance, he has caught fish, to give them to his grandfather (1962, B13-B14).

Often the visit involved a transformation of the seeker and a journey with the manitou. Jenness recorded a particularly detailed journey ascribed to a man named Ogauns who traveled through six layers of the cosmos on the back of an eagle (1935, 55). Rogers reports the experience of a boy who traveled under the water with a giant turbot (1962, D7). And Vecsey offers thirteen accounts of visitation journeys including the following recorded by Hallowell.

> When I was a boy I went out to an island to fast. My father paddled me there. For several nights I dreamed of a chief who

finally said to me, "Grandson, I think you are ready now to go with me." He danced around me as I sat there on a rock. I glanced down at my body and noticed I had grown feathers. I felt just like a golden eagle. The chief had turned into an eagle too and he flew off to the south. I spread my wings and followed after him. After a while we arrived at a place with many tents and people, the summer birds. After returning north I was left at my starting point. The chief promised to help me whenever I wanted it (Vecsey 1983, 138).

On Manitoulin I was told that the puberty vision quest had not been practiced for at least three generations. It is not unlikely, however, that the practice will be revived in its traditional form, especially as people do continue pilgrimages to Dreamer's Rock and do receive visions and guidance there. The Elder William Trudeau recalled the requisite traditional practice in some detail, stressing the necessity for forming a relationship with the "right sort of guardian, a manitou whose power would not overwhelm the seeker.

And the people, when they were bringing up their kids, if they had a boy they had to tell him to fast for about 10 days; every one of them was brought up like that, not a single one was left out—hoping that when they fast that they'd get a vision or a dream, whatever, from some of the creatures that live on the planet—but not necessarily a big one. They tried to avoid that, like maybe a great big snake or polar bear or whatever—a big animal. They avoid that as much as they could.

And when they fast those young people they really look after them. They took them to a certain place where they stayed and this guy would stay there for 10 days. If he doesn't have a vision before that he's gotta stay for 10 days and every day an older man would go up and check on him and ask him if he dreamt something or had a vision of some kind. Every morning he'd do that, and if the guy happened to dream about or have a vision about one of those big animals he'd tell him to quit right away, right now, and they'd sort of scrape their tongue, they'd pull the tongue out and they used a cedar knife to scrape it out . . . Because if they don't get rid of that early the one who had that vision or dream is gonna live with that monster—I might say a monster—for the rest of his life and a lot of times they wouldn't live very long, either, maybe about 4 or 5 years after they make their fasting.

But it was better for them—like maybe little insects if they could get help from those little insects or flies or birds or small animals, things like that, they had better use for those while they were living. They needed them most of the time, like maybe hunting or fishing or maybe traveling, or trying to hide from somebody else like the Iroquois people, you know the way they killed each other in those days. So they could hide, they were able to hide their family too when they had that power. So there was a reason for that (Personal Communication, 1988).

Throughout discussions with my consultants I found that while the traditional puberty quest appeared to be dormant, reports of meaningful dreams were still quite frequent. Kitty Bell recounted such a dream, a visitation by the soul of her brother.

I never dreamt of my brother when he was alive. But after he died, that's when I started dreaming of him. One time he came and I didn't know this but when someone dies the spirit world sends someone to come and meet you to go back with. And I guess that time my sister—her baby was in the wrong place [a tubal pregnancy] and had to be aborted. The same day she was in the hospital and I was sleeping and again I dreamt of my brother and he came in here like he was in a rush. And he looked so beautiful, his hair looked so nice, he always had real long hair, eh? I think he had about a hundred girlfriends! Anyway he was in a rush and I could see that he was going somewhere. I said, "Wait! I'm so delighted to see you. Let me get my tobacco." I had to give him tobacco and I got it and I gave it to him. And I said, "Hug me, just hug me." And he hugged me and then he said, "I have to go now. I came for a reason" (Personal Communication, 1988).

Mrs. Bell knew that her brother Jimmy had come to guide the soul of her sister's baby, and later she was able to soothe her sister by recounting the experience.

Traditional Ojibwes believed that when a woman slept, her free-soul traveled in a world that was characteristically distinct and yet, as we have noted, essentially continuous with the waking world.[6] This is not to say that Kitty Bell did not differentiate between sleep and wakefulness, but that meaningful dreams were included in her memory of pivotal autobiographical events. Meaningful dreams, like waking visions, include premonitions and, especially, important meetings with the souls of the dead and manitouk. In former times there was a proscription against relating dreams, the feeling being that, once revealed, the dream would lose its power. While this proscription appears to have been relaxed on Manitoulin, I have no reason to doubt that there were many meaningful dreams which dreamers kept to themselves. (This would clearly be the case among those involved in bearwalking practices. One's sources of power, dreams, and medicines were always kept closely guarded lest they be stolen and turned upon their former owner.)

Unlike visions, dreams were and are not generally courted, but in every other way dreams have the same status as waking visions. The Ojibwe word for dream, *naabndanwin*, is, in fact, the same as that for visions. And manitouk, as Hallowell noted, may go by the name *pawaganak* or dream visitors. This is so because they are so often met in dreams:

> Moreover, it is a dogma that most of these pawaganak are *only* seen in dreams... This is why the testimony of the man who *dreamed* of *pinesi* [Thunderbirds] was needed to verify the account of the boy who had *seen* pinesi, instead of the other way about (1934, 389).

BEHAVIOR

Whether met in myth, vision, or dream, or in the phenomena of the natural world, the manitouk invariably act as persons. They have volition, they move and speak, and they may take, according to their power, a variety of forms. Further, as the category of the animate would seem to indicate, animals, plants, and objects should also be treated as persons. They may or may not be *powerful* persons (manitouk), but as one can never be sure, all "things" are given the benefit of the doubt. Thus the traditional Anishnaabe always behaved toward phenomena in the natural world as if he were dealing with his fellows. He entreated the elements, spoke to his game, and propitiated the dangerous waters. His behavior included a respectful attitude toward the world and the extension of kin terms to its particularly beneficent aspects. Vecsey summarizes the traditional Ojibwe attitude.

> When an event took place in the universe—a branch put a person's eye out; a storm roiled a lake—the Ojibwas' first response was to ask *who* caused it (Lahontan 1905, 2: 446). They lived in a very personal universe (1983, 72-73).

I noticed this same attitude among my consultants on Manitoulin. Invariably, when speaking of the Thunder and Underwater manitouk, my acquaintances referred to these symbolic realities as if they were people. Both William Trudeau and Raymond Armstrong always employed personal pronouns. It was, for instance, never *something* but always *somebody* who lived under the water. Armstrong once cautioned me about swimming in Lake Manitou.

> It's okay to swim there but the guy who lives in that lake doesn't like you to stay in too long. You should go maybe ten or fifteen minutes and then get out. He gets tired of people splashing around in there (Personal Communication, 1988).

I would reiterate that such usage does not indicate a naïve romanticization of impersonal forces. Hallowell found that the Saulteux Ojibwe rejected scientific explanations of thunderstorms not because the theories were too complex but because the notion of impersonal forces did not reflect their own experience of thunder and lightning (1975, 155). Norval Morriseau, an Ojibwe shaman and artist, tells a story that reflects the lived reality of personal causality in his world.

> Where did the white man get his electric power from—the thunderbirds? This is a general belief among the Ojibwe. "At one time", said this same Ojibwe elder, "I went west and came upon some white men making a golden serpent that was hollow inside. About an hour after the serpent was put out in the prairies, thunderclouds were seen to come over in its direction. This snake was made so that the thunderbirds would be attracted to it and have some lightning caught inside the hol-

low part." When the thunderbirds saw the serpent they dropped from the heavens showers of lightning. Some of it got caught inside the hollow part and when there was enough the white man took the lightning and made it into electric power (1977, 5-6).

It has been suggested that the harshness of the threatening sub-arctic environment and the loneliness of the long winter months led the Ojibwe to develop a dependence upon other-than-human persons. Since fellow humans were frequently both weak and in competition for food, the traditional Ojibwe was "told to seek a patron and companion among supernatural beings" (Landes 1938, 19). Further, this patron manitou was to be found among a host of other manitouk who might kill humans if they had the chance. Bebon might freeze them, Mishebeshu might drown them, the *windigo* might eat them, the ogimaa of the deer and moose might keep their charges from reach, and even the Thunderers, usually protective entities, might strike their homes with bolts of lightning. I mention these things in part because it would be wrong to give the impression that the Anishnaabe cosmos was or is some kind of enchanted fairyland. While it is an en-souled reality, not all souls are good, not all persons are to be trusted.

Today we find that the natural caution of the Ojibwe people is frequently translated into a suspicious attitude that sometimes serves to poison relationships. Freed to a large degree from fears related to the natural environment, Ojibwe people constantly project their personal anxieties onto others. They fear bearwalkers, blaming them for illness, accident, and even bad luck. I was told more than once that successful members of the community must always be careful lest they open themselves to the envy of a sorcerer. And while bearwalkers do sometimes pursue people, the charges seem to be made somewhat indiscriminately. Simple gossip on the island was often tinged with threats or perceived threats, and alliances and feuds among families were common.

In a strange way, I, as an outsider, benefited from this environment. Since I was peripheral to the community I was not generally perceived as threatening. And despite the fact that I am a member of the majority society, which continues to oppress Native people, I was shown great generosity and a surprising amount of trust. My feeling is that I was often used as a kind of sounding board for complaints, accusations, and self-justifications. Possessing neither a vested interest in the drama of the reservation nor any real power, I did not fall into any established camps. In short, I was only a visitor, not a dweller on Manitoulin Island, on the greater island that is the Anishnaabe world.

In summary, the context in which we find the Thunder and Underwater manitouk consists of a multileveled cosmos. The island of the earth, while it has its own meaningful horizontal directions, must always be understood as one layer in a hierarchical system. Manitouk who dwell on, above, and below the island travel frequently and necessarily affect human life. The manitouk, met in dream or vision and remembered in myth, are persons with all the attributes of human beings: they have wills, they can move and speak, they respond to entreaty but also act according to their own needs and wants. Like humans manitouk may be nurturing or threatening and should be treated with both respect and caution. Unlike most humans they always have great power and so can metamorphose at will. Therefore nothing in the sensible world should be taken at face value, for manitouk are recognized not by their appearances but by their behavior. Likewise, objects and human beings are suspect and must be watched for signs of unusual power or even malevolence. If one "lives well" (bimadiziiwin) this world has its rewards, but nothing can totally guarantee success in a life-world where a multitude of conflicting wills are constantly at work. It is, therefore, incumbent upon humans to form respectful and reciprocal relationships with powerful persons for it *is* guaranteed that no one can live well all alone.

In the next two chapters we will analyze how the Thunder and Underwater manitouk exist and operate in the scheme described. We will examine their names and forms, observe their behavior in the natural world, meet them in myths and in reports of dreams, and listen to their voices in all these spheres. In short, we will attempt to understand just what sort of "people" they are.

NOTES

1. The conjuring shaman "is usually a male diviner who 'reveals hidden truths' while in communication with the manitou in a shaking tent" (Grim 1983, 65). Here Grim is following W. J. Hoff-

man, who included mention of the *jessakid* or *Tsisaki* shaman in his large study of the midewiwin (1891, 157-58).

The conjuring lodge or shaking tent was constructed of birch bark and/or canvas wrapped around poles joined at the top. The jessakid went into the tent alone and called upon various manitouk, whose visits caused the structure to shake. Subsequently, observers could hear the voices of these visitors as they conversed or sang with the shaman. The shaman sought their help in locating lost people or items as well in prognostication.

While the practice is now quite rare, it was most common until the early part of this century. For nineteenth-century occurrences see Brown and Brightman (1988). For the most thorough study in the twentieth century see Hallowell (1942).

2. For his most concise and lucid statement on the personalistic nature of the Ojibwe world see Hallowell (1975).

3. "For example, /*mistikw*/ (animate) meaning live tree or live wood, is distinguished from /mistikw/ (inanimate) meaning dry pole or dry wood. In practice these distinctions are not always clear and one speaker may refer to a pole in the animate while another will refer to it as inanimate. /Asiniy/ (stone) is another word where the gender distinguishes two alike entities, live and dead stones. In this case, the gender of the stone is less easy to specify by observable traits. For both words, /asiniy/ and /mistikw/, there are many instances where two speakers will refer to the same referent as though it had a different gender" (Craik 1982, 29-30).

4. For a full text of this tale see W. Jones (1919, 207-40).

5. We should note that while women, as well as men, could and did embark on vision quests, it was not *required* of women and was less frequent among them. The belief was—and is—that women are already "complete" humans because they have the power to give life.

6. The traditional Ojibwe understanding of the soul is a structural intuition in which the self is experienced as being constituted by three parts: the body, the ego-soul (the part that leaves the body upon death), and the free or shadow-soul (the dream or traveling part).

III

THUNDERERS

"We saw a Thunderbird a few summers ago.
Ho! A huge bird it was—a lot bigger than the planes that you
see go by today. Many of the people at Shoal Lake saw it go by.
It didn't flap its wings, not even once. It was white on
the underside and black on the top. Ho! A big, big bird.
There were some great big thunderclouds making up a storm
and out of the clouds came this great bird."
—James Redsky (Esquekesik),
Great Leader of the Ojibway:
Mis-quona-queb, 1972

From late spring until the first snows of winter thunderstorms regularly roam the Northern Great Lakes. They travel roughly west to east, usually in large groups at the head of a passing cold front. Less frequently they pop up singly during the course of a hot spell, expend some of their energy, and move on across the water. Their season here is circumscribed by a winter that normally loosens its grip in May only to return by October. Like the flora of this area, the storms bloom for an exceptionally short growing season. And like the animals and humans of the Ojibwe life-world, they travel the earth as organic entities in their own distinct forms.[1]

While thunderstorms are no more frequent or violent in the Great Lakes than in many other parts of North America, the Anishnaabeg maintain the belief that storms visit them more often than they do anyone else. While collecting tales among the Chippewa of northern Michigan, Richard Dorson engaged in an unfortunate conversation with a native storyteller, John Sogwin. It seems that when Sogwin asked Dorson if they had thunderstorms in South America Dorson answered at length in the affirmative. His answer served to silence Sogwin.

> On the way back to his camp Oscar explained that I had cut John off short on the point of a real storytelling streak...If John's question had produced the proper flat denial, he would have gone on to say that thunderstorms occurred only around the Great Lakes, where the thunder gods had taken the Chippewa under their especial protection. Then he would have given illustrative stories. But I had spiked his guns. I was heartbroken (Dorson 1952, 20).

The point here is that Sogwin was not so much insisting upon a claim regarding the occurrence of storms in his world as attempting to establish the special nature of the Anishnaabe *experience* of these storms. Thunderstorms don't just happen in this life-world; they signal the arrival of powerful people, Thunderers or Thunderbirds, who have a relationship with human beings. The Thunderers, possessing wills like all people, intentionally follow a path which allows them to overfly and so oversee the island of the Anishnaabeg. As Sam Oswamick told me, "That's why the Indians believe there are Thunder spirits. They help people, you know, looking all over, seeing everything's going on all right. That's why they travel around." As they look below them, the Thunderers sound their voices, not merely for show but in order to communicate with human beings. And while Thunder may well speak elsewhere, it doesn't speak Ojibwe.

It should be noted, however, that claims of exclusivity regarding the Ojibwe experience of Thunderbirds require some qualification within the matrix of North American Indian beliefs. Thunderbird beliefs are widespread and are especially prominent among the near neighbors of the Ojibwe, the Sioux. The Ojibwe do not reject the beliefs of other tribes; to the contrary, and especially with the rise of Pan-Indianism, they both accept and respect the observations of these groups. Just as Indian people share a fundamental kinship with one another, so too the Thunder beings of North America are related. Yet the distinct tribal identity of each group is also held by its Thunderbirds.

The *wakinyan* of the Sioux are not identical to the *animikeek* of

[handwritten marginal note: Thunderbirds oversee the island]

the Ojibwe despite the fact that they are also said to cause the storms and hunt the water monster (Sioux *unktegila*). The wakinyan are reported to have once been giants on the earth whose spirits, upon their death, were changed to Thunderbirds (Fire and Erdoes 1972, 238). Or alternately, they are the descendants of Wakinyan/Heyoka, the dual destroyer and restorer Thunder being (Dooling 1984). The Ojibwe Thunderers have no such origins or lineage and, most importantly, no relationship with the heyokas or clowns that are so prominent among the Sioux (Black Elk and Nierhardt 1932, 192). There are no ritual clowns among the Ojibwe, only people who mirror the behavior of Nanabush in their everyday lives.

Undeniably wakinyan and animikeek have a recognizably similar structure. Both entities are responsible for thunderstorms, both appear as gigantic, frequently eagle-like birds, and both enjoy positions of power and prestige within their respective worlds. But as particular instantiations of religious patterns they are not interchangeable. In any comparison one must be careful not to mistake an alignment for an equation, and while this particular study might possibly serve as a first step toward or a component of a larger discussion of North American Thunderbird beliefs, we must be careful not to wander from one life-world into another. In this life-world, on this island, it is the Anishnaabe Thunderers who act and speak from out of the storm.

In order to meet these Thunder beings, or Thunderbirds, we must learn how to call them, we must understand their names. While animikeek is the most common and inclusive name given to the Thunder manitouk, they are also known as pinesiwak, pawaganak, and atisokanak, depending upon both the area and the circumstances. In the Ojibwe life-world one's name is no arbitrary moniker. Among the traditional Ojibwe, names were given to children by relatives or tribal elders who had *dreamed* the name. This name had tremendous spiritual significance for its holder inasmuch as it partook of the power realm of dreams and signaled a close relationship between child and namesake (Hilger 1951, 35-39). While each person might collect a number of names and nicknames over the course of her life, only the birth name described above and a name received during the course of a vision quest "truly identified the essential person and were usually kept secret, hidden for the same reason that other extensions of the person received protection" (Vecsey 1983, 61). On Manitoulin I encountered only a few people who revealed non-English names to me. These names were, however, nicknames or honorific titles. Raymond Armstrong was, for instance, named *Ginozhe* (large fish or pike) as a youth because he was such a strong rower in the fishing boat. He was also given the title *Nigankwam* (first thunder) by an Alcoholics Anonymous group because he had shown leadership. Leland Bell had the Ojibwe name *Bebaminojmat* (storyteller) because he is quite articulate and humorous. I will not assume, however, that dream or vision names no longer exist on Manitoulin, for if they do, it is not likely that they would have been shared with me.

We have observed how the traditional proscription against telling stories in the summer months was founded upon the belief that in articulating the names of the manitouk one was actually conjuring them. The name partakes of the essence of that which it names, for it is not a sign, but a symbol. Thus the various names may all tell us something about the nature of these manitouk: how they appear, how they act, and how they relate to human beings. By analyzing their names we are, in effect, analyzing these symbols through their own symbolic forms.

This method is not really as oblique as it may sound. Ricoeur has said that it is in language that one discovers an entry into the labyrinthine complex of multivalent symbolism. While the symbols reach far beneath the semantic level, they remain opaque as long as they remain unarticulated. To speak the symbol, especially in the narrative structure of the myth, is to crack a door to "the shadowy experience of power" (Ricoeur 1976, 69), to begin to make intelligible that which is apprehended in immediate experience and that which resides in our memories and our dreams. In speaking the names of the Thunder manitouk we not only make them present, then, we begin to interpret them as animikeek (Thunderers), pinesiwak (birds), pawaganak (dream visitors), and atisokanak (grandfathers or tales of the grandfathers). This is a first step into the world that the symbols present and the world in which they reside. As Samuel Makidemawabe said, "To say the name is to begin the story" (Norman 1982, 49).

ANIMIKEEK

The most common and comprehensive name given to the Thunder manitouk is animikeek, the plural form of animiki, (*nimkii* on

Manitoulin), meaning "Thunders, Thunderers or Thunderbirds." If one wishes to say that there is an electrical storm in progress, one uses the verb form of the name, *animikika* or *nimkiigog*: "it is thundering, there is thunder, there are Thunderers or Thunderbirds." There is also a word in Ojibwe for lightning, *wassmowin*, derived from *waskoneg* (to give off light) but it is almost never used to describe a storm.[2] This is because wassmowin names only a piece of the thunderstorm, a product or effect of the animikeek. In describing the manitou patrons of shamans, Ruth Landes says, for example, that "sometimes Thunder's associate was Lightning, though natural lightning was considered a function of Thunder's activity" (Landes 1968, 48).

While the relationship between animikeek and wassmowin appears to reverse the cause and effect sequence that is readily observable during an electrical storm, the reversal is not unusual. In English we usually speak of thunderstorms, not lightning storms, even though we know full well that the thunder is but an echo of the electrical charge that precedes it. Knowing scientifically that lightning is the active member of the team does not seem to affect the way in which we describe the natural phenomenon that is a storm. What is most interesting about the relationship between animikeek and wassmowin is the fact that the Ojibwe language gives a different ontological status to each. Animikeek is an animate noun, wassmowin is inanimate; i.e., Thunders are persons in the Ojibwe cosmos, lightning is not. Further, the word animikeek has something of a *double* status in that it names both the storm and the maker of the storm. Animikeek are often said to cause the sound of thunder by moving their huge wings and the flash of lightning by opening and closing their eyes. Alternately they produce the thunder when they speak, the lightning when they hurl bolts and/or stones to the ground. We will explore these acts of the animikeek in due course. For the moment, however, we concentrate upon what it means to say that thunder, the creative force of sound, both rules and defines the storm.

For the Ojibwe, the thunderstorm is not just an auditory phenomenon, it is the act of a manitou person: it is a speech event. Whether the thunder is caused by the Thunderbird's wings or by his mouth is relatively unimportant. What matters is that the storm is experienced as a communication from manitou to human being. Hallowell recalls an experience of such a speech event.

An informant told me that many years before he was sitting in
a tent one summer afternoon during a storm, together with an
old man and his wife. There was one clap of thunder after another. Suddenly the old man turned to his wife and asked,
"Did you hear what was said?" "No," she replied, "I didn't
catch it." My informant, an acculturated Indian, told me he
did not at first know what the old man and his wife referred to.
It was, of course, the thunder. The old man thought that one of
the Thunder Birds had said something to him. He was reacting
to this sound in the same way as he would respond to a human
being, whose words he did not understand (Hallowell 1975,
158).

While the speech of animikeek is not always clear it is intelligible, or at
the very least potentially intelligible. And humans may exhibit their
own powers by their ability to translate what is said. This was certainly
the case with the traditional jessakid or conjuring shaman. While the
manitouk who visited the shaking tent of the conjurer sometimes spoke
in ways that were understandable to observers outside the tent, often
they conversed in unknown languages or with a volume that was too
low for observers to catch (Brown and Brightman 1988, 147, 153-54). It
was the responsibility of the jessakid to translate in such circumstances. Interestingly enough his powers of prophecy, conjuring, and
translation were said to be a gift bestowed upon him by the animikeek
(Hoffman 1891, 157).

I did not meet any Ojibwes on Manitoulin who claimed to understand what the animikeek said during the course of a storm, but most
agreed that something, usually a warning of some kind, was communi-
cated by the Thunder. Since the animikeek are hunters in search of underground or Underwater manitouk, Thunder tells humans, who are
not the objects of the hunt, to head for cover lest they be struck by
stray shots. These stray shots are normally the misdirected work of
young Thunderers, who we will discuss later in this chapter. I would
add, however, that I was told that lightning does not strike Indians—
only white people. This statement reflects both the special relationship
which Anishnaabeg hold with the Thunderers and a certain amount of
anger which is, understandably, directed at whites. A Fox Indian related the following to William Jones.

The Thunderers are kept busy with watching over us . . . They grow angry at the sight of the wrong done to us. With great effort they restrain themselves when they behold the people driven to an extremity, when they behold the people enduring wrongs beyond all endurance. Naturally there must be an end of this thing; it will be on a day yet to come. The Thunder manitous will no longer withhold their patience. In that day they will crack open this earth and blow it to pieces. Where the white man will be hurled, no one knows and no one cares. After this, the manitou will then create this world anew, and put the people back into it to live again. In that day they will no longer be pestered with the white man (W. Jones 1911, 213-14).

People do not normally engage in a dialogue with the animikeek, except of course when they meet them as pawaganak or dream visitors. Instead contemporary Anishnaabeg, like their ancestors, continue to make offerings of tobacco to the Thunderers as a sign of respect and as a form of entreaty. Virtually every Ojibwe with whom I spoke was familiar with this practice, first recorded by Allouez in 1667 (Thwaites, ed. 1896-1901, 50:287) and most engaged in it themselves. Basil Johnston (1982, 33-36) relates a traditional tale of some men who foolishly approached the very nest of the Thunderbirds without a tobacco offering: "Voices could be heard chanting above the mountain's rumblings. 'Who dares without tobacco? Who dares without offering? Tobacco will allay our anger. Tobacco will clear the cloud.' " One young man who did not turn back fell to his death and the Thunderers left the place until Anishnaabeg remembered to make appropriate offerings.

Normally tobacco is placed directly in the fire of a wood stove or burned on top of the oven or in an ashtray or smudge pot reserved for this use. But the formality and even form of the ritual varies with the individual. Steve McGraw told me of his mother's rather unusual and casual practice, which he witnessed as a child. Whenever a storm would come by, especially at night, she would sit up and smoke cigarettes, always lighting one first for the Thunderers and placing it in the ashtray as an offering. Raymond Armstrong contended that this sort of offering was really no good at all as it did not show proper respect for the animikeek.

Armstrong instructed me in the details of tobacco offerings when I expressed some uneasiness about thunderstorms. While on Manitoulin I lived in an old two-story farmhouse near Lake Manitou that sat in the middle of a field. Often the storms that seemed to travel along the lakeshore would shake the house severely, and since it was the tallest structure in the vicinity it was not entirely unlikely that my house could be struck by lightning. I told Armstrong that this vulnerable position sometimes made me a bit nervous. He said I shouldn't worry, but told me that as soon as I "heard them [the animikeek] coming" I should get some tobacco and put it in the wood stove. A handful was a good amount, he said, and he, like many other people, kept a special pouch of tobacco for this purpose. If I had no loose tobacco it was all right to use one of my cigarettes, but I had to open a new pack and remove the tobacco from the paper before burning it. Then I should ask the Thunderers to move on and not stop over my house. If they showed signs of stopping I should burn more tobacco and ask again. It was also not a bad idea, Armstrong advised, to bury some tobacco in the yard for extra insurance. He had some buried in his own garden, partly to prevent lightning strikes and partly to attract the attention of eagles, whose presence was essential to his family's well being.

Sam Oswamick also related a story of a woman who buried tobacco for the Thunderers.

> I know one lady told me a little story. Her grandmother used to put tobacco in the garden in the ground when the thunder comes. She would put tobacco in there and cover it up. That's it. And this time she forgot so the Thunders stop right there. They were there. They didn't move. So she remembered that. So she got this little girl to put tobacco there. So that little girl ran up there and put tobacco in there and come back. And they heard the thunder crack, the lightning just came up there, you know, and away, they're gone. I heard that it was a pretty old lady, the one that did that. That's the one that told me. It's a true story.

The burning or burying of tobacco should not be understood as purely preventative medicine, however. When one burns tobacco for any reason one exhibits respect, as tobacco is not only prized but, along with cedar, sage, and sweetgrass, is considered a sacred plant. In all traditional ceremonies, tobacco, sage, sweetgrass, and cedar are placed on the central fire. Meeting lodges are frequently roofed with cedar boughs and sweetgrass is used in a preliminary purification ritual. Cedar is also a purifying plant, and both Angus Pontiac and Sam Oswamick told me of the traditional practice wherein a dreamer who had dreamt of unwanted manitouk (Underwater creatures, for example) would have his tongue scraped with a cedar knife to rid him of the dream. The traditional offering of tobacco to an elder is still appropriate, and I made a practice of giving gifts of cigarettes or chewing tobacco to consultants. When Leland Bell planned to end a lecture I had arranged with a tobacco offering, he told me that I should buy the tobacco and hand it to him before the ritual. If he had not received it as a gift, the ritual would not be efficacious, he explained, and would be perceived as "just play-acting."

When tobacco smoke rises one's words may rise with it. But unless one has the proper frame of mind, the proper attitude, the ritual is useless and no communication takes place. No Ojibwe person ever told me that she feared the Thunderers but all told me that they respected them.

> My dad used to tell me that as soon as you get a storm in the spring, put tobacco in the fire and talk to them. Whatever you want to happen, just say that. That's what he used to tell me. They'll strike you if you don't respect them. I heard a story; I wonder if it's true or not. One of them said something about a thunderstorm. So he went outside and that lightning came around like this, around his head. That's what happened (Sam Oswamick, Personal Communication, 1988).

While many Ojibwes with whom I spoke were quite obviously aware of and accepted scientific explanations for storms, they continued to experience them as essentially personal phenomena, as animikeek. The animikeek are real to them because their experience of the storm is the experience of a 'noema,' i.e., the intentionality of Anishnaabeg consciousness constitutes the storm experience as a meaningful object,[3] or in this particular case, a meaningful subject. It is not that traditional Ojibwe people anthropomorphized the natural world; they did not somehow artificially *attach* meaning to their experience. The meaning was already there, inextricable from the experi-

ence. And contemporary Anishnaabeg, brought up with the experience of animikeek, would have to self-consciously extract this meaning,
re-figure the experience—in a sense kill the Thunderbirds—before
they could stop hearing their voices. One of the ways in which white
people are said to have developed electricity is through such a murder,
an extraction of the energy of the storm from the Thunder manitouk:
"The Ojibway elder also said that one time the white men took off for
the thunderclouds on a plane and when they got up there they shot at
the thunderbirds, took only the heads, put them in huge pots and the
juice of the heads was turned into electric power" (Morriseau 1965, 6).

We have discussed the pre-eminence of sound in the Ojibwe experience of Thunderstorms as animikeek, how that sound is understood as speech, and some ways in which humans can respond to that
speech. It is important to note here that I have used the plural form,
animikeek, almost exclusively because in each storm one usually experiences the visits of several Thunderers. Animikeek rarely travel alone,
and when one listens to a storm one can hear that each Thunderer has a
different voice. Accordingly, they are sometimes given names that are
descriptive of the sounds which they make (their modes of speech) or
the way in which they seem to move. Diamond Jenness gives the most
complete roster of animikeek, twelve in number (1935, 35). Jenness
understands these animikeek to be "invisible thunders," fundamentally different from Thunderbirds. I believe he is mistaken in this opinion, obviously confused by the fluidity of Thunder forms. As he says
himself, "Strangely enough, alongside of this belief in invisible thunders, the Parry Islanders possess the totally different concept of a thunderbird; and the same Indians will subscribe to both notions without
remarking any contradiction" (37). In other words, if you ask an
Ojibwe, "Is the Thunder the storm, or is it a bird? Can we see the
Thunderers or are they invisible?" he is likely to reply, "Yes, yes, yes,
and yes," for the various appearances of Thunderers are elaborations
rather than contradictions.

My language tutor, Raymond Armstrong, was familiar with eight
of Jenness's names, all of which, he told me, were old words seldom
used today. Armstrong agreed generally with Jenness's translation, offering the following interpretations:

1. *ninamidabines*—The chief or boss of the Thunders who sits
    quietly above, "like an overseer."

2.   nigankwam—First Thunder. This name was given to Armstrong at an AA conference as a sign of his leadership.
3.   *beskinekkwam*—Thunder that's going to hit.
4.   *anjibnes*—Jenness calls this "the renewer of power." Armstrong saw it as the "transformer or changer" (from *andji*, meaning "change").
5.   *besreudang*—The echoer.
6.   *bodreudang*—Approaching Thunder.
7.   *bebomawidang*—Searching Thunders, Thunders which seem to advance and retreat.
8.   *zaubikkwang*—The rainbow which appears after a storm.

Armstrong did not think this last one could properly be called a Thunderer. He said that the rainbow was always born from a rock immersed in a lake. This conception and its connection with thunder was a bit unclear. Possibly the presumed rock was one that had been struck by lightning.

These names help to illustrate both the attention that traditional Ojibwe people gave to the Thunderstorms and the precision with which they recorded their experiences in language. It is a mistaken notion to assume that an experience of the world as "peopled" is a product of a consciousness which is unable to differentiate itself from its environment. The Anishnaabe life-world is undifferentiated only to the extent that humans are not understood to stand radically outside of the natural world. They stand within a world of interconnecting relationships, a cosmos populated by a variety of personalities who sometimes cooperate and sometimes engage in conflict. The experience of thunder involves the careful observation of the behavior of people who are different from ourselves and who, within their own society, exhibit various personalities. To say that we are all people is not anything like saying we are all the same.

PINESIWAK

While animikeek is the name that encompasses all the personalities of the Thunderers there are, as I mentioned earlier, still other names given to these "people" as a group. The first of these, pinesiwak, is most often used among the Northern Ojibwe and the Cree (Brown and Brightman 1988; Hallowell 1975; Ray and Stevens 1984; Rogers 1962).

But everywhere the word or its variations (*pinesak, binaysihwuk, bineshik, bneshiinhak, binesheehnuk*) is translated as *birds*. Hallowell describes the 'empirical' alignments of bird and storm that are expressed in the symbolic reality of the Thunderbird.

Thunder as birds

> The belief that Thunder and Lightning are the manifestations of a huge hawk-like bird (pinesi) may at first seem a preposterous idea, without the slightest empirical evidence in its favor. But consider the following facts. In April, when pinesi first appears, it inevitably comes from the south. This is likewise the month when the birds begin to arrive from the same direction. In the fall, thunderstorms move towards the south at the same time that the birds begin to disappear in this direction, following the Milky Way which stretches across the heavens almost north and south and called the "summer birds' trail." And these birds, like pinesi, have disappeared by the end of October, are absent all winter, and only reappear the following spring.
>
> Here we have a perfectly rational inference made from the common observation of concomitant phenomena—summer birds and thunderstorms. They are not independent variables. They always occur together. Therefore, they are somehow related (Hallowell 1934, 394-95).

This analysis of the origins of Thunderbird beliefs runs the risk of reducing the symbol to its purely etiological function and by extension casting religion in the role of a kind of pseudo-science. Hallowell is himself quick to note that such 'empirical' evidence is but a piece of a complex belief system that lends validity to the experience of the Thunderbirds. Yet it is not unfair or inaccurate to say that the avian character of Thunder manitouk is strongly indicated by their behavior patterns. In addition to sharing similar seasonal migratory tracks, Thunderers, like birds of prey, travel through the sky on currents of air, striking the earth in search of food. Further, the traditional Ojibwe believed that songbirds predict the arrival of their huge and powerful cousins through their own restless behavior before a storm (Coleman, Frogner, and Eich 1962, 105). And when a thunderstorm appears especially violent, some people say that it is because the Thunderbirds are flying too low. James Redsky says that when this happened, his father would shoot at the sky.

I saw my dad do this one time. He got the muzzle loader and
fired into the air to scare them up. Boy! It was lightning and
raining. Coming down! Coming down! They were so low you
could almost hear their wings flapping; they were too low. No!
Nothing. It did not work. So he said, "I'll try shooting up again
a little later." Then he loaded up his gun the second time and
shot it into the air again. You know the storm died right away;
it went off into the east. (Redsky 1972, 111).

I was also told that if one looks closely at thunderheads one can see the
wings and the head of the pinesiwak (Angus Pontiac, Personal Communication, 1988).

The Thunderbird is frequently depicted as an eagle or eagle-like
bird and along with Mishebeshu frequently appeared as a motif on
traditional bags and pouches—especially medicine pouches. Some
contemporary artists and crafts people continue to represent the Thunderbird in this stylized and static form while others, like the artists
Francis Kagige, Randy Trudeau, and James Simon Mishibinijima, in-
fuse their images with the strength and majesty they observe in the
eagles that fly over their homes (Southcott 1984). When I asked the
Elder, William Trudeau, if he thought these images were accurate, he
said that they were, so far as he knew, having never seen a Thunderbird himself. He was, of course, drawing upon images he had perceived through myths, images which sometimes paint the Thunderbird
as a kind of Thunderbird/man. "It looked something like a bird and
it looked something like a man in places, like his legs, you know, and
part of his body, but the face is something like a bird's face with a
beak and wings on the sides" (William Trudeau, Personal Communication, 1988).

Carl Ray has painted this sort of Thunderbird person occasionally
as has Tim Restoule, yet in both of these cases the figure is actually that
of a human-like person with wings, quite like an angel (see Ray and
Stevens 1984, 87-88, and Southcott 1984, plate 14). This image of the
Thunderer as an angel-like creature was most prevalent among the
Passamaquoddy, an Algonquian tribe of the northeast United States
(Leland 1884, 259-67). These Thunderers are described as "very like
human beings; They used bows and arrows and had wings. But these
wings can be laid aside, and kept for use. And from time to time their
chief gives these Thunders orders to put them on and tells them where

Menomini Nettle Bags with Thunderbird
and Mishebeshu Motifs
Public domain artifacts
From *Patterns of Power*
Reproduction courtesy of The McMichael Canadian Collection

Thunderbird Quillbox
Annie Pangowish
From the author's collection
Photo by Fred Maize

to go" (263). Like Jenness, who appears to have been stymied by the variety of thunder forms among the Ojibwe, Leland maintains that these Thunder men cannot be the "same" as the Thunderbirds. And for reasons which he fails to make clear, Leland asserts that the Thunder men tales are of Eskimo origin (265).

The variation in these depictions causes no controversy, in part because of the generally non-dogmatic nature of Ojibwe religion, and also because of the tendency toward metamorphosis which was discussed in the previous chapter. Consultants were firm on the point, however, that while the eagle and Thunderbird may well resemble one another, the former may only serve as a sign for the latter. Some eagles may indeed be manitouk (often messengers of Kitche Manitou) but they do not cause the storms. Angus Pontiac summarized the prevailing attitude toward artistic representations of the Thunderbirds. He sees the art as a kind of myth-making, an ongoing process rather than a record of codified beliefs: "The artists are great story-tellers. If you can only understand the pictures that they draw, it means a lot. I'm not an artist. I speak what I know and that is where it ends."

The Thunder manitouk as pinesiwak or Thunderbirds are closely associated with the winds. While Vecsey understands the four winds and the Thunderbirds to be entirely different entities (1983, 73, 75) other sources record that they were one and the same (Coleman 1937, 37-38; Coleman, Frogner, and Eich 1962, 102; Howard, 1965, 92). I would tend to agree with Vecsey, for while Winds or Directions and Thunders are related, they each have their own discrete mythologies. The Winds or Directions are said to be the guardians of the four corners. They are named clockwise from the East: Waubun, Zeegwun, Ningobianong, and Bebon (Johnston 1976, 161-63). Nanabush is said to have placed these guardians at their posts (Chamberlain 1891, 206-7). Thunderbirds may well act as messengers of the Winds, but this is not their primary function and the formal separation of Winds and Thunderers is an interpretation that is in keeping with both traditional and current directional orientations among the Ojibwe. For while the Thunderbirds are sometimes said to ride the wind from different directions, their home is generally found in the west.[4] I would add that these questions regarding the identity of Winds and Thunders serve to further illustrate the interconnected and fluid nature of the Ojibwe world and of symbol systems generally. In this particular mythic world, a world full of traveling and metamorphosing persons, it is especially difficult to delineate clearly the parameters of symbols.

Naturally enough, given their existence as pinesiwak, the Thunder manitouk are believed to live in huge nests, usually built upon large inaccessible mountains: "The Ojebways believed that the home of the Thunder-bird was on the top of a high mountain in the West where it lays its eggs and hatches its young like an eagle" (P. Jones 1861, 86). One such place is Mt. McKay, a butte just to the west of Thunder Bay, Ontario. This forested mountain is crowned by a flat top supported by sheer rock cliffs, and while local Ojibwes regularly hold powwows under its shadow, few attempt to scale the cliffs to its sum-

Mt. McKay, Ontario
Photo by the author

mit. It is considered a sacred place and, especially when clouds obscure its top, people still consider the Thunderbirds to be in residence
there. Jones also makes special mention of the La Cloche Mountains
just to the north of Manitoulin, which are currently referred to as the
pathway of the animikeek. This is because thunder seems to sound
loudest when it crosses these quartzite mountains. "It is on these
mountains the poor superstitious [sic] Indians say the thunder-gods, or
eagles, have their abode, and hatch their young" (43). Such mountains
appear to be appropriate places for Thunderbirds to live, and the observation of eagle nests in these places reinforces the idea.

However, naturalistic explanations are, again, merely one layer
of the multileveled body of "evidence" that supports Thunderbird beliefs. The deeper levels are to be found when we call the Thunder
manitouk by their other names: atisokanak and pawaganak. One may
observe and even hear the manitouk in the storm but only in myth and

dream do they display the full power of their personalities, for only in these arenas are they met face to face.

ATISOKANAK *(grandfather myths)*

The adsookaaneg (Manitoulin dialect) or atisokanak (Saulteux dialect) alternately served as the legitimating structure for symbols realized in dreams and were expanded and elaborated upon by the personal experience of dream contacts. Hallowell maintains that the myths were not understood as a corpus of narratives but as the retelling of the acts of the manitouk. This retelling among traditional Ojibwes became a kind of reenactment, a ritual circumscribed by seasonal proscriptions, and in practice constituted an "invocation" of the manitouk. According to Hallowell, atisokanak should not be translated simply as myths or stories:

> A striking fact furnishes a direct linguistic cue to the attitude of the Ojibwa toward these personages. When they use the term atiso'kanak, they are not referring to what I have called a "body of narratives." The term refers to what we would call the characters in these stories; to the Ojibwa they are living persons of an other-than-human class. As William Jones said many years ago, "Myths are thought of as conscious beings, with powers of thought and action." A synonym for this class of persons is "our grandfathers" (1975, 150).

Given this interpretation of atisokanak, the story is simply the form or outer shell of the personal structure of the myth, that stage upon which manitouk, pawaganak, atisokanak, act. In this context we can accept Hallowell's alignment of atisokanak and grandfathers, especially inasmuch as we know that words themselves have life in this world, and animate nouns appear to exist not as linguistic objects but as subjects. Just as animikeek are the Thunder and make the Thunder, so too atisokanak, because they speak the grandfathers, are the grandfathers.

Thunderers as atisokanak and pawaganak present us with a detailed picture of their attributes, behavior, and society. In myth and dream their relationship with Anishnaabeg is characterized by three patterns: (1) humans go to meet them; (2) they come to meet humans;

and (3) in the closest interactions of all humans marry and/or are transformed into Thunderbirds. William Trudeau told me a story of the first
kind of meeting, one in which ten humans took the initiative to visit
the Thunderers. This tale of the atisokanak is told frequently and in a
number of forms, sometimes being recounted as a recent event, but
more often as a journey taken long ago (Copway 1850, 109-13; Dorson
1952, 39; Jenness 1935, 37; P. Jones 1861, 86; W. Jones 1919, 191-95;
H. Smith 1906, 219-20). While details differ, a few themes appear to
recur. First, the humans normally begin their trip on account of curiosity: "They had a notion to go up and see the people who were making
all that noise in the sky" (Trudeau, Personal Communication). "A long
time ago the Indians decided to find out who was making that big noise
and light up in the sky" (Dorson). "Now, once two youths said: 'Come,
let us fast, that we may see what it is like at yonder place where the
sound is heard!' " (W. Jones). Almost invariably the expedition is pre-
ceded, as W. Jones' version notes above, by a vision or dream. It is this
dream that not only provides the impetus to resolve curiosity but gives
the seekers their map to the Thunderers' home.

> Upon arrival, the humans frequently discover a nest: "After
> fasting, and offering my devotions to the thunder, I with much
> difficulty ascended the mountain, the top of which reached to
> the clouds. To my great astonishment, as I looked I saw the
> thunder's nest, where a brood of young thunders had been
> hatched and reared. I saw all sorts of curious bones of ser-
> pents, on the flesh of which the old thunders had been feeding
> their young; and the bark of the young cedar trees pealed [sic]
> and stripped, on which the young thunders had been trying
> their skill in shooting their arrows before going abroad to hunt
> serpents" (P. Jones 1861, 86).

As we can see—or I should say hear—the nest of the Thunderbirds
tells us something about their behavior and social structure. We understand that they eat serpents and that they exist in family groups.
William Trudeau added that they had friends as well as relatives who
ate with them, a communal pattern which they shared with humans.
But perhaps most interesting is the existence and character of the
young Thunderers, immature manitouk who must learn the skills of
their elders.

While the mature Thunderers, those who are properly understood as atisokanak, protect Anishnaabeg from underground and
Underwater manitouk with their lightning strikes, the immature members of this group are often both foolish and dangerous. They have not
perfected either their flight or their strikes and sometimes their behavior is rather pitiable.

> On the reservations at Fond du Lac and White Earth, we were
> told the story of the young thunderbird who struck the side of
> a hill and broke his wing. He was then caught between the
> precipices. When he tried to free himself, he kept on striking
> against the rocks, and he repeatedly broke his wing as he did
> so. This explains the continuous flash of heat lightning (Cole-
> man, Frogner, and Eich 1962, 102).

More often, and unfortunately so for humans, the young Thunderers
wreak havoc with their wild shots and generally unruly behavior.

> In the moon of berries, when the young thunderbirds go by,
> they cause destruction because they don't know any better.
> They are like children and this is the fault of the young birds,
> not the parents. When they go by in August and September,
> they are pretty rough on the Ojibways. They knock down trees
> with lightning from their beaks. Houses are struck and
> smashed also. The older thunderbirds try to correct these fool-
> ish young birds, but they do not learn because they are so
> young (Redsky 1972, 110-11).

This destructive behavior is never understood as malevolent. Sometimes it appears completely unavoidable. In Mel Madahbee's painting
(Chapter 5), for instance, we see the young children of the Thunderbirds hatching from the clouds. As their elders guard them, the cloud
eggs crack open, spewing bolts of lightning toward the lake. Fortu-
nately, in this case, it is Mishebeshu who bears the brunt of the attack.

    With few exceptions, then, the destructive force of the mature
grandfathers is seldom unleashed upon humans without good reason.
Normally travelers to their nest find that they are well received and
transported safely home. In William Trudeau's narration, the Thunderbirds, who see that humans cannot eat the snakes that they relish,
provide venison and moose meat for their visitors. And when it is time
for the humans to leave, the Thunderers transport them:

By the time they [humans] got up most of the other bunch [Thunderers] were gone, except two, so they started to cook something to eat and while they were cooking, that old man came up to them and said to them that he was gonna help them out to get back home although they didn't tell him yesterday that they were going, but he knew. And the old guy says that these two boys that I have over there will take you home. It took 11 days to get here and now if you start real early in the morning you'll get there round about noon today. And they were kind of surprised but they accepted the help.

So when they were ready there was a tree out there close to where they were camping and there was a deerskin [hanging on] a branch to get it dried up. That old guy [Thunderer] went and got that deerskin and he threw that on the fire. After that deerskin was burnt up there was only a little ball about this size, a little black ball and he says "This is the earth, I made it smaller. When you leave here it will only take you til noon to get there even though it took you 11 days to get here." So after they were ready and they told them that they were ready to go, these two guys came up, they just made a circle all holding hands, they never even realized they were up in the air. All of a sudden they could feel that they were standing on solid ground, you know, and I guess their eyes kind of opened up, or maybe they were sleeping, I don't know, but they recognized they were on their own ground. So everything went well when they went to see their grandfathers (Personal Communication, 1988).

There are instances, however, when humans who act in particularly cruel and foolish ways incur the wrath of their grandfathers. In Peter Jones's version of "The Visit to the Thunders," a group of warriors comes upon two nestling Thunderers. They torment the babies with their arrows, ignoring the warnings of one of their companions:

The foolish young men would not listen, but continued to teaze [sic] and finally killed them. As soon as they had done this a black cloud appeared, advancing towards them with great fury. Presently the thunder began to roar and send forth volumes of its fiery indignation. It was too evident that the old thunders were enraged on account of the destruction of their

young—soon, with a tremendous crash, the arrows of the
mighty thunder-god fell on the foolish men and destroyed
them, but the wise and good Indian escaped unhurt (1861,
86-87).

Once again we see the price which one may pay for disrespect in the
face of the power of atisokanak. Basil Johnston warns that the grandfather thunders are angered by neglect (1976, 27) and Andrew Blackbird
offers what he calls a moral commandment: "Thou shalt not mimic or
mock the Thunders of the cloud, for they were specially created to water the earth and to keep down all the evil monsters that are under the
earth, which would eat up and devour the inhabitants of the earth if
they were set at liberty" (Blackbird 1887, 103).

PAWAGANAK

The word pawaganak means dreams or dream visitors and, especially
among the Northern Ojibwe groups, is used somewhat interchange-
ably with manitouk. We have discussed both the power and "reality" of
dreams in the Anishnaabe world and how the formation of a relationship between human and manitou or pawagan, which occurred in
dream vision, was essential to the traditional Ojibwe's identity and survival. But apart from meeting one's special guardian spirit, the dream/
vision world offered one the opportunity to speak with and travel to the
homes of various manitouk. These dreams existed in a dialectical relationship with the myths: legitimating and being legitimated by the
tales of the grandfathers.

While the Thunderers visit Anishnaabeg whenever they pass
over in the storms, as pawaganak or dream visitors they enter most
directly into the life of the individual. When they do so, they bring
gifts of power and/or healing to human beings. Frequently, among the
traditional Ojibwe, this power involved increased skill or luck in hunting. Vecsey maintains that this hunting medicine applied only to birds
(1983, 75), yet John Tanner recorded the following Hunting Chant in
the early nineteenth century: "I can kill any animal because the loud-
speaking Thunder helps me; I can kill any animal" (James, ed., 1956,
359). Or the Thunderbirds might serve as the special guardian to a shaman who had sought this pawagan's attention through a vision quest.

We have already discussed the translation skills which Thunder imparted to the jessakid or conjuring shaman. Norval Morriseau describes a Thunderbird Medicine Society wherein members received a medicine dream, i.e., the ability to create and use sacred medicines. In this instance the medicine involved the use of light blue eggs: "When a Thunderbird medicine-man prepared medicine he would scrape the egg and some of the powder would be placed in a small pail. Sometimes small medicine eggs were used whole in the medicine pots. These were used for curing the sick" (47-48). The exact nature of these eggs—whether they were thought to be the eggs of actual Thunderbirds—is unclear. They do call to mind, however, another medicine object provided by Thunderers, the thunderstone.

Beliefs concerning thunder or rain stones are found in many cultures and these stones are often thought to be meteorites and/or minerals bearing magnetic properties. There is a cigar-shaped fossil called a belemnite which was apparently once thought to be a thunderbolt or stone. And fulgurite, a glassy rock, is a true thunderstone in that it is produced when lightning strikes sand or exposed rock. Mircea Eliade discusses the symbolism of thunderstones, saying that their supposed celestial origin and the belief that they fall during rainstorms leads to their ritual use as "rain-bringers." For the Anishnaabeg, they may serve another function—protecting one against the power of the storm. Eliade's remarks on the power which inheres in such stones are relevant to the Anishnaabe experience, however.

> The power of these stones never originates in themselves; they
> share in a principle or embody a symbol, they express a cosmic
> "sympathy" or betray a heavenly origin. These stones are the
> *signs* of a spiritual reality beyond themselves, or the instru-
> ments of a sacred power of which they are merely containers.
> (1965, 226-27).

For the Anishnaabeg these stones are small spherical objects which the Thunderers hurl to the ground. William Trudeau told me that the stones hit trees and whirl around the trunk, leaving a spiral scar in the bark. If one digs at the roots of such a tree, one may be lucky enough to find the stone. Tanner records a similar belief in which the stone is said to be a small ball of fire. He adds that while he searched for such balls, he never found them (James, ed., 1956, 123-24). Ray-

mond Armstrong was also familiar with this phenomenon and claimed
to know someone who had once owned such a stone. He said that it was
small and heavy and gave its owner "power." Armstrong was not clear
on the nature of this power but it seemed to be a general sense of well-
being. Other sources hold, however, that the thunderstone served primarily to protect one from lightning strikes. Frances Densmore (1929)
reported, for instance, that

> a charm which was believed to cause an approaching thunder-
> storm to recede consisted of a spherical stone. This specimen
> was obtained from Mrs. Razer and had been in her possession
> 14 years, and had been used successfully by her . . . Mrs. Razer
> said that "the thunder bird likes this stone as a hen likes the
> egg she has laid and will not hurt it." She said that if a thunder-
> storm threatened, the proper procedure was to put this stone,
> with a little tobacco, on a birch leaf, anywhere out of doors
> (113).

Diamond Jenness records a particularly interesting variation on
the theme of thunderstones. In his account, Jonas King told him of the
existence of small, weightless balls with which the Thunders or Winds
control the weather. A man who found such a ball received great
power: "he could throw a stone at the trunk of a tree and bury it out of
sight in the wood. Two medicine-man, one a wabeno and the other a
mede, stole it from him at different times, but they could not retain it,
for the ball returned irresistibly to its owner" (1935, 34). In the next
chapter we will see how the Underwater manitouk also provided medicinal rocks to Anishnaabeg, albeit not always as willingly as do the
Thunderers. In their case the stone is a particular mineral—copper
garnered from their own horns.

Another important tangible gift of the pawaganak or Thunders is
the much rarer gift of a feather. Sam Oswamick told me the story of a
dream visit by Thunderers to a man who was ill with tuberculosis. In
this tale the man is rewarded for helping the Thunders to kill the underground monster. Oswamick's words speak best for themselves:

> So one time there's a sick man and he couldn't go with his dad
> to make for shore to camp because he's sick, you know, with
> T.B.—spitting blood. So they left him home. So while he was

there—it was in spring, you know—and a guy came in, and he wanted him to go out with him and help him out. Well, he said he couldn't go anywhere, "I'm sick, that's why I'm here." So he cooks a meal to come out with him. So he finally says, "Alright, I'll go." So he takes his bow and arrow and when they got outside that guy told him, "Step where I step." So he follows that guy and he steps right there and he kind of felt that he was going up in the air. So they walk in the air until they met those other guys, the other young men. And so they start to travel.

Finally they got to the place where that big monster is. He lives in the sand, you know. And that monster he's doing something bad—he kills people that pass there. So when those thunders and lightning hit that monster, the earth opens up like this and it comes back again, because it's sand, you know. So they couldn't get him. So when the earth opens that's the time he shot it with his bow and arrow. So they got him out, maybe it was a snake or whatever it is—it's a big monster. They put him out and kill him. And the boss said—there's a boss, you know—he told them that somebody should take this man back where you got him and give him something, for helping us out. So they bring him back. Finally they got to the house where he lived and that man told him, "After I'm gone come and look where I left." And that man just disappeared in the clouds. So he stayed there thinking about what happened and he went outside and looked. So he found a feather, thunderbird feather. He picked it up. "I guess this is the one that was given to me," [he said]. So he felt different. He felt so good he ran around. "Well, I guess I'll go down and see my dad and my mother." So he started walking.

So they were outside there, those sisters and brothers, so when they saw him coming they took off, they were so scared, you know. They ran to their camp. "We saw him coming. I guess he's dead already. That's his spirit we seen over there." They were so scared. So he got in there. Everyone was so scared and he talked to them. "It's me." So he told them the story and his dad told him, "They're Thunders."

That's why the Indians believe there are thunder spirits.

They help people, you know, looking all over, seeing everything's going on all right. That's why they travel around. That's
why those Indians have faith in that feather. They believe in
that. So those white people they don't believe in that. I heard
them saying it.

The Thunderers as pawaganak do not always, or even often, give
such concrete keepsakes to those whom they visit. Often they leave
nothing but the memory of their visit, a memory which is more than
enough to heal one's sickness and/or change one's life. Angus Pontiac
related such an experience to me. Confined to his hospital bed following a gall bladder operation, Pontiac developed a fever. He had a vision
in which the room filled with smoke. Standing in the smoke were two
figures: "Two old-timers well dressed in leather jackets, jet black hair
well combed. They looked at me real stern. They didn't say a word.
They just looked at me." At this point Pontiac glanced out the window
and saw that it was storming. The lightning flashed, the thunder rolled,
and he heard his name called three times. This was the voice of the
grandfathers, the same pawaganak who manifested themselves in human form before his hospital bed. Pontiac said that following his recov-
ery he told an older person about the dream/vision. This man told him
that if he had heard his name called once more, a fourth time, he would
have died and been taken up by the Thunderbirds.

This was a profound experience for Pontiac and one that has
made him extremely cautious, or as he put it, respectful toward
storms. Whenever a storm develops when he is driving his van, Pontiac immediately pulls to the side of the road and sits quietly until it
passes. This is more than the act of an overly wary driver. Pontiac says
that the thunder grandfathers are "looking after" and "protecting" him
and so he accords them this respect. His behavior is not just a precau-
tion but an obligation and is quite similar to the attitude described by
an Ojibwe to Inez Hilger over forty years ago: "We were taught to
show respect for the Thunder; we were told to sit down and be quiet
until the storm had passed over. It was just like God going by" (Hilger
1951, 61).

We have seen that the Thunder manitouk, usually hidden within
the clouds, may occasionally be seen as pinesiwak flying overhead or
nesting with their young. Sometimes they appear as humans, winged

like angels, or, as in Angus Pontiac's dream, they present themselves as relatively ordinary men. Up until now we have spoken of them as exclusively male and this is generally the way in which they are described, although, given the absence of male/female gender-specific pronouns in the Ojibwe language, one should be careful not to jump to conclusions. However, the Thunderers are consistently referred to as grandfathers. This does, indeed, make sense inasmuch as the Thunder manitouk that one encounters are primarily engaged in hunting. Like traditional Anishnaabeg, the males of this society travel around in search of game, leaving the females to tend the family camp and care for the young and the elderly. In Trudeau's version of the visit to the home of the Thunderers he notes that this is precisely what the female Thunderers were doing: "They were kind of surprised at what they saw, you know, and there was a young lady, a young one with the old man and an old woman." Occasionally, however, humans have met female Thunderbirds, and these meetings provide the closest and most profound interactions possible with the manitouk; the Anishnaabeg marry the Thunderbirds and because of this union they sometimes metamorphose into Thunderbirds themselves.

There is a tale called *Mutcikiwis* or First Born in which eight brothers are joined by a mysterious woman who cares for their camp when they are away (see Skinner 1919, 293-95 and W. Jones 1919, 133-50). Mutcikiwis is annoyed because the woman chooses the youngest brother over him, and so he shoots her with an arrow. The woman metamorphoses into her true form, that of a manitu penasi or Thunderbird, and flies away. Consequently the youngest brother follows her trail, finds her home, passes a son-in-law test, and returns to his brothers with Thunderbird brides for each of them.

In a variation of this tale offered by Norval Morriseau the conclusion is different. The youngest brother, here called *Wahbi Ahmik* (White Beaver), again loses his beloved Thunderbird woman (*Nimkey Banasik*) to the arrow of his brother, *Ahsin* (Stone). Wahbi Ahmik sets off to find her but before he goes he scolds his brother:

> "Now my brother Stone," replied White Beaver, "I am indeed mad enough to kill you, even if you are my blood brother. You are a very foolish man and very evil. Even though I am mad at you, still in a way I am sorry for you. My brother Stone, tell

me, did it ever come to your mind what or who Nimkey
Banasik was? Could you not think what her name meant—
Great Thunderbird Woman? I had meant to tell you but I did
not do so right away because I knew you did not like her. This
woman could have been the one to boost future generations, if
her blood and ours had been mixed together by means of a
child. For this woman was a thunderbird in human form. Nimkey Banasik had six sisters. With them we could have founded
a great civilization. Now it is too late. And from this day forward Indians to come, from generation to generation, will
know that it was you who stopped that progress (1965, 7-8).

Subsequently Wahbi Ahmik finds Nimkey Banasik and the other
Thunderbirds and decides to stay with them. He has a problem, however, as he cannot stomach the food (horned snakes) upon which the
Thunderbirds thrive. Therefore a medicine Thunderbird prepares a
potion from two light blue medicine eggs, and having ingested it
Wahbi Ahmik is metamorphosed. Morriseau concludes: "Ojibway belief states that this Thunderbird is still heard up in the great heavens
and I myself have heard it twice in my lifetime." Wahbi Ahmik's transformation is unique in that unlike the metamorphoses that shamans
and dreamers experience his is a permanent change of nature rather
than a temporary shift of form. Like all Thunder beings he may live forever, joining the ranks of the grandfathers.

In his closing remark Morriseau reminds us that Thunder manitouk beliefs are legitimated by and experienced in a number of arenas.
Having told the tale of the grandfathers whose daughter visits human
beings as a bird, Morriseau substantiates the story further by claiming
to have heard the voice of Wahbi Ahmik in the storm. In other words,
the Thunderers who live at many levels of consciousness are
atisokanak, pawaganak, pinesiwak, and animikeek in turn and at once.
They are experienced in the natural phenomenon of the storm, in the
memory of myth, in the sacred objects and marks that they leave and in
testimony offered by those who have met these people in vision and
dream. Each experience, each story, each representation in art, each
name of the Thunder manitouk at once refines and extends the belief
system. This is the nature of the symbol, that which both reveals and
obscures by reason of its very depth. In the Anishnaabe life-world one

may often have the sense that just as the microscope of analysis is placed over a symbol, that microscope takes on the quality of a kaleidoscope. Like the metamorphosing entities of this world, symbols grow and shift and meld together into patterns that change at the slightest touch. The Thunderers form a complex of beliefs which cannot be manipulated or constricted into an equation of signs.

The meaning of this symbolic reality comes most distinctly into focus when held against the contrasting and equally fluid symbol of Mishebeshu. For while the Thunderers are generally understood as protectors of the Anishnaabeg, the full force of their personalities appears most unmistakable when they are acting against the Underwater/Underground manitouk. And it is in this role that they truly fulfill their protective relationship with human beings. Before discussing this aspect, however, we must complete the analytic stage of our interpretation by looking closely at the antithesis of the Thunderers. We will have to meet Mishebeshu in his own world, leaving the clouds to submerge ourselves in the waters.

NOTES

1. Lyall Watson makes the point that the scientific observation of thunderheads yields a description of their structure which is quite easily translated into a metaphorical statement that the storm is a kind of person: "A thunderstorm is a living thing, an organism with a definite and easily recognizable form. It stands on a foot of cool hard rain, with a heel of drizzle and a toe of rolling squall, feeling its way slowly forward step by step. Drafts of warm air rise all about its body, flaring out at the head into an anvil of ice and hail. The anatomy is characteristic and well-defined. Morphologically it is divided into what can almost be called functional body parts" (1984, 48-49).

2. The only exception which I have found in literature or field studies is in George Copway (Kah-ge-ga-gah-bowh) (1850, 124): "In the Ojibway language, we say 'Be-wah-sam-moog.' In this we convey the idea of a continual glare of lightning, noise, confusion—an awful whirl of clouds, and much more."

3. Husserl (1962, Chapter 9, "Noesis and Noema," 235-59). Erazim Kohak gives an example of the experience of the noema in everyday life: "As I dive precipitously for a dime-store ring which my daughter, then aged two, gave me in another life a quarter century ago, I do not experience myself as anxiously rescuing a tin trinket to which I attach considerable sentimental value. That may be the account I give in retrospect, but the lived experience is one of *my precious ring* rolling toward the sewer. The lived reality is not ring + sentimental value but rather the noema constituted in experience: this precious ring" (1978, 128).

4. There is an exception to this pattern. Among the most northerly tribes, the home of the Thunderbirds, as well as the land of the dead, lies not to the west but to the south (Hallowell 1934, 394-95).

IV

MISHEBESHU

Sure I saw the water monster!
Why do you think I got back here so fast?
Yes, that was me
sitting in a tree by the lake
wishing myself into a walking stick
and making cracking-leaves sounds
and making wishes on myself.
That's when I saw him!
I couldn't think straight so thought crooked,
which is how I got to be
a snake
come winding out
and safe at home.
All because I saw him.
       —Jacob Nibenegenesabe in
       Howard Norman, The
       Wishing Bone Cycle, *1982*

On the eastern side of Manitoulin Island, across the bay from the peninsula of Wikwemikong, lies a small village called Manitowaning. The oldest white settlement on the island (1838), Manitowaning takes its name from the Ojibwe *Munidowaning* (den of the manitou) or *Mnidoowaanzhig* (at the spirit's lair). This picturesque town would appear to sit upon a particularly blessed spot where the shoreline curves gently around a sheltered bay teeming with bass, pike, splake, and even the occasional sturgeon. Tourist publications will tell you that just as Manitoulin (from *Mnidoomnisig*) means Island of the Manitou and refers to the traditional home of Kitche Manitou, Manitowaning describes the Great Spirit's favorite haunt. These sources are wrong. Manitowaning does not belong to Kitche Manitou but to another, entirely different and entirely frightening person: Mishebeshu, the great underwater monster.

Just off the town pier where an old ferry is docked, the water takes on a deep shade of blue signaling a sudden increase in depth. All my native consultants agreed that a big hole is cut into the lake bottom here and this hole is said to lead to an underwater cavern in which the monster shelters. This is the real Manitowaning, the den of the manitou. William Trudeau, in speaking of the hole, said: "The older people, the ones that fasted real good, they know that there's a *mnidoo*, a *mnidoowhash*, that's what the people called it, that place. Now we call it *Mnidoowahning* in Indian, Manitowaning in English." Many people, including James Simon Mishibinijima, claim to have actually seen the monster swimming in the bay.

> The water serpent we saw once, a long time ago, a long time ago—I was about fourteen I think and carrying a gun. The gun worked, but the specific time we saw it, down in Wikwemikong Bay there—it was about fifty yards off the shore—and the darn gun won't work. At first we thought it was a big sturgeon. It had a triangular back and was about forty feet long. I went to see William that time, the William we talked about [William Trudeau], and another one who's passed away already named Dominic. We talked about that serpent and the way he said it was, "That's a gift to your eyes" (Personal Communication, 1988).

James Simon had painted this gift to his eyes and in our conversation he spoke of the creature as both a specific animal (in this case, a serpent) and as the manifestation of a manitou, Mishebeshu. This apparent contradiction regarding the nature of what he had seen—was it a peculiar animal or a powerful other-than-human person?—is, in fact, fundamental to the nature of the Underwater manitou(k). Mishebeshu appears to be at once the name of a particular mythic personality and a descriptive term for his various manifestations and associates. It would be convenient to assume that Mishebeshu is the ogimaa or owner of all underwater creatures, both ordinary and extraordinary (Vecsey 1983, 76), a kind of "spirit prototype" (Landes 1968, 22) that describes, determines, and controls the nature and behavior of fish, water snakes, and the like. While Mishebeshu does appear to serve this function, his power extends far beyond the control of underwater "game." The Underwater manitou may have been entreated for success in fishing, but most frequently he was asked simply to allow humans to travel on the water in safety, for he controls the water itself as well as all creatures which "people" it. As we shall see, he also possesses powerful medicines that are effective in a number of spheres.

The name Mishebeshu means literally Great Lynx and may be used as "both a generic word for a class of malignant aquatic feline beings, and the proper name for the ruler of the species" (Brown and Brightman 1988, 109). My consultants extended the name even further to include not only these great water dwelling lynxes but water serpents and monster ground snakes. In this instance, as in all my analyses of the Ojibwe life-world, use of the term Mishebeshu must be governed, finally, by prevailing Anishnaabe usage. And while usage here appears somewhat inconsistent, one must resist the temptation to systematize or circumscribe artificially the application of the name. To the Anishnaabeg, Mishebeshu is at once a manitou and a class of manitouk, the ogimaa of all underwater and underground creatures, and any of these creatures that might be termed extraordinary. He is not a person with a plurality of forms like Nanabush but a kind of "plural person" who is met within a complex of symbols and realities.

The particularly feline character of Mishebeshu, as expressed in his name, does require some elaboration, however. While the dragonlike form is not a constant in the Anishnaabe experience of Mishebeshu, he is described in the earliest sources as a "fabulous animal" (Allouez 1664-67 in Thwaites 1896-1901, 50:289, where the name is given as *Missibizi*), "The Great Panther" (Perrot 1654 in Blair 1911-12, 59, *Michipissy*), "the great tyger" (Charlevoix 1761, 2:142), and "a sea tiger on which they put fins" (Pachot in Kinietz 1965, 287, *Bichi-Bichy*). Some modern and contemporary studies continue to characterize Mishebeshu as a feline monster (Brown and Brightman 1988; Howard 1965; Ray and Stevens 1984; Redsky 1972). Redsky, for example, describes Mishebeshu as an

animal that Indians used to offer tobacco [to] and worship
highly...The *mishe-beshoo* is a huge, brown cat. It has

webbed feet for swimming and lives in great big caves or holes
in the ground. It acts something like a bear; it gathers moss
and grass and places it in a hole where it hibernates until
spring. This animal is always seen in the water or close to it
(120-21).

However, these characterizations seem to be based upon his name and
his appearance in traditional accounts, for current firsthand experiences are invariably of a water serpent, usually horned and always of an
immense size.

Allouez recorded that Mishebeshu was never seen "except in
dreams" and if we take his statement to mean that the Great Lynx form
was only met in dream, then it may well be an accurate appraisal. Of
course for the Jesuit the dearth of waking experiences served to rein-
force the unreality of what he called the "pretended deities" of "a false
and abominable religion" (Thwaites 1896-1901, 50:285, 287). Like most
Europeans of his time, Allouez failed to appreciate the nature of the
Ojibwe dream experience which, by providing access to the power of
manitouk, gave meaning to one's life and actually introduced one into a
world of heightened rather than diminished reality.

Still, the question of Mishebeshu's existence in myth and dream
as a Great Lynx or cat remains. Attempts have been made to explain
this symbol but they fall short, relying as they do upon strained alignments between hissing cougars and snakes and/or hypothesizing a re-
figuration of European images of the lion. Selwyn Dewdney suggests
these explanations in *The Sacred Scrolls of the Southern Ojibway*
(1967). He postulates that the association of lynx with snake "was a natural outcome of the animal's uncanny capacity to vanish from sight
combined with a venomous hiss. By paleo-logic ... the Lynx was the
Snake and vice versa" (124). Later he suggests a theory about "the origin of the word 'lion' as an English translation of *Misshepeshu*. Un-
doubtedly, wherever British influence penetrated North America, native eyes examined the pictographic devices on British coins, treaty
documents, and flags with great curiosity. Noting a catlike animal with
sacred projections around the head, neck, breast, and tail, particularly
the *length* of the tail, they must inevitably have associated it with Misshepeshu" (125). Given the Ojibwe antipathy for the British, it would
have been appropriate to identify the leonine symbol of their oppres-

sors with that of a malignant manitou. The *inevitability* of such an identification is questionable, however.

Further, Mishebeshu was also called a panther or tiger, a fact
which led Charlevoix to draw an erroneous conclusion: "[I]t must be
observed that the true tyger is not to be found in Canada; thus this tradition [of an underwater cat] is probably of foreign extraction" (1761,
142). These observations have little to do with the nature of Mishebeshu and are, in fact, just speculations born of confused translations.
The reality is that *beshu, beshoo, bizhiew*, and all its other ortho-
graphic variations signifies a lynx, the largest feline with which the
Ojibwe have contact. There are stories, however, of cougars or mountain lions in the area of Manitoulin, and the name is likewise applied to
these as well as to all great cats of the world. That Mishebeshu is a
michi or *mishi* (great or big) member of the group indicates not only his
huge size but his great power and generally extraordinary nature.
Dewdney comes much closer to the point when he concentrates on the
evocative or exploratory meaning of the symbol rather than on its etiological function: "Were there not creatures inhabiting the deep waters
more deadly and dangerous than any of the fish species? How should
they be named? 'Great Fish-Monster'? 'Snake-Fish'? 'Underwater
Lion'? How does one name one's deepest, unspoken fears?" (1967,
125).

None of my consultants knew of any reason *why* they thought of
Mishebeshu as both a huge water cat and a serpent. Mishebeshu is
just, in the original sense of the word, a true monster (from Latin
monstrum, "something marvelous") sharing the worldwide mythic patterns of dragons and supernatural serpents. He is extraordinary and his
parts exaggerated, misshapen, or forged together from two or more animal species. Perhaps Mishebeshu was traditionally understood as a
Great Water Cat to indicate not only his ferocity but the fact that he is
like no one else we will ever meet.

In analyzing the Thunderers we called their names in order to
conjure their presence. Our entry into Mishebeshu's world must go by
way of another path. In part, this is because of the traditional proscription against speaking the name of Mishebeshu during the warm
months when he is active and not imprisoned under the ice. While
most contemporary Anishnaabeg do not believe that the use of the
name will actually bring the monster to one's door, there is still a gen-

eral reluctance to speak his name. My own consultants, while not strictly avoiding the use of the word Mishebeshu, were disinclined to mention it. Sometimes their reluctance would take the form of an initial denial of firsthand knowledge, later to be succeeded by tales of the monster. This was especially true among older persons like Mamie Migwans, whose son, David, said, "My grandmother always said not to talk about him" (Personal Communication, 1988).

The Ojibwe have a profound fear of this manitou(k), an attitude which is wholly unlike the caution and respect accorded the Thunderers. In part this is due to the fact that, while immeasurably powerful, the Thunderers have an alliance with the Anishnaabeg and are somewhat predictable, especially in their response to propitiation. Further, one may always hear the Thunderbird coming; he does not take you by surprise. The Underwater manitouk, in contrast, hide themselves and act in unpredictable ways. They usually come upon you when you least expect or want them, like long-suppressed fears and memories welling up from the unconscious mind. In seeking these manitouk one travels in a dangerous world where lakes grow suddenly rough and streams are transformed into a series of dangerous rapids and whirlpools.[1] Mishebeshu is the uncanny element in this world, the hidden form beneath the ice, which may suddenly crack in winter. He is the one who pulls boaters and swimmers to their deaths and the one who makes the ground go soft beneath your feet. Raymond and Delores Armstrong, Mamie and David Migwans, and Blake Debassige all spoke of the power of the monster to drown people. Debassige's painting of Mishebeshu ("One Who Lives Under the Water") was inspired, in part, by the near-drowning of his own brother. The Armstrongs also spoke of the great danger of swamps and quicksands on the island. And James Simon explained Mishebeshu's role in such places: "Sometimes when the land goes soft on you, he's been there. One time there's a road and then all the sudden the whole road is soft—he went across there. He's wet and he's heavy. They say he moves like a leech on the land." Unlike the storms of the Thunderbirds, the natural creations of Mishebeshu seem to have a thoroughly unnatural quality about them.

As a causative agent in the Anishnaabe life-world, Mishebeshu exerts his will however and whenever he sees fit. Like the Leviathan, this monster is distinguished not only by his watery home and gigantic proportions and powers but by his ultimately impenetrable mystery.

We are reminded of Ahab's search for Moby Dick, the great white whale who, when met, is still unknowable.

> Dissect him how I may, then, I but go skin deep; I know him not, and never will. But if I know not even the tail of this whale, how understand his head? Much more, how comprehend his face, when face he has none? Thou shalt see my back parts, my tail, he seems to say, but my face shall not be seen. But I cannot completely make out his back parts; and hint what he will about his face, I say again he has no face (Melville, *Moby Dick*, 1851).

Our analysis of Mishebeshu is a kind of pursuit, then, a hunt for a creature that we fear we will catch. In adopting an attitude of simultaneous attraction and repulsion toward Mishebeshu we echo the prevailing Anishnaabe sentiment toward him: he who is at once "a gift to the eyes" and a thief of life. In this analysis, as in all our researches, we conduct our search through myths, dreams, and waking experience. And we begin by first looking upon images which are drawn from those areas, images which attempt to show us the shadow, if not the face, of Mishebeshu.

The Manitoulin artist Blake Debassige has painted Mishebeshu and calls his work simply, "One Who Lives under the Water." The most well known rendering of the monster, at Agawa Rock on the North Shore of Lake Superior, shows him in bodily profile with his face turned from the viewer. It is from this pictograph that Debassige, Mel Madahbee, Mamie Migwans, and Anne Beam took their inspiration. The original image done in red ochre sometime before 1850 is attributed to Myeengun, a mide shaman who undertook the long voyage from the south shore of Lake Superior to Agawa on account of a vision. Mamie Migwans gave me a different version of this painting's creation: "It's said that they used Mishebeshu's blood after they killed him. The Thunderbirds, they killed him. They used the blood to paint all those pictures." One aspect of Mishebeshu's mystery is indicated by Migwan's assertion: "The Thunderbirds, they killed him." Over and over in the myths we are told that Mishebeshu has been killed and yet he continues to resurface. Like the rough water, Mishebeshu, who is one and many, will always return.

There are many other feline depictions of Mishebeshu, both in

One Who Lives Under the Water
Blake Debassige
Acrylic on canvas
Reproduction courtesy of The Royal Ontario Museum

the form of pictographs and on birch scrolls. Tanner reproduced some of these drawings from the scrolls of the mide society, (James 1956, 345 and 377) as did Coleman in her study of decorative designs (1947, 67). Included in Coleman's collection of underwater/underground "animal spirits" is a particularly striking image of Mishebeshu taken from a Menominee bark-fiber bag very like the one reproduced in Chapter 3. An almost identical representation appears in Covarrubias's collection (1954, 278) in which, oddly enough, he identifies the pattern as a cat, presumably an ordinary cougar. This misidentification is especially strange given the fact that the figure is clearly horned and has an elongated tail. Both tail and horns are indications of Mishebeshu's immense power. He uses the tail not only to travel swiftly through water but to roughen the lakes and rivers and to strike the boats of unwary and/or

Mishebeshu Pot Using Agawa Rock Painting Representation
Anne Beam
From the author's collection

disrespectful humans. The horns here, as in all traditional Ojibwe drawings, are signs of extraordinary power. In the mnemonic scrolls of the midewiwin, a powerful shaman is easily identified by his horns, and in one of Hoffman's scrolls from Red Lake, a shaman compares himself to the water monster even while he entreats him: "The place that is feared I inhabit, the swift-running stream I inhabit...I have long horns...you [Mishebeshu] to whom I am speaking...See me, whose head is out of water" (1891, 291-92).

We will explore Mishebeshu's role in the medicine society and his problematic status as a pawagan, later. For now let us emphasize

signif.ce
of horns.

that while horns may be affixed to any figure in order to denote power, only Mishebeshu *always* has them. So great is his power that he is almost never challenged except by the Thunderbirds and, in a somewhat disastrous encounter, by Nanabush. The presence of these power horns may have contributed to a false equation between Mishebeshu and an entity known as *Matchi-Manitou* (evil manitou). Matchi-Manitou is sometimes understood as a shadowy underworld figure who stands in contrast to Kitche-Manitou (P. Jones 1861, 83), but the name is properly used as a generic term for a group of malevolent beings that includes the Windigo and Mishebeshu (Cooper 1933, 101).[2] The attachment of this descriptive name to a particular manitou was probably due in part to the influence of Christian missionaries. Vecsey notes this influence and is of the belief that Matchi-Manitou was of post-contact origin, an Ojibwe re-figuration of the Christian devil (1983, 82). We should note that the Jesuits often saw the devil in Ojibwe religion, especially in the activities of the jessakid or conjuring shamans. They assumed that the manitouk who visited the shaking tents were demons and classified Ojibwe beliefs concerning pawaganak as demonology. They were slightly kinder, albeit equally inaccurate, in their appraisal of the Montaignais as practitioners of a "rudimentary Manicheism" (Moore 1982, 77-97). Under missionary influence Matchi-Manitou and Mishebeshu, he of the long tail and horns, were conceptually merged with the Christian Devil.

> [I]t is alleg'd that the Savages are acquainted with the Devil. I have read a thousand Ridiculous Stories Writ by our Clergymen, who maintain that the Savages have conferences with him, and not only consult him, but pay him a sort of Homage. Now all these advances are ridiculous; for in ernest, the Devil never appear'd to these Americans... [T]hese Ecclesiastics did not understand the true importance of that great word Matchi Manitou, (which signifies an Evil Spirit, Matchi being the word for Evil and Manitou for Spirit;) For by the Devil they understand such things as are offensive to 'em, which in our Language comes near to the signification of Misfortune, Fate, Unfavourable Destiny, etc. So that in speaking of the Devil they do not mean that Evil Spirit that in Europe is represented under the figure of a Man, with a long Tail and great Horns and Claws (Lahontan 1905, 447-48).

Lahontan's words raise an important question regarding the nature of evil in the Ojibwe life-world and one which is directly relevant to our discussion of Mishebeshu. Contrary to the reports of the Jesuits (Pomedli 1987), the traditional Ojibwe and related Algonquian people apparently exhibited a developed ethical sensibility that included a concept of sin.[3] The goal of Anishnaabe life was and still is bimaadiziwin (living well), or "life in the fullest sense, life in the sense of longevity, health and freedom from misfortune" (Hallowell 1975, 171). One may only live well if one maintains good relations with human and other-than-human persons. Therefore, traditional bad conduct or *madjiijiwe baziwin* involved the failure to keep up one's side of a healthy relationship and could be punished through misfortune and illness (Hallowell 1967, 269). Typical sins against humans were: excessive greed and failure to share one's food and belongings, excessive pride and the misuse of power, homicide, cruelty, and sexual perversions. Sins against manitouk included disrespect or neglect of the manitouk and the mistreatment or misuse of animals and plants (Vecsey 1983, 149).

It was not a purely utilitarian attitude which informed traditional Ojibwe ethical standards. Humans were not merely concerned with protecting their own interests, for a system of interconnecting relationships led to a recognition of mutual responsibilities among all persons. Very powerful shamans might obtain great advantages for themselves, but inasmuch as they exhibited excessive power and misused others, they were hated and feared rather than respected (Landes 1968, 43-47). Being a glutton could transform one into a windigo, and even excessive fasting for visions was a punishable offense. There is a well-known tale, "He Who Over-Fasted," in which a young boy who has fasted successfully many times is repeatedly urged by his father to fast again. Finally the boy is taken from his father, for he is changed into a robin and flies away.

> Accordingly the name of the bird is the chirper or the robin, the one that was once a human being. And this is what the people say: "When the sound of the bird is heard, the omen is not good," so they say. One will meet with something [baneful] if one hears the cry of the bird saying: "I feel a foreboding." Like a human does the bird speak (W. Jones 1919, Pt. 2, 309).

All these sins were harmful because they unbalanced the earth, a precarious island which had been made to float upon a flooded world. Standards of good and evil are better understood here as standards of balance and imbalance, control and chaos. Mary Black has suggested that Ojibwe behavior is governed by a "power belief system." In this system, "power is a relation between a person and his environment, including but not limited to, other people." The goal of life is to establish individual autonomy, here defined as "freedom from control" within a hierarchy of helpful and harmful power-persons. In short, the "good" is identified with a state of "being in control" and the "bad" with "being out of control." Anyone (human or otherwise) who unbalances the life-world, or who weakens an individual or causes her to feel helpless is "bad." "Indians do not 'push others around' and 'Indians do not want to be pushed around,' to quote an actual statement" (Black 1977, 141-51). In this context, Mishebeshu is clearly a kind of cosmic bully who both disrupts the waters and uses his power to torment humans. As the person responsible for the primordial Deluge, he is evil inasmuch as he is the paradigmatic unbalancer of the world. Mishebeshu is not, however, the source of all evil or even misfortune, merely a person possessed of great power and a malevolent will.

To return, then, to images of this person, we find that he is frequently depicted in another form which excites Christian imaginations to conjure the devil. As a serpent Mishebeshu appears, again, in traditional pictographs, mide scrolls, and contemporary artwork. The portraits are very much like those found among both the Eastern Algonquians and the Plains tribes, often resembling an elongated lizard with a spined back, a huge tail, and horns. However, while his form may appear to be that of an amphibian, Mishebeshu is always described as a reptile. All snakes, it is said, were originally derived from him. The following account is given by the Timagami Ojibwe.

> A man was one time walking along and he came to a lake which he wanted to cross. But he had no canoe, and so he walked along the shore until he saw a big Snake lying in the water with his head on the shore. "Will you carry me across?" asked the hunter. "Yes," answered the Snake. "But it looks cloudy and I am afraid of the lightning, so you must tell me if it thunders while we are crossing." The hunter got on the Snake's back

and they started to swim across the lake. As they went along,
thunder began rumbling, "kax kax," and the lightning flashed.
"Mah, mah, listen!" said the Snake in fear. "I hear something."
Just as they reached the shore, when the hunter could leap to
safety, a stroke of lightning hit the Snake and broke him into
numberless pieces, which began swimming about and finally
came to land. The great Snake was not killed, but his pieces
turned into small snakes which we see all about to-day (Speck
1914, 71).

snake

Oddly enough, snakes are rather rare in the northern woods and venomous ones are now practically unknown.[4] But they make striking and
frightening appearances in myth. We might recall, for instance, the appearance of the snake as the mother's consort in the "Rolling Head" or
"Bad Mother" stories. The serpent also has a place in stories told of human journeys to the land of souls. On the way one must cross a bridge,
a slippery log, which is suspended over a raging river. The log is sometimes transformed into a snake which may throw you into the water as
you attempt to cross. If you do fall you will never reach the land of
souls but will, instead, haunt the riverbanks or, alternatively, disappear altogether. When met in waking experience snakes are, not surprisingly then, generally viewed as undesirable creatures. They are
clearly aligned with Mishebeshu and their habit of dormancy during
the cold months might well contribute to the complex of belief which
inhibits the manitou's activity during the winter. Just as hawks and eagles are not identical to the Thunderbirds and yet share some attributes with them, so too common ground and water snakes may be said
to share the behavioral world of Mishebeshu.

When depicted as a serpent in the mide scrolls, Mishebeshu is
often placed at the entrance of the midewegun or lodge. His role here
is normally that of an obstacle under which an initiate must pass in order to reach a higher mide degree. Dewdney reproduces a chart of the
fourth degree in which Mishebeshu appears as both a lynx and serpent
blocking the doorway near which supportive bison and bear manitouk
also stand. The successful entrance into these higher degrees would
seem to entail an entry into the medicine realm of Mishebeshu. "Only
the combined rites of candidates and priests reinforced by the supportive manitos were able to force these snake-monsters to arch their backs

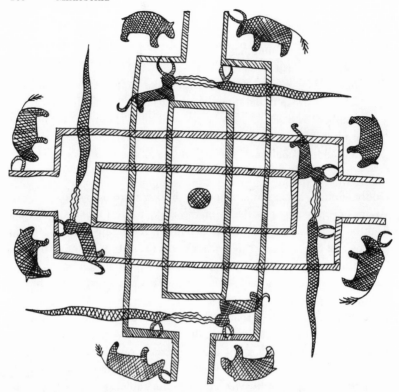

Fourth Degree Mide Chart
Reproduction courtesy of University of Toronto Press

and allow the candidate to pass safely under" (Dewdney 1967, 94).[5]
The medicines of the Underwater manitouk may prove effective
when properly used. Recall the medicine song recorded by Hoffman,
above; Tanner also includes such a song in which the shaman asks for
the help of Mishebeshu in healing a patient. Here the remedy includes
the swallowing of snakeskins or a long cord which the shaman then
pulls from the stomach of his patient. Because of its association with
the Underwater manitouk, this is considered an extremely powerful
cure (James 1956, 376-77). But the mide members who reach the
higher degrees are in danger of becoming perverted by an excess of
power. In fact, the members of the highest degrees were routinely un-

derstood to be practitioners of bad medicine. Although Mishebeshu may not have been solely or even directly responsible for the transformation of healers into malignant sorcerers, his symbolic appearance at the door to higher—and more dangerously seductive—degrees is consonant with his role as a dark power in the Anishnaabe world.

While the post-contact origins of the Midewiwin have been established to the satisfaction of many scholars, contemporary Anishnaabeg continue to maintain that the Mide society expresses an archaic form of Ojibwe religion. What matters here, though, is not the resolution of this argument, but the acknowledgement that mide symbolism, whether of pre- or post-contact origin, is most certainly consonant with the very oldest beliefs concerning the manitouk. Thunderbirds, bears, and otters are most often depicted in scrolls as helpful, enabling agents while the Underwater manitouk generally hinder one's progress. Likewise, traditional visions of the former manitouk, especially of the Thunderbirds, were met with much rejoicing, whereas dreaming of manitouk of the lower world was an unpropitious event and the dreamer's tongue would be scraped with cedar in order to free him of the dream's influence. Kohl (1860, 236) records that dreamers would build beds on trees in order to avoid dreams of the underground or Underwater manitouk.

There are, however, some exceptions to this rule. Mishebeshu could be courted by shamans eager to share in his great power, but such alliances with the monster carried great risks for human beings. Kohl relates a myth concerning a man who dreamt of Mishebeshu.

> The man of whom he was speaking had once dreamed ten nights in succession that a voice spoke to him, saying that if he wished to have something very fine, which would make him happy, he must one night strike the water with a stick and sing a certain verse to it. He told this dream to his friends, who, however, dissuaded him, and said, "Do not go, my friend—do not accept it."

Against this good advice the man went to the lake and beat it with a stick, calling for Mishebeshu to show himself. The water swirled, forming a great whirlpool, and waves broke the shoreline, nearly drowning the man. Finally the waters grew still and the water-king emerged from the placid lake in the form of a mighty serpent. "What wilt thou of me?" he said. "Give me the recipe," he replied, "which will make me healthy, rich, and prosperous." "Dost thou see," the snake said, "what I wear on my head, between my horns? Take it: it will serve thee. But one of thy children must be mine in return for it."

The Indian saw between the horns of the water-king something red, like a fiery flower. He stretched out his trembling hand and seized it. It melted away in his finger into a powder, like the vermilion with which the Indians paint their faces. He collected it in a piece of birch bark, and the serpent then gave him further instructions.

These instructions allowed the man to manipulate Mishebeshu's gift in order to cure illness and obtain good fortune. However, a terrible price was paid for this power, for the vision seeker's wife and children all died and the man, "who gave way to such bad dreams was, for a long time, rich, powerful, and respected, a successful hunter, a much-feared warrior, and a terrible magician and prophet, until at length a melancholy fate befell him, and he ended his days in a very wretched manner" (1860, 423-25).

This tale, while reminiscent of the well-known "The Fisher and His Wife,"[6] is more than just a cautionary fable in which one learns (or *doesn't* learn) the value of modesty and moderation. Here the assignation between monster and human takes place within a culturally sanctioned context, the vision quest. The goal of this quest, the attainment of power, is a profoundly religious one, and in this case the man errs not only because he overreaches himself but because he underestimates both the power and the malevolent will of the religious object, Mishebeshu.

Other seekers have had more success in their dealings with the underwater monster. Radin reports a tale, "The Boy Who was Blessed by a Serpent," in which a vision seeker is told by his pawagan that he will never be killed. The old man supervising his fasting tells the boy, "That is a very good blessing. Accept it, for the serpent will take good care of you" (1914a, 52). Yet in the next sentence we are told that the serpent proved somewhat fickle: "The young man was helped by this blessing until he became a very old man, then the serpent deserted him" (1914, 52). Unfortunately, we are not told what services the serpent required from the boy in exchange for his protection and whether the desertion was a betrayal or the result of the dreamer's failure to participate fully in the relationship.

To return briefly to Kohl's tale of the man who met Mishebeshu, the monster's medicine gift was a vermilion-like powder taken from between his horns. This substance was more frequently said to be copper, the horns and sometimes the entire body of Mishebeshu being covered in the metal (Howard 1965, 105; Radin and Reagan 1928, 145). Copper was quite familiar to the traditional Ojibwe, and, despite its abundance in the Great Lakes area, it was always held to be a sacred and powerful mineral. Allouez reported that copper was said to belong to the Underwater manitouk: "One often finds at the bottom of the water pieces of pure copper, of ten and twenty livres' weight. I have several times seen such pieces in the Savages' hands; and, since they are superstitious, they keep them as so many divinities, or as presents which the gods dwelling beneath the water have given them, and on which their welfare is to depend" (Thwaites 1896-1901, 50:265). Raudot said that Mishebeshu, whom he called *Michibichy*, was believed to guard copper mines on the shores of Lake Superior (Kinietz 1965, 376). And on Parry Island, where the Underwater manitou went by the name of *Nzagima*,[7] medicine men would scrape either the body or the horns of the monster.

> Only certain sorcerers could see it, sorcerers who during their childhood fasts had been visited by Nzagima in the guise of a man, and instructed to offer tobacco and to summon it when they needed its aid. Such a sorcerer, in later life, would sit on a sandspit on a cloudless day (for Nzagima dreads the thunder), and summon it with a medicine-song accompanied by a drum. A black hell-diver would appear, followed by a white; then a black loon, likewise followed by a white loon. Finally the serpent itself would rise to the surface and draw its long body over the sandspit, awaiting the man's request. The sorcerer might ask for a medicine to cure rheumatism, or to kill some enemy. Then the serpent would quiver in a certain spot, and the man would scrape off his medicine there with a wooden spoon or a knife, wrap it in birch bark, and deposit it in his medicine bag (Jenness 1935, 259).

To attempt to take the substance without permission, to steal from Mishebeshu, was to risk his wrath. And if one chose to partake of the monster's power, any lack of caution would result in death and destruction. Unlike the thunder stones cast by animikeek, Mishebeshu's medicinal minerals carried with them a huge responsibility, for in accepting them one entered into a pact with the monster.

The obvious question which arises here, given Mishebeshu's great power and malevolence, is how may one avoid incurring his displeasure? Certainly, as regards dreams and medicine, strict avoidance of the monster was one's best insurance. But Mishebeshu's influence extended beyond these areas into one's daily life. Bodies of water are, after all, his element, and in Ojibwe territory the inland seas of the Great Lakes are complemented by many thousands of lesser lakes. In Ontario alone there are more than 250,000 such lakes, each a potential home for the monster, or, given the plural application of Mishebeshu, monsters. Some of these lakes are believed to be more dangerous than others, that is, more favored by Mishebeshu, and are avoided altogether. A missionary, Reverend F. Frost, visited such a lake near Nipigon, saying that it was avoided by the Indians on account of "the unnatural color of the water" and the belief that it was inhabited by a "sea serpent." He added that "the Indians go to it in winter, but never in summer . . . They would not think of embarking in a canoe upon its surface for any consideration" (Frost 1904, 133).

While on Manitoulin I visited two such mysterious lakes, Whitefish Lake on West Bay Reserve and Quanja Lake on Wikwemikong. Both are rather small but are said to be very deep, perhaps even bottomless, and both are distinguished by their unnatural color. Whitefish, just off the main road through West Bay, is a narrow and very dark lake that is infrequently fished due to the beliefs surrounding it. One old resident of West Bay, Abel Beboning, told me that he had once seen "a giant snake" on the shore there and had run away from it. Raymond and Delores Armstrong both said it was best to avoid the place. And Mamie Migwans at first disclaimed any real knowledge of Mishebeshu, but later recounted an experience that her father had at Whitefish.

> M.M.: My father saw something once—at that lake there— Whitefish Lake. My father used to go fishing there all

the time. That's where he always liked to fish. Once he came running home because he saw something there that scared him. He said the water went black and it started going around.

T.S.: Like a whirlpool?

M.M.: Yes, a whirlpool, and it was black. But he didn't see nothing—he ran right home and he told us never to go there.

T.S.: But he didn't see Mishebeshu?

M.M. (laughing): No, but he saw something. He didn't *wait*. And my mother always told us not to go there. He used to fish there all the time but after that he never went back.

Mamie Migwans volunteered that she was afraid to go into the water and always had been. She and her son David added that the whirlpool meant that the monster was coming up out of his hole. Raymond Armstrong added his own story of a similar occurrence at Whitefish Lake: "My grandmother and grandfather, when they used to net fish there, like Mamie told you, they seen this whirling there around the water. And they could have went down with the boat if they were any closer and they had to get away as soon as they could." When I asked the Armstrongs what they thought it was that could cause such a whirlpool, Delores replied, "It's probably whatever it is going down." Raymond had a more enigmatic answer, "I don't know. Maybe it's anger."

All four added something to their stories which both surprised me and made me understand the activities of Mishebeshu a bit better. I had been confused both by the plural nature of Mishebeshu's name and by accounts which have him, as one entity, disappearing in a small lake and apparently moving to another. The Migwans and Armstrongs told me that they believed there were caverns and tunnels beneath all the lakes on Manitoulin, and possibly under all the lakes in Canada. Mishebeshu is said to live in these caves and travel via the complex of passages.[8] On Manitoulin, the hole at Manitowaning is the main conduit from the Georgian Bay; hence its favored position as the "den of the manitou." When I checked this story with other consultants, they were all in agreement, and once they discovered that I had heard of the

network, they elaborated upon Mishebeshu's use of it. The belief in
these tunnels also clarified the monster's occasional appearances from
under earth as well as water.

It was stories of Mishebeshu's tunnel system that led me to visit
Quanja Lake on the isolated south end of Wikwemikong. I had heard of
the lake many times but was unable to pinpoint its location. William
Trudeau and Sam Oswamick had both told me that it was connected to
the hole at Manitowaning and that the monster was said to go there frequently. As proof of his story Trudeau added that representatives of
the Game and Fishery Department had found fish which they had
tagged in Wikwemikong Bay swimming in the waters of Quanja. All
consultants agreed that Quanja was a "bad" lake, very deep at one end
and oddly colored, and while they had not seen Mishebeshu there
themselves, others had. Further, Angus Pontiac said that people who
were interested in "bad medicine" went there to prepare and collect it.

Pontiac agreed to take me to Quanja but we made no definite
plans, and when I stopped by his home to collect him he had, unfortunately, gone moose hunting on the North Shore. I had a friend with me
who was visiting the island and, as Pontiac had given me general directions to Quanja, we decided to try to find it on our own. On the way we
received more directions from a few people we met on the old logging
tracks but somehow we still kept taking wrong turns that dead-ended
in the bush. (That all these turns were to the left, in a "sinister" direction, was a symbolism that was not lost on us.) We did finally find
Quanja late in the day. It was a rather odd place, at once striking and
yet disturbing. The strangest thing about the lake was the radical difference in depth that one could see from the shore. On our side, the
only one easily accessible by land, the lake was extremely shallow, just
one to two feet, and banked by a sandy beach. The far shore was ringed
by forested cliffs, and on that side the water was a very deep green-
blue. The drop-off from shallow to deep water was so extreme that it
appeared as if a line were drawn straight down the middle of the lake
between the light shallows and the dark depths. What the lake recalled
more than anything was a water-filled crack or ravine which had overflowed its banks on our side. We saw no signs of the monster and, since
it was getting dark, we stayed only long enough to take a few pictures
and collect a rock from the shore.

Frost described his own experience with a "bad lake," and the impression made on him is strikingly similar to my own reaction to Quanja.

> It was truly a wonderful sight; the water was, indeed, a pecu-
> liar color, a glittering, lustrous, greenish blue, not like the
> color of the water at Bermuda, or the blue of the Mediterra-
> nean, nor like the water in the harbor at Barbadoes, nor a mix-
> ture of these. The Indian was right when he said it was ghastly.
> It was a beautiful color, yet somewhat repulsive. I have never
> seen a blue snake, but it was the same color a snake would be,
> supposing it were blue. It was intensely brilliant, glittering in
> the sunshine; it looked like a pigment, yet it was quite white,
> of course, when taken up in a vessel or in the hand. It might
> have been the descriptions of the Indians that had affected my
> imagination, or the contagion of superstition, but I do not won-
> der that they were struck with the unusual appearance of the
> lake. It was not the sunshine that made it that peculiar color; it
> was not the reflection of the sky. It was the same when cloudy;
> it was the same always, in the daytime, probably (1904,
> 135-36).

There are many other lakes which appear to be special homes for Mishebeshu. Some of these lakes are well known. Howard reports the general avoidance of Devil's Lake in North Dakota by both the Ojibwe and the Lakota (1965, 5) and Morriseau says that Lake Nipigon was once frequented by Mishebeshu but "the last offerings were made to the demigod about thirty years ago. Now the offering rock is bare, for the water god *Misshipeshu* moved away" (1965, 27-28). However, as often as not the monster is only glimpsed if he is, in fact, seen at all. The bad lakes seem to be distinguished less by the frequency of monster sightings than by their own physical characteristics. These characteristics may include: dark or oddly-colored water; relative inac- cessibility; great depth or extreme differences in depth; a lack of fish; frequency of rough-water conditions; and the presence of whirlpools, strong currents, or undertows. This last set of characteristics, fre- quently responsible for boating accidents and drownings, is an indica- tion that the monster is present, perhaps hunting Anishnaabeg.

On Manitoulin, where the lakes are both cold and deep, the bod- ies of drowners have been known to sink, often irretrievably, to the

bottom. Drowning is considered an especially terrifying and even unnatural form of death by Anishnaabeg, and when bodies are not found
they say that Mishebeshu has taken the victims. Both David Migwans
and Raymond Armstrong said that they believed the monster to be responsible for many drownings. Armstrong explained: "Something will
pull them. Sometimes they're never found and that's when the monster will take them." It is unclear what Mishebeshu does with his victims. Morriseau claims that the manitou lives on the flesh or the souls
of humans (1965, 27) but most consultants felt that he ate fish. Often an
absence of fish in a lake is attributed to the monster's presence.

The monster's activities are not confined to particular lakes, however. As the many people who are Mishebeshu may travel at will
through a network of tunnels, they are likely to turn up anywhere.
Mishebeshu is believed routinely to tour the Great Lakes where he has
been sighted by white people as well as by Indians.

> Last year, a CP newspaper item, dated Detroit... July 23,
> 1948, reported: "While men yelled and one woman fainted
> aboard the passenger liner City of Detroit III, a sea serpent
> slithered through Georgian Bay. That was the report of an eye-
> witness, Bess Munroe... She described the serpent as a 60-
> foot, green-and-purple scaly monster with a huge horned
> head. The description was confirmed by more than a dozen
> passengers and several of the ship's crew (Barbeau 1952, 116).

Certainly these tales of monster lynxes or serpents are likely to be met
with some skepticism, especially when people seldom testify to having
had more than a glimpse of the monster. Yet from a phenomenological
standpoint, a posture in which we 'believe in order to understand', stories of Mishebeshu, like stories of the Thunderers, must be viewed
without the distortion of belief which skepsis invariably effects. I saw
no monsters in the lakes yet my personal lack of 'empirical' evidence
cannot override the reality which these creatures have in the Ojibwe
life-world. A. Irving Hallowell put it succinctly.

> [There] are water monsters living in the lakes and swamps and
> some of the Indians have seen them. Thunder Birds and mon-
> ster snakes, then, are important items in the behavior environ-
> ment of these Indians. Since from our point of view thunder is

part of their physical environment and monster snakes are not, we might be inclined to make a distinction between them. But if we do this we are making *our* categories a point of departure. We are assuming them as a universal norm. I prefer to consider both the Thunder Birds and the monster snakes as part of the behavioral environment of these Indians and to ignore any such distinction. Both are "real" in the sense that they have actual affects upon behavior (1942, 6).

It is important to remember, too, that as Hallowell also pointed out, the lifestyle of the Sub-Arctic and Woodlands hunter was not only —— physically but intellectually demanding. Traditional Ojibwe people observed the natural world with great care and precision because an accurate understanding of one's environment was essential to one's very survival. These people were neither vague nor romantic in their descriptions of the world, and their complex understanding of natural phenomena is reflected in their language. The many descriptive names given to Thunderers on account of the different sounds which they make is a case in point. In short we must assume that traditional Ojibwes did not report unusual creatures where they did not exist. Even today, tales of monster sightings are catalogued according to who sees the creature and *how* she sees it. William Trudeau, while expressing his belief in the monster's existence, took care to debunk what he saw as false sightings by people who were incautious or prone to exaggeration.

> Well, a lot of times, like so many stories that I hear about, the people right here on the Reserve they tell stories to other people that they think they saw a great big snake out there on the lake or maybe around the Bay here or someplace else, you know. But the problem is they don't bother to find out what exactly was that thing that was standing up there out on the lake. The minute that they notice it looked something like a snake they run away. I have a couple of ideas. The first and the most frequent thing that people see is a fish, a sturgeon, a big sturgeon. Another thing is a log standing up in the water. The current takes those logs, moves them quite a bit. I know for sure there's something out there—it's not a log, it's not a fish, it's something bigger than a fish. A sturgeon could be about 13

feet long but still there are other things out there much bigger than that. I know for a fact.

Trudeau added that he had never seen Mishebeshu himself and his unwillingness to lay false claim to an experience is illustrated by the following story which he told me. At about the age of twelve Trudeau had been up to Toad Island in the Georgian Bay picking blueberries with his family. The water was quite rough and so the group waited until the wind died down at dusk in order to start for Killarney, where they were to sell the berries. Trudeau and his family were in a sailboat that was being towed behind a gas-powered vessel when they encountered the monster. But since Trudeau did not see Mishebeshu *with his own eyes* he does not count this experience as an actual sighting, merely as a kind of brush with the creature.

And when we got out to the open water, after we left those shoals, you know, now we're out in deeper water. I was maybe about twelve years old at that time. I was the youngest of the family and my sister Rebecca and me played in the boat. There was a centerboard right in the middle of that sailboat and on both sides of the centerboard my mother put some blankets there where we could lay down there and have a sleep. At the front end of the boat, that's where all the berries are, so we were playing here and I guess we were laughing sometimes, I suppose we were crying sometimes, too. And all of a sudden our mother started to tell us to keep quiet. It was already dark. Oh, we didn't bother, we just kept playing, you know, and all of a sudden a lot of water came in the boat just like that on both sides of the boat. And we sort of look around at each other, we don't know what's happened. I thought maybe somebody took a bucket and threw that water because we were making noise, but everybody was looking very serious and nobody said anything. Not realizing that there was something going on, not us anyway, but the older people, my mother and my dad, you know, they knew. By the time that water came up they'd already realized there was something behind us, maybe about ten or fifteen feet from the boat.

And that thing that was there never left us, from way out there, maybe about five miles from the lighthouse that's on the other side of Killarney. That thing never left us, it stayed there for the whole time and the moon came out, there was a little light, you know, and they could see it back there, and the old man figured it out that whoever it was must have had his head right under the boat and blew that water that came in. He did that twice. After we were told that we should keep quiet for the second time we did keep quiet on account of what happened. Then another bunch of water came in after awhile. So the head must have been right underneath the boat somewhere. That old man was sitting at the back end, that same boat was pointed at both ends and they had a rudder hooked on there, on the back end. And he says after we got to Killarney that the rudder was really shaking at times. We never saw it. What they told us after was it looked like maybe a cup, smooth, maybe about five inches of it sticking out of the water, that's how they noticed it, and there was little waves out there following the boat. There was an older lady in that other boat, the one that was towing us, and of course we didn't bother to holler at them.

So after we got to Killarney the old lady that was there, she lived in Killarney for a long time, she had a house there and raised her family. She was married to one of the Solomons that lived in Killarney. When they told the story of what they saw and what happened, "Oh, you should have told me", the lady said. "I should have fed him some bread, flour. All you have to do is scoop up the flour in the bag and throw it in the water and he would be gone just like that." She never mentioned that something similar had happened before but she knew what she would have done.

The act of propitiation which the old woman would have performed is consonant with the traditional offerings made to Mishebeshu. Apart from food, the gifts of choice included tobacco, which was either smoked before a trip or thrown into the water. Inez Hilger who did her field studies from 1930 to 1940 found the practice common. In the words of her consultants: "My aunt always strews tobacco on the water, all around the boat, before leaving the shore in order to drive away the evil spirits"; "Early in the spring when we make our first trip on the water we throw a pinch of tobacco in the lake"; "Some white men drowned here in the lake and that did not happen for nothing. Some things are sacred to Indians and white people who make fun of it can expect to be punished. Whites have laughed at Indians putting tobacco in the lake. We put tobacco in the lake whenever we go swimming, or when we want to cross the lake" (1951, 62). Sometimes copper objects and provisions were thrown into the water as well and dogs (usually white ones) were ritually sacrificed to the owner of the waters (Henry 1901, 169, and Kohl 1860, 60).[9] Unlike the tobacco offerings, which are still routinely made to the Thunderers, these gifts to Mishebeshu are seldom, if ever, proffered now on Manitoulin. People appear to have forgotten the practice even while they retain a firm belief that monsters people their lakes. In William Trudeau's tale, which occurred sixty-five years ago, only an old woman seemed to be aware of the proper propitiation. However, the respect which always accompanies offerings to the Thunderers is still accorded to the Underwater manitouk. Just as young people are told to keep quiet when the storms pass overhead, silence is appropriate when one ventures into Mishebeshu's world. Many Anishnaabeg feel it is unwise to draw attention to oneself when out on the lakes.

> Whenever we got in the boat we always kept quiet in the boat. We kind of whisper to one another if you're going to say something, if you're way out in the lake, way out in the bay someplace. It's different if you're close to the dock, then you can yell as much as you want, like young children (Raymond Armstrong, Personal Communication, 1988).

We must be aware, however, that no gift or sign of respect can bend Mishebeshu's will if it is fixed. Like the deep waters his ways are opaque. The monster may ignore you or he may choose to drown you or steal your children for reasons known only to himself. As a relatively powerless person, a human being, there is little that you can do to dissuade him. Blackbird tells the tale of a woman whose child was stolen by the water monster. Powerful conjurers assembled in order to divine the whereabouts of the child, who could be heard crying beneath the ground. They finally discerned an underwater passage that led into the heart of a nearby hill and managed to dig down to the monster's lair. The Mishebeshu (there were two) ran away in the face of these exceptionally powerful and determined Anishnaabeg. The people found the child but failed in their mission, for the baby who had been stolen was dead (Blackbird 1887, 82-84). The infant's mother had been incautious and had laid the baby near the water at the doorstep of Mishebeshu's home. In effect, she figuratively and literally invited disaster.

This story illustrates the extreme precariousness of Anishnaabe life in a cosmos where all places and all things serve as potential homes or disguises for powerful persons. Just as one cannot isolate the Thunderers from the thunderstorms, so too the symbol of Mishebeshu is embedded in the context of a natural phenomenon or feature. The water, which provides essential sustenance and transportation to Anishnaabeg, has always been recognized as a liminal area of their life-world. Ultimately, humans do not belong in the water and they may only hope that their presence on or near it will at least be suffered by the manitouk who dwell there. Unlike the Thunderers, Mishebeshu is never called grandfather for he does not help humans. Certainly he may offer great power to some but this power always comes at a great price. It is given neither freely nor with any affection, not in the way that a grandfather would give it. While *matci-manitouk* like the windigo and Mishebeshu share in a fundamental personhood with humans, they are not family members. Their defiance of ordinary rules of behavior between kinfolk and friends is an indication of their fundamental strangeness and malevolence. While humans await the visits of the Thunderers and court their attention, the most that they ask of Mishebeshu is to be ignored, to be given safe passage from his home back to their own.

In the previous chapter I said that the symbolic reality of the Thunderers formed a complex of belief akin to a kaleidoscopic vision. In the world of Mishebeshu we find instead a monster symbol who hides himself amidst a labyrinth of shifting currents and subterranean passages. The monster speaks to us only with the dull roar of an angry lake, and analysis is frustrated by the inaccessibility and obscurity of the places in which this symbol resides. We catch only glimpses of his form, and these brief encounters do little to illuminate his features. Our knowledge of him is more an emotion than a thought, a feeling of uneasiness that someone, a person (or people?) who we will never understand, is *down there.* Likewise, the Anishnaabeg can neither penetrate Mishebeshu's realm nor stand alone against him when he chooses to surface. Only the Thunderers have the power and will necessary to right the imbalance that is the inevitable product of Mishebeshu's acts.

In the final chapters I will explore not only the ways in which Thunderbirds and Underwater manitouk meet but the foundational events which led to the formation of the present earth. As we begin the reconstructive phase of interpretation, putting together the pieces which analysis has yielded, we will remember that Nanabush performed an analogous yet inestimably more significant act of re-creation. He fashioned a fragile island so that humans might have a place to stand, above the threat of the waters and under the protection of the sky.

NOTES

1. Mishebeshu is frequently associated with rapids and is said to live in them (see Kinietz 1965, 328, and Southcott 1984, 71). Rogers notes that the identification between Mishebeshu and rapids was so strong that to dream of rapids was, in effect, to dream of the Underwater manitouk (1962, D.6).

2. The windigo is one of the most feared manitouk, especially among the northern Ojibwe. He is represented as a giant ice monster and/or cannibal. This manitou is said to have once been a human who, in the throes of starvation imagined that his family was a group of beavers. He ate them all and was subsequently condemned to wander the earth as a windigo. The windigo acts as both a specter of starvation and a warning to those who are excessively greedy. Gluttons may be eaten by windigos or become windigos themselves. References to the windigo are numerous. For tales see Johnston (1976, 165-67), Colombo (1982), and Howard Norman (1982). For a psychological study see Morton Teicher (1960).

3. Vecsey (1983, 148-50) makes a convincing case for 'sin' as a conceptual reality in the traditional Ojibwe life-world.

I am reminded, here, of Paul Ricoeur's analysis of the categories of defilement, sin, and guilt (1967). Given Ricoeur's thesis regarding these progressive stages of responsibility and internalization, one might assume that the Ojibwe notion of sin, occurring as it does in a mythic/ritual vision of the world, would be properly termed 'defilement' in his scheme. A brief comparison will show, however, that while 'evil' in this world is, in fact, well described in terms of Ricoeur's second stage of analysis (i.e., the traditional Ojibwe notion of evil especially as it is expressed in the Re-Creation Myth is the nightmare of a primordial chaos), human actions would seem to share in the symbolism of sin. Sin here is an act which has both positive and negative aspects. While it takes up the "infection and dread" of the symbol of defilement, the Ojibwe notion of sin is not the violation of a taboo but of a proscription which has been formulated in order to assure good relations between humans and those persons who control the ultimate conditions of Anishnaabe life. Ojibwe sin is nothing less than an *act* which violates a relationship formed between the self and other persons, both human and other-than-human. "It is not the transgression of an abstract rule—of a value—but the violation of a personal bond" (Ricoeur 1967, 54).

While the negativity of sin, the estrangement of the self from the manitouk, is not the radical estrangement which one finds in the Judeo-Christian context, the traditional Ojibwe who lost contact with manitouk was a pitiable person, as helpless as a baby in the face of the world. I would also add that the Ojibwe concept of human nature was quite different from that which Ricoeur describes. Their inherent weakness was not a 'faulted' nature but merely a lack of power within the hierarchy of a peopled cosmos. Even today, many Christian Anishnaabeg express profound discomfort with the idea of the Fall.

4.   Frank G. Speck (1923, 273) reports the absence of venomous snakes in the Northeast. Long recorded a large snake population in southern Canada near Quebec including rattlers, turkey snakes, and blackwater snakes (Quaife 1922, 199-201). But recent studies indicate that venomous reptiles are nonexistent in the Northern woods. The harmless milk snake does appear in Ojibwe territory, however, and it is often mistaken for a copperhead (*Audubon Society Nature Guides: Eastern Forests*, 1987).

There is some disagreement as to the presence of rattlesnakes along the North Shore of Lake Huron, but the name of a town at the northwestern edge of Manitoulin, *Sheshegwaning* (place of the rattlesnake), indicates that they once inhabited the island. All consultants agree that there are no rattlers anywhere on the island either now or in recent memory. The only common snakes (*gnebig*) appear to be the small, harmless garter snake and perhaps some non-venomous species of water snakes.

5. The Midewiwin has a number of progressive degrees, each of which provides more knowledge and power to the initiate. Hoffman (1891) recorded four degrees but both Warren (1885) and Landes (1968) testify to the existence of eight. Dewdney indicates that there can be as many as sixteen.

6. This is the tale in which a man releases the magical fish he has caught in return for a promise that all his wife's wishes will be granted. The wife, in her greed, exceeds the boundaries of the agreement and all good fortune is lost. See Stith Thompson (1976, 134).

7. I have been unable to obtain a translation of this name. None of my consultants were familiar with the word. Raymond Armstrong thought it might be associated with *zaagwigan*, a word for lake, or perhaps it means the *agima* (ogimaa) of something.

8. The Zuni have a similar belief in such underground waterways. See Ruth L. Bunzel (1929-30, 467-544): "The cosmology of the Zunis is extremely fragmentary. The earth is circular in shape and is surrounded on all sides by ocean. Under the earth is a system of covered waterways all connecting, ultimately, with the surrounding oceans. Springs and lakes, which are always regarded as sacred, are the openings to this system. On the shores of the encircling ocean live the *Uwanami* or rain makers. They have villages in the four world quarters. The underground waters are the home of *Kolowisi*, the horned serpent" (487). We should note that the rainmakers are thundercloud beings and there is an extensive priesthood attached to them. Their purpose is, clearly, to provide moisture for crops and not to attack the horned serpent who, in this mythos, appears as a guardian of the springs and symbol of flood and fecundity. He is celebrated in ceremonies and is not understood to be a malevolent person like Mishebeshu. My impression is that any relations between Uwanami and Kolowisi are not at all antagonistic and that the two reside and act within a unifying symbology of life-giving water.

See Bunzel, 513-16. Of course, in the desert world of the Zuni agriculturalists, water is necessarily seen in a very different way than it was by traditional Ojibwe hunters and fishers. On the Anishnaabe island, water is omnipresent, and while it provides a source of food, it is more often experienced as a threat or a barrier.

9. Kohl (1860) offers an explanation for the sacrifice of the dog, saying that an Indian told him "the dog is our domestic companion, our dearest and most useful animal . . . It is almost like sacrificing ourselves." Morriseau agrees: "For this cat [Mishebeshu] had to be pleased; it lived on human flesh or souls, but also accepted offerings of white pups about six months old to replace human souls" (1965, 27). Morriseau adds that the monster did not require this special offering very often.

The color white was always associated with special significance and/or power in the traditional Ojibwe world. White is, naturally enough, the color given to the northern quarter of the world, a region from which winter and dreaded windigos come. The ogimaa or owner of an animal species was frequently said to be white—perhaps a reminder of the rarity of albino animals—and Mishebeshu himself is described as a white monster in some versions of the deluge myth (see William Carson 1917, 491, and Chamberlain 1891, 200).

V

STORM ON THE LAKE

"My great-grandfather used to tell us that the
[thunder]birds were our friends, and would kill the snakes and
the dragons. You remember Jehovah said, 'I will send a bird
to kill the dragons.' So at a certain length of time the clouds
pass over a place and you see the fire going into the water.
The birds are killing the dragons."
  —*Elizabeth Philemon in*
  Richard Dorson,
  Bloodstoppers and
  Bearwalkers, 1952

To this point I have intentionally spoken about the Thunderers and
Mishebeshu in some isolation from one another in order to explore
their various symbolic forms in depth. In what I have called an analytic
phase we entered the Ojibwe life-world and met these persons within
their own homes, looking first up and then down, listening for their
voices and searching for their shadows. Now, as we enter the final
phase of interpretation, the dialectical or synthetic movement of our
hermeneutic is both pre-figured and echoed by a parallel movement of
the symbols.[1] The Thunderers and Mishebeshu come together right at
the limits of their respective realms; the monster breaking the waters
of the lake just as the Thunderbirds dive toward it. This meeting is effected in a middle ground, at the level of the Anishnaabe island, and
constitutes an event which is witnessed in waking experience, dreams,
and myth. At the moment of this event, all that we have come to understand about the manitouk is amplified by the very force of their
meeting.

In this coming together of the symbols there exists a tension not only between manitou and manitou but between event and meaning as well, for contained in the relationship and in the myths which describe that relationship is both an experience *and* an interpretation of that experience. While the 'transformative' power of human consciousness, the intentionality which forms perceptions into noema, is always with us, the experience of the symbol is, in effect, the experience of a world built upon and within the context of tradition. While tradition determines and circumscribes the symbols here—one wishes to dream of the Thunder manitouk and avoid dreams of Underwater manitouk; Thunderers are grandfathers, Mishebeshu is not—the symbols are always multi-valent. And the experience of the plethora of meanings contained in each symbol can only be increased when symbols meet, when their worlds metaphorically, and in this case literally, collide with one another.

The text of the myths of Thunderers, of Mishebeshu, and of the two together is "writ large upon the face of the earth," so large, in fact, that one actually *reads* the myths in the clouds, on the lake, and in the terrifying battle that ensues when storm and water come together. In 'reading' these myths, I have, heretofore, concentrated upon the events, the experiences of Anishnaabe people, drawing the symbols out from that experience and studying them as closely as possible. Now I may release the symbols from analysis and in so doing also relax the brackets I have imposed upon myself and the reader in the spirit of phenomenological inquiry. In this chapter, as we witness the interactions of these persons, we will read the myths differently, concentrating more explicitly upon the way in which humans interpret these persons and their acts. We will see how the self-reference of the traditional Anishnaabeg allowed them to make their own world somewhere in between the worlds of height and depth. In the final chapter this self-reference will prove pivotal, and only then will we turn from reflection upon Anishnaabe experience toward the responsible 'appropriation' of that experience.[2] Such explicit and self-conscious interpretation is appropriate at this point, for here we are trying to fit the pottery shards together, to rebuild and reunite the symbols which yearn to meet in a dialectical and often deadly dance.

In interpreting the relationship between Thunderers and Mishebeshu we turn, once again, to the now familiar categories of authority:

firsthand experience and testimony (including the testimony of art), myths, and dream/visions. As we refer to accounts of the cosmic battle between the manitouk it is important to clarify my use of the term 'dialectical' in describing the relationship that we will see enacted. When I say that the relationship here describes a dialectic I mean several things. First, I wish to reject the prevailing and largely underdeveloped thesis that these persons are the tutelary spirits of a dualistic system. Howard's description of the *Bungi*, or Plains Ojibwe, is exemplary.

> The dualism implied in the Thunderbird vs. Underwater panther struggle is common to the philosophies of many Midwestern tribes, particularly of the Algonquian stock. The Thunderbirds represent the sky and upper world, light, and good; while the Nambiza represent the lower world, darkness, as in dark waters, and evil. In the Indian concept man has within him both qualities, and both forces must be placated (1965, 5).

Clearly there is a dualism present here just as there is in all myths and symbolisms which revolve around the axes of sky and water.[3] And in the Ojibwe life-world such oppositions do describe one aspect, a structural level, of the interchange between the manitouk. However, as we have seen, the Thunderers and Mishebeshu are exceedingly complex beings whose forms and wills are mutable. Further, we are not dealing with two *independent* principles but, as we will see later in this chapter, two *mutually dependent* persons. And while there is a general attitude among the Ojibwe which assigns good qualities to the heavens and places evil in the waters, it is in no way a strictly dualistic system.[4] We have seen that young Thunderbirds sometimes attack humans and that the Underwater manitouk are, on occasion, sought for their medicinal powers. And the fact that metamorphosis is such an integral part of the Ojibwe life-world leads us to believe that no relationship, no direction of the cosmos, is invariable. More important, however, is to understand that the battles between these manitouk are not experienced as contests between good and evil, light and dark, right and wrong, but between the forces of balance and imbalance, as embodied in powerful persons. These persons are much more than signs to be placed on opposite sides of an equation. They do not, as Howard says, *represent* opposite directions and qualities. Such an interpretation, at the level of allegory, merely scratches the surface of a relationship which, as we shall see, not only expresses a conflict but provides a necessary and complementary element in the lives of the manitouk and of the Anishnaabeg.

Far from being a simple vertical clash between the powers of sky and water, the relationship of the manitouk can be understood as dialectical inasmuch as it expresses a continual movement between two contradictory symbols. In the next chapter we will see how this contradiction merges into a higher truth or synthesis both through the actions of Nanabush, the ally of the Thunderers, in relation to Mishebeshu, and in the creation of the Mide society under the auspices of the two manitouk. For now we observe the circularity of this relationship by turning to the interpretation offered in the work of some Ojibwe and Cree artists.

David Migwans, a Manitoulin potter and artist, has painted the struggle between the Thunderers and Mishebeshu. In his work the battle is joined in a circular movement wherein the two manitouk are literally locked in combat. This is not an especially unusual depiction, and we find a similar circular pattern in works by the Cheyenne artist Dick West and the late Cree painter Carl Ray. Migwans explained his vision of the mythic battle, saying that the conflict serves to keep a balance in the world, for in attacking the monster the Thunderers check the imbalance which Mishebeshu causes. Yet no matter how many times the Underwater manitouk are attacked, even killed, they always return. As Migwans put it, quite simply, "Nobody ever really wins" (Personal Communication, 1988). And the circle which they inscribe can be read as a symbol of their eternal and inevitable reunion with one another.

This reunion, this unending strife, is also a kind of communication or discourse, albeit a rather violent one. This communication is apparent in Carl Ray's work on the subject. While Ray titled his painting *Conflict Between Good and Evil*, we can see that something more than a battle of polarities is happening here. Southcott, in her artistic analysis of this piece, follows the familiar assignment of symbols indicated in the title, saying that the "Thunderbird represents good, the waterspirit evil." Her interpretation of the visual elements continues:

Conflict between Good and Evil
Carl Ray
Acrylic on canvas
Reproduction courtesy of The McMichael Canadian Collection

> An ovoid vortex of whirling lines converges into a cluster of flailing claws and paws. A waving line of communication leads from one mouth to the other. Finer lines connecting the two figures seem to represent animosity made visual. It is a masterpiece of Anishnaabe graphic design, imitative of the water surface patterns made by swirling currents in a river, or wave patterns on a northern lake when wind and waters collide (1984, 23).

Here we see how the text of the mythic relationship is read first in the artist's image and at another level in the natural phenomena which the image recalls. The manitouk not only speak to each other but mirror one another in their conflict.

Likewise, Mel Madahbee's painting, while more static in form, includes the same sort of reflective imagery. We see the shattering of the Thunderbird eggs reflected in the lightning and in the jagged shapes of the mature bird's wings. Mishebeshu's back recalls the waves that surround him, and his spines and horns gesture back to the lightning strokes, cracking eggs, and sharp feathers above him. In the monster's tail the symmetry is amplified into an identification as the lightning and Mishebeshu's spines meet and actually merge into one another. The lightning could even be growing upward from his tail, forming an inverted tree.[5] In a similar vein, the colors which Madahbee has chosen unify the world of sky and water, moving downward from a deep, purplish hue through progressively lightening blues, just to the level of the clouds. Here the artist switches to a dark red, reflected as a pink in the background waters. This pink darkens as it nears Mishebeshu until in the foreground it becomes purple, slightly lighter than the highest portion of the sky but exactly the same color as the clouds on which the Thunderbirds nest.[6]

The reflective imagery of these paintings should not be taken to indicate that the Thunderer and Mishebeshu are antagonistic twins or even, in the Jungian sense, a self and shadow pair. Certainly, as Howard noted above, Indians recognize the dual qualities which exist in the human heart and insist upon the necessity of balancing one's inner conflicts. Yet such a recognition is, in no way, exclusive to Native North American consciousness. What is particularly characteristic of the traditional Ojibwe is the belief that humans are, in fact, structurally and functionally *tripartite*. Traditional beliefs hold that each person not only possesses but is made up of an ego soul, a free or shadow soul and a body. The two souls are located in different parts of the body, the ego soul residing in the heart and the free, traveling, or shadow soul being located in the brain. "Neither of these souls was the entire person, according to the Ojibwas. Neither constituted a personality-soul or a unified soul. Each soul had an existence on its own, apart from the body; however, both acted in harmony with the body." The ego soul "provided intelligence, reasoning, memory, consciousness, and the ability to act" (Vecsey 1983, 60). The free soul is the part of the person that travels in dream and vision and that acts as a scout for the hunter or warrior. "When a man is travelling his shadow goes before or behind him; normally it is in front, nearer to his destination. It often causes a

Animikeeg and Mishebeshu
Mel Madahbee
Acrylic on canvas
From the author's collection
Photo by Fred Maize

twitching of the hunter's eyelids, informing him that it has seen game ahead" (Jenness 1935, 19). Interestingly enough, then, the character of each soul is exactly the reverse of what Euro-Americans might expect, the seat of reason being the heart and the seat of perception and instinct being the brain. Jenness says, "translated somewhat imperfectly into the terms of our own psychologists, [the free soul] is the sensation and perception that precede reasoning and knowledge" (1935, 19).[7]

Unless all discrete elements are present and functioning well, the human is something less than a person. In contemporary Anishnaabe art, painters working in the ancient x-ray style indicate integrity of being and honesty by a line connecting the heart (ego soul) to the mouth. This device, called a heartline, is most noticeable by its absence. In the painting *Racism* by Blake Debassige, for instance, the figures of white racists are empty of both hearts and heartlines. As Debassige described it, "I wanted to make a comment about people seeing themselves, how they really look and how they look at me" (Personal Communication, 1992). Traditionally, inner conflicts were often thought to be the result of a lack of cooperation between the souls. As Jenness described the condition:

> Occasionally the shadow may divide or become double; one part may wish to co-operate with the [ego] soul and body, the other seek to travel or go hunting. The man then becomes a centre of conflicting desires. His two shadows contend for the mastery, his struggling [ego] soul remains aloof from the body awaiting the issue, and the body itself falls sick. There is generally no cure for this condition and the man dies (1935, 20).

This ailment was not always the result of mere intrapsychic conflict. Malevolent shamans could, and still do, steal or disrupt one of the souls in order to cause sickness or death. The shadow soul of a baby is considered highly vulnerable to such attacks, perhaps because the infant has just begun to integrate as a person.[8] This integration, like the battles of the manitouk, is an ongoing process, a life-long balancing act.

With these preliminary observations regarding the dialectical character of the relationship between Thunderer and Mishebeshu and the need for balance of the tripartite self in mind, let us turn away from artistic images and back toward the event in which the symbolic representations are born. We need to understand exactly how this battle is joined in order to flesh out the pattern that we have sketched. In all battles, in all lake storms, it is the Thunderer who is understood to be on the offensive. Swooping down upon the lake the Thunderbirds attack in more than one manner. Their most obvious weapon, lightning, is often understood to be the hurling of thunder stones upon the water. These stones often strike and kill the Underwater manitouk, whose bodies may later be found floating upon the water. Norval Morriseau relates a tale in which the evidence of the Thunderers' victory was clearly seen. As in a story included in our previous chapter, Mishebeshu steals a baby that has been carelessly left at his doorstep.

> About half an hour later both returned to find their baby gone. By the shores of Lake Superior paw prints were seen and they were Misshipeshu's prints. The baby had been taken, cradle and all, into the water and into the underwater caves. What could the poor Indians do? Despite the loss of their child the

Indian spoke, "I will play my medicine drum and ask the thunderbirds to destroy the cave, including Misshipeshu."

From the heavens appeared a great thunderbird that threw lightning into the caves and rocks. Misshipeshu was forced to come out. As the demi-god was about to leave, the thunderbird struck the ground and Misshipeshu died from the lightning.

Meanwhile the couple fell into a coma, not knowing what really had taken place. When they awoke later they found their child's cradle floating on the surface of the water, their child dead with two holes in his head, and Misshipeshu's head floating around, the rest of his body having been eaten (1965, 31).

This tale includes several elements with which we are already familiar. First, Mishebeshu is able to take the baby because its parents did not exhibit sufficient caution. In this life-world, nothing should be taken for granted, for persons appear suddenly and every lake serves as a possible home for the monster. The underwater passages are here, the symbols of Mishebeshu's "hiddeness" and of his ability to travel quickly and unseen between waters. Anishnaabeg may call upon the Thunderers for protection and they will answer, acting decisively against Underwater manitouk. Even so, the baby is lost, for the monster has great power and this world is not a forgiving one to those who are foolhardy.

We have not, however, seen such a battle between the manitouk before. And one of the more interesting points in this story is Morriseau's assertion that during the course of the struggle the couple "fell into a coma" and so were not able to witness the actual moment when the Thunderbird took Mishebeshu and devoured his body. This inability to see the Thunderbird carrying out the second phase of his attack is not unusual. Often the event is obscured in fog. "It was said that they [the Thunderers] lived on the spirits of the deep or darkness. When they dived down into the water and brought up the wicked spirits in their claws, in order to carry them away to their home in the skies, the whole place was enveloped in fog" (Coleman 1937, 37). Ojibwes on Manitoulin talked about the clouds coming down "real low" right after lightning had struck the water and just before the Thunderer seized his prey. While one could not see the Thunderbird through the shield of cloud or fog, one could catch a glimpse of the monster as it was dragged up to the heavens. Delores and Raymond Armstrong recounted two such events.

Delores: You know Jeremy's story when they were caught in a storm up there [Whitefish Lake]? A big thunder came, eh? It was lightning and stuff like that. And then they saw this—well, there was a big clap of thunder, eh—and then they saw this thing going around and around way up in the air. And they said it looked like a big snake.

Raymond: That's the thunder. Thunder will come. Thunder will take certain things out of the lake or out of the bay. It's just like in Wiky. I wonder why William [Trudeau] didn't tell it. Maybe he didn't hear about it. Anyways, a friend of mine's grandmother told us this. She was sitting by her window one day, I guess, one stormy day. She knew it was gonna be storming so she was sitting close to the window. It was getting dark and she went and sat close to the window so she could see what she was knitting. She was knitting, I guess, a pair of socks for one of her boys.

And this is when the Thunder came. It started to rain and thundering and she could see the lightning at the bay from on top of the hill where you were—you must have seen the bay where Bill lives. It's very close. You could see the bay pretty good. And this is where the lady was sitting. There used to be an old log house there, and this old lady sitting on that chair knitting away. And she seen all kinds of fire, lines of fire going back and forth at that bay—like as if it was searching. Every now and then there would be a big Thunder. At one time there was a big Thunder. At one time her whole house shook. And she could hear some of her stuff falling from the noise of the Thunder that she heard. And she looked out the window and that's when she seen this all fog, it was all fog, water. And she seen this big thing. They used to say it was about seven or eight feet wide in diameter that was going up in the sky. And she saw the tail end of it. It was going like this [a whirling movement]. It was a big snake—maybe fifty, sixty feet, or a hundred feet long. I don't know how big they are. And she *al-*

ways told her boys, don't stay out in the bay long (Personal Communication, 1988).

The detail with which Raymond Armstrong told this story, setting the scene in which the old woman was knitting not just anything but *"socks for one of her boys,"* is common to many of the tales which I heard. Such detail succeeds not only in lending veracity (it happened just this way) but in heightening the immediacy of the account. Further, Armstrong places me at the scene—"You must have seen the bay where Bill lives. It's very close. You could see the bay pretty good." And as I listened I did, indeed, place myself on the hill where William Trudeau's house sits and let the images play themselves out before me from that vantage point. The first thing that occurred to me was, "this sounds/looks like a huge waterspout" and yet I was quickly forced to discount or, at least, qualify this "natural" explanation. I remembered that I had been told about waterspouts in the bay, notably by Trudeau, who was a retired fishing guide. These spouts were usually seen quite clearly and while considered dangerous to boaters were not understood to be the work of manitouk. Clearly my Anishnaabe acquaintances, with their fine eye for detail, differentiated between these phenomena. In postulating a "rational" explanation I was, in fact, confusing two disparate events and falling prey to the muddled, undifferentiated thinking that was once so often erroneously ascribed to "primitive" peoples.

At the end of his story Armstrong added that following the event, the fish, once absent there, had returned to this part of the lake. The Thunderers, having purified the waters by purging them of a monster, had benefited the Anishnaabeg and restored a balance to the bay. This purifying role of the animikeek is clearly defined throughout myths and personal testimony. Leland Bell saw such purification as the primary function of the Thunderers (Personal Communication, 1988). Others agree and say that the Thunderbirds were specially created by Kitche Manitou to cleanse the world not only by ridding it of the monsters but by bathing it with rain (Blackbird 1887, 103; Hoffman 1890, 244).[9] Mishebeshu, in turn, works his imbalance through decimating the water game, drowning Anishnaabeg, and, on at least one occasion, flooding the earth. While the manitouk are clearly at cross-purposes, the interdependence of the symbols is apparent even in their conflict. Mishebeshu needs the moisture provided by the storms in order to survive, for without it his world would literally disappear. And as we will see shortly, the Thunderers might well starve without the food which monster snakes provide. In the fog that cloaks their struggle, air and water mingle at a middle point, and a new symbol is thus suspended as a visible reminder of conflict and interdependence in this remarkably fluid world.

The Thunderers, as grandfathers, work constantly to protect Anishnaabeg both from cosmic imbalance and personal harm. At the end of this chapter we will see how their protective power is transmitted to humans who have seen the grandfathers as pawaganak or dream visitors. Even though grandfathers do love and protect their grandchildren, they are not completely unselfish people. Unlike the water manitouk they do not exact Charon-like tolls or bribes in exchange for service, but, as we have seen, they do require attention and respect, often in the form of tobacco offerings. Further, their attacks on the malevolent monsters are self-serving inasmuch as they feed upon the flesh of Mishebeshu and all of the ground and water snakes associated with him. We recall William Trudeau's tale from Chapter 3 in which the Thunderbirds were found in their nest eating a huge snake. And certainly the monster serpent which they took from Wikwemikong Bay would have provided them with quite a feast. Weather lore further reflects the dining habits of the Thunderers. Killing frogs or snakes is said to bring on a storm, especially if one lays the snake on its back, thus exposing its belly both as a taunting gesture and as a tempting morsel for the Thunderbirds (Hilger 1951, 106; Morriseau 1965, 16).

Thunderbirds eat the serpents in part because they have a taste for blood. And, oddly enough, some accounts say that they once preferred human blood to that of monsters. Copway relates a tale in which young Thunderbirds are killed by a man who has been abducted by their parents. Wrapping himself in the skin and feathers of one of the murdered babies, he flies home in triumph. According to Copway, this victory, and the subsequent influx of people along the shores of Lake Superior, pushed the Thunderers farther to the West, in much the same way that the Ojibwe and Sioux were progressively dislocated by Europeans: "Their nests are now built on the *Ahsenwahgewing* (Rocky Mountains), in the far West, and at times they are heard passing through the air towards the East, on their way to the sea, for they live upon fish and serpents, since they have been subdued by man" (1850, 113).

There is also a short Cree tale in which *bokogeesihwok* (black flies) trick the Thunderbirds into striking trees. Anyone who has spent the month of June in the Northern Great Lakes area will be familiar with the virulence of black flies and their seemingly insatiable thirst for blood. Caribou herds have been known to stampede and are said to be driven mad by the swarms of tiny insects. On this particular occasion a group of black flies were looking for a warm place in which to spend the fall and decided to go up to the nests of the Thunderbirds.

> The nests of the thunderbirds were located high in the mountains toward the setting sun. Upon their arrival at the nests of the thunderbirds the black flies were asked many questions by the chieftain bird. The chieftain bird noticed the Bok-o-geesih-wok were full of rich red blood
>
> "Where did you obtain the blood in your bodies?" commanded the thunderbird. One of the black flies flew up and said, "Oh, great thunderbird, we get blood from the tall trees in the forest."
>
> That night there was a great storm as the thunderbirds aimed bolts of fire at the tall trees in the woods.
>
> Whenever my people see trees split by lightning bolts, they tell us that it is the thunderbirds looking for the blood of the Indians (Ray and Stevens 1984, 92).

These stories are exceptions to the general rule which governs the behavior patterns of the Thunderers. And it should be noted that both tales are said to have occurred long, long ago, before the present earth and the relationship between Thunderers and Anishnaabeg was formed. But if there is any truth to these tales, if the Underwater manitouk do indeed take a place on the Thunderers' table once reserved for Anishnaabeg, then the continued survival of Mishebeshu and of all reptilian creatures would seem to be an essential element of the Ojibwe life-world. We do, in any case, know that a strong protective bond was forged when the Thunderers allied themselves with Nanabush at the time of the Deluge and Re-Creation. This bond, a covenant between grandparents and grandchildren, is, as we have seen, still a strong influence in the lives of contemporary Ojibwes. It is so strong, in fact, that most Ojibwe people would question the veracity of these tales, especially inasmuch as Anishnaabe identity itself is tied so closely to the mythology of the protective Thunderers. Among Christian Natives, the Thunderer is so central to spirituality that he is retained in this foreign context and often aligned, even merged, with the symbol of the Holy Spirit. An example may be found in the Catholic Church at West Bay, which is built in the round style of a medicine lodge. Here, where one would expect to find the dove of the Holy Spirit, a Thunderbird pattern is affixed in the skylight over the altar, its wings spread protectively.

This survival of the spirit of the Thunderbird within a foreign religious context is testimony not only to the strength of Ojibwe symbols but to their flexibility as well. Angus Pontiac, who did not identify himself as Christian, held that the validity of Ojibwe Thunderbird and eagle mythologies was reinforced by references to eagles in the Bible. His theory was that such cross-cultural references strengthen rather than dilute Ojibwe beliefs (Personal Communication, 1988). Without surrendering their identity and what they consider to be the uniqueness of their own symbols, contemporary Ojibwes tend toward a holistic understanding of both symbols and religions. Inasmuch as they hold that all things and persons in their own world are interconnected, they extend this web of relations to the whole earth. They see themselves to be, in a way, like the lakes of their own life-world, connected by unseen passages, first to one another, then to other tribes and peoples, and, ultimately, as rivers and underground channels reach the oceans, to the entire population of the world. In my conversations with Kitty Bell, for instance, I found remarkable examples of this kind of global consciousness. Mrs. Bell, a member of the newly revived midewiwin was especially interested in the curative aspects of all religions. She welcomed visitors of all kinds and told me, with some laughter, of a group of New Age witches who had sought her out and spent the afternoon with her. Mrs. Bell felt that Manitoulin held a special kind of "spiritual charge" that attracted people from all over the earth. The island was, for her, a kind of spiritual meeting ground for various cultures, all of which held some particle of truth, some insight that might yet save the world from destruction. Her vision was, in fact, somewhat apocalyptic, and she spoke often of the need to reinstitute a physical and spiritual balance not only on the earth but within the entire universe.

To return to a particular relationship in this cosmic tapestry, we see that while the Thunderers and Mishebeshu fight one another they also depend upon each other for their survival. It is an odd and, for

Mishebeshu, who is usually on the losing side, rather unfortunate marriage.[10] The Thunderers seem to have little or no trouble subduing the monster but, to his credit, and like the game animals of the Ojibwe world, Mishebeshu appears able to regenerate himself constantly. His eternal survival at once frustrates the Thunderers—who would rid the cosmos of him for their grandchildren—and nourishes them as a continuing food source. On rare occasions Mishebeshu has been known to triumph in this war. Only two such victories come to mind. In the first, the victory of Mishebeshu is seen as a very bad sign. Norval Morriseau relates an experience of his ancestor, Little Grouse.

> When he reached a certain place thunder was heard again. He looked in amazement to see a huge, big Misshepeshu with remains of bits of meat and bones on top of the rocks. Thinking it was a sign of some misfortune he went on his way. This foretold his death, for one year later my ancestor died (1965, 85).

In the second tale, a Cree narrative told by the artist, Carl Ray, Thunderbirds attack a great crayfish that may or may not be another form of Mishebeshu. It is a special protector of Ray's family, having once saved his mother from drowning, and the tale seems to be the special property of his family on account of the very unusual beneficial relationship which his people formed with the monster. Because of the personal nature of the story, and the beliefs about Thunderers and the Underwater manitouk which we have seen expressed elsewhere, I would take Morriseau's version to be more consistent with prevailing attitudes.

> My uncle, Abraham, has said that only one creature in the world was capable of defeating the thunderbirds, and this was the giant crayfish. This underwater creature once fought a thunderbird. The *binay-sih* caught the crayfish out on a sandbar and hurled lightning at it, but the bolts just could not penetrate the hard shell of the crayfish. When the thunderbird came lower, the crayfish grabbed the big bird with its claw and dragged the thunderbird under the water and drowned it (Ray and Stevens 1984, 94).

Mishebeshu's victories are few, perhaps in part because he is almost always outnumbered by his adversaries. In his battles with the Thunderers, Mishebeshu—despite the fact that his name denotes a

plural person—is most often seen as standing completely alone, an individual fighting against a group. This solitude may be read as a sign of
this manitou's great power and of what we have called his uncanny nature. We should note that the only other manitouk who invariably live
and travel alone are the dreaded windigo and the mournful and frightening pauguck. For while the traditional Ojibwes prized independence, they were also radically aware of the need for communal actions
and alliances both in hunting and in war. Further, they turned to the
manitouk early in life, pleading for visions which would ensure a strong
and lasting relationship between themselves and more powerful other-
than-human persons. Even when Mishebeshu left his isolation and
chose to engage in such a guardian relationship with humans, the character of the interaction frequently stood outside the normal patterns of
human-manitou relationships. As we have seen, the monster asked too
much of his human companions, treating them as if they were his ser-
vants rather than his grandchildren, and often demanding their souls
or the lives of their families. It is not surprising, then, that
Mishebeshu's great victory, the primordial deluge, is effected in the
context of a myth wherein he is not alone but instead acts as ogimaa in a
lodge full of monster serpents and lynxes.

Mishebeshu does, however, score another, rather indirect, victory in this war. There is one unusual tale, found in William Jones'
collection, in which a human uses the antagonistic relationship to take
revenge upon the Thunderers who have destroyed his village (1919,
241-45). In this myth, "Floating-Net-Stick," the eponymous hero lives
with his people near a huge lake. The fishing is very bad and Floating-
Net-Stick, the ogimaa of the group, devises a plan whereby the people
might increase their catch.

> And the chief said: "Then make you a small lake by the shore of
> the sea. And let there be a small [underground] passage out to-
> wards the sea."[11]
>
> Now, it is true that they did what they had been told by
> the chief. And after they had finished the little lake, "Now in
> this place do you remain, in this [underground] passageway."
> And one floating-net-stick he made, whereupon he said to the
> people: "Under the water will I go to fetch the fish, for by this
> very place will I bring them to the little lake. And when you

see that they are filling up the little lake there, then shall you close up the place of the [underground] passageway."

The plan proves successful and the people catch fish easily in the small lake. Their time of happiness is short-lived, however, for the Thunderers attack their village and kill everyone but Floating-Net-Stick. The ogimaa is furious and goes around asking various manitou rocks for help.

> Then at last there was one unknown kind of black metal that must have been very strong, and it was by it that he was promised help. And so what he said to it was that it should look like a great serpent. And so truly that was what the black metal looked like. Thereupon over there at one side he hid himself. And during a thunder-storm the Thunderers beheld a large serpent lying there, whereupon they struck at it. But the black metal did not shatter into pieces. [He watched it] till he could scarcely see any lightning, for all their fire had the Thunderers used up. At last [the Thunderers] sprang upon that metal, but they could not make an impression upon it.
>
> And when Floating-Net-Stick saw that [the Thunderers] had no more fire, he then made an attack upon the Thunderers; he seized hold of one by the foot. "Are you the one who destroyed my town?" And so there upon the iron he flung it till he slew it.

Following his victory over the Thunderers, Floating-Net-Stick returns to his village, and through the ritual shooting of three arrows toward the sky, he first reanimates the bones of his people and finally resurrects them entirely. By these acts he validates the natural phenomena of these small lakes with their connections to the larger water and establishes the rights of Anishnaabeg to fish in them.

This story illustrates some important points regarding the symbology of the relationship between Thunderers and Mishebeshu. First, the symbolism, like the persons of this world, shows up in unexpected places and in unexpected forms. One might wonder why the Thunderers attacked the Anishnaabeg, whom they are normally sworn to protect. But the fact that these particular humans built *underground passages* between the lakes places them structurally within the world of

Mishebeshu. While the monster is never mentioned here, we know that he uses such passages, traveling through them and often sheltering in them when he wishes to avoid the attacks of the Thunderers. What appears to be just a clever engineering feat, if we do not know Mishebeshu's habits, takes on added meaning and becomes a symbol of the monster when we are familiar both with his activities and with the structure of the Ojibwe cosmos. It is not surprising, then, that Thunder attacks the Anishnaabeg. For humans are meant to live on the island of the earth, and just as it is risky to travel to the nests of the Thunderbirds, so too venturing beneath the ground or water signals a challenge to the accepted boundaries of the world. Only the most experienced and powerful shamans travel routinely through these layers. In this case the Anishnaabeg prevail only because Floating-Net-Stick is both personally powerful and able to enlist the aid of an extraordinarily powerful mineral-person. In using the powers of the black mineral against the Thunderers, Floating-Net-Stick depends upon the ability of all persons to metamorphose: "And so what he said to it was that it should look like a great serpent. And so truly that was what the black metal looked like." Here, once again, the mythology of Mishebeshu is invoked, and, because we know of the antagonism between Thunderbirds and serpents, we know that it is inevitable that this trick will work. The Thunderbirds will not give up striking this "snake" until they are exhausted because they simply cannot do so—it is their nature to strike until they are spent. Note too how the events here parallel those in Ray's tale of the crayfish. Like the crayfish, the metal serpent's impenetrability frustrates the Thunderbirds' attack. And in both cases, the Thunderbird is dragged bodily from his world—the air—into a lower one, where his powers appear to fail him. In robbing the Thunderers of their power, Floating-Net-Stick shows us the ability of the Ojibwe to manipulate their symbols. For not only do the persons and symbols transform themselves in this world, but humans, steeped in the complex from which such symbols arise, may mold and juxtapose images and forms. Such manipulation allows them to fool immensely powerful manitouk, and this trickery, which we usually see employed by Nanabush, is highly respected. It is, itself, a form of power and one particularly suited to persons who are as relatively weak as human beings. This same sort of cleverness was exhibited by the black flies, who, despite or perhaps because of their tiny size, tricked the Thunderbirds and so preserved their own food supply.

We have said before that this beautiful world of vision and dream holds within it great darkness and terror. However, we should not forget that humor, especially expressed as trickery, is an elemental ingredient as well. Even in the face of the majesty of the Thunderers and Mishebeshu, Anishnaabeg retain a certain sense of the absurd. This playfulness, even irreverence, indicates a sophisticated and self-conscious appropriation of the symbols by which the Ojibwe experience of the world is expressed, and it puts the lie, yet again, to antiquated theories that would have us believe that "primitives" stagger through life under a burden of superstition and confusion and tremble before forces which they but dimly comprehend. Traditional as well as contemporary Ojibwe people seemed well aware of the complexity and limitations of their religious beliefs, and their detailed understanding of the manitouk led them to ridicule themselves when they recorded extraordinary experiences with something less than precision. The following tale, collected by W. Jones in the late nineteenth century, illustrates this attitude.

THE HORNED STURGEON

Once some people got into [their canoes] to look for sturgeons; some spears they had; far out at sea they went. And while looking down into the water, every now and then they beheld a sturgeon, whereupon they thrust a spear at the sturgeon. By and by a certain man was heard saying: "Oh, behold the form of this sturgeon! It has horns in the same manner as a moose!"

Thereupon all came in canoes to see how [the sturgeon] looked. "Verily, it is horned!" they said. "That is a manitou sturgeon!"

Accordingly they smoked, some tobacco too they put into the water. When they had finished smoking, they went away.

Now, another canoe [of people] went thither, and they saw [the sturgeon]. Then, taking up his spear, [one of] the men thrust it into the sturgeon. And when they brought it up from the water, then they beheld a bald eagle clinging fast to the head of the sturgeon. Thereupon heartily did all the people laugh (1919, 289).

Here the symbols of sky and water are indeed joined but in an absurd and ultimately meaningless way. And the message seems to be that anyone who can't tell the difference between an Underwater manitou and a sturgeon with a drowned eagle on its head is very foolish indeed.

Yet laughter does nothing to rid the world or one's consciousness of the clear and present danger of Mishebeshu. Therefore Anishnaabeg turn again and again to the Thunderers to act against the monster. Usually the Thunderers are entreated, with words and offerings of tobacco, to attack Mishebeshu. This "calling-down" of the Thunderers stands in contrast and in complement to the entreaties with which we are already familiar, whereby humans ask approaching grandfathers to pass by quickly. Barnouw offers the following example of a successful entreaty on the land.

> In 1942 an Indian informant told Robert Ritzenthaler that he was once chased by a big supernatural snake about six or seven inches in diameter. He managed to reach home and told his wife to fill his pipe for him. Then he smoked and called upon the thunderbirds for help. Soon some clouds appeared in the sky; then a thunderbolt came down and killed the snake, which was close to the house. Since one of the thunderbirds carried the snake away, no one else saw the carcass (1977, 226).

Oddly, rough water, one of Mishebeshu's great weapons, is also a product of the salvational actions of the Thunderers. However, the wild seas of a storm-tossed lake, while potentially dangerous, are not considered malevolent, in part because one simply doesn't venture onto a lake in a storm. Anyone can see that the Thunderers are hunting and only an idiot would place herself between them and their prey. And because the Thunderer responds to tobacco offerings with great consistency, anyone unlucky or unwise enough to find herself on the lake in a storm may be relatively confident that the Thunderer will answer her prayers for safety. This is not the case with Mishebeshu who, as we have seen, can be unpredictable even when he is appeased. He may take your offering very nicely and leave you alone or he may decide, without provocation on your part or warning on his own, to open a whirlpool in front of your canoe or a quicksand before your feet. Mishebeshu's manipulation of the water is far more dangerous than the maelstrom of the lake storm because it seems to come from nowhere, just like the manitou himself. And when a storm strikes the water, the ferocity of the event is always tempered by the knowledge that the grandfathers are thrashing a great and terrible enemy.[12] Further, the power contained in this struggle may actually be transmitted to a witness. John Paul, the powerful and somewhat controversial shaman from Birch Island Reserve, claimed to have received his foundational vision in this way, "on a boat in the midst of a thunderstorm." The vision was said to have been "induced by a lightning flash" (Paper 1980, 197).

This leads us to another way in which the Thunderers may attack the Underwater manitouk. Rather than joining the battle directly, Thunderers have been known to empower Anishnaabeg, who in turn may take up their grandfathers' roles in this dialectical relationship.

NOW GREAT-LYNX

Long ago people used to see something in places, especially where the current was swift. The people feared it; and that was the reason of their practice of sometimes throwing offerings to it in the water, even tobacco. Now, once yonder, at what is called Shallow-Water, was where some women were once passing by in a canoe. Accordingly there happened to rise a mighty current of water, nearly were they capsized; exceedingly frightened were they. While they were paddling with all their might, they saw the tail of a Great-Lynx come up out of the water; all flung themselves up into the forward end of the canoe in their fright. Now, one of the women that was there saw that the canoe was going to sink; accordingly, when she had gone to the stern, she raised the paddle in order to strike the tail of Great-Lynx. And this she said: "While I was young, often did I fast. It was then that the Thunderers gave me their war-club." Thereupon, when she struck the tail of Great-Lynx, she then broke the tail of Great-Lynx in two. Thereupon up to the surface rose the canoe, after which they then started on their way paddling; and so they were saved (Jones 1919, 259; see also Barnouw 1977, 132-33).

The storyteller in Barnouw's version, Pete Martin, stipulates that the paddle was made of cedar (a sacred wood) and that the words spoken when Mishebeshu was hit were, "Thunder is striking you." He also adds that when the monster's tail was struck, a piece of it came off. "When they picked it up, it was a solid piece of copper about two inches thick." Like all copper garnered from the Underwater manitouk, this specimen had beneficial properties and in this case was to provide luck in hunting and fishing.

This tale contains within it three pivotal relations: Anishnaabe/Mishebeshu, Anishnaabe/Thunderer, Mishebeshu/Thunderer. The human being, threatened from below and aided from above, would appear to be hopelessly trapped between opposing categories. The power of the woman's Thunderbird dream, however, allows her to stand against the nightmare of Mishebeshu. Her paddle, a tiny weapon, acts as if it were a thunderbolt because she strikes with the assurance of her vision. This dream has effectively freed her, allowing her to partake in the power realm of the Thunderers and, like them, move against the monster with strength. In effect, by participating in a relationship with the Thunderers the woman temporarily escapes her customary relation (victim) to Mishebeshu and steps into the dialectical dance of the manitouk. While all humans are not so blessed by the Thunderers, all Anishnaabeg may partake of what is, in effect, their birthright. Their inheritance is that of a traditional world view in which a precarious island lies cradled between cloud and water. This island is plagued by storms that give humans life because they act against a force of death. And the apparent force of the lake storm is, in this world, a loud and brilliant dance whose steps lead, always, toward balance. When the woman hit Mishebeshu with her paddle she was at once assisting the Thunderers in their movement and being guided by them. And because they know that the Thunderers protect them, Anishnaabeg, who reciprocate with respect and gratitude, may be allowed to stand safely in the eye of the storm, in the midst of this eternally whirling dialectic. They should not go down into the depths and they are only rarely taken up into the clouds, but they can travel freely, if always cautiously, upon their own land.

The fluidity of their metamorphosing world and the constant tension that suspends it remind Anishnaabeg that this landscape was once wrested from the waters. Both this land and the medicine which sustains the humans who inhabit it were produced in the context of a cosmic struggle. Nearing the end of our journey after understanding, we return to the beginning, in order to discover the event and meaning that both precede and fulfill the symbols of Thunderers and Mishebeshu.

NOTES

1. By dialectical or synthetic movement I mean the phase of interpretation in which remembering gives way to reconstruction, experience to reflection. This is, in essence, a reference to Paul Ricoeur's "balanced contemporary hermeneutic [which embodies] both the deconstruction and demystification of myths, on the one hand, and their reappropriation and reaffirmation, on the other" (Pomedli 1987, 276). Ricoeur's model for his hermeneutic, a circle, moves, he says, "from *living in* symbols toward thought that *thinks from* symbols" (1974, 297). This circular journey carries interpretation beyond the recognition of 'motifs', beyond comparativism, and toward a place where the disengaged observation of the phenomenologist receives its reward. This reward is the 'second level naïvete', the opening of new horizons of meaning and value—in short, the conversion of consciousness.

2. The word, "appropriation" here refers to the point at which the interpreter looks beyond the horizon of understanding toward that of relevance, of belief: "But then I must quit the position, or better, the exile, of the remote and disinterested spectator in order to appropriate in each case an individual symbolism. Then is discovered what may be called the circle of hermeneutics, which the simple amateur of myths unfailingly misses. The circle can be stated bluntly: 'You must understand in order to believe, but you must believe in order to understand' " (Ricoeur 1974, 298).

3. For a cross-cultural study see Eliade (1965, chap. 2 and 5). For a not always accurate but frequently thought-provoking analysis of beliefs in the Americas, see Brinton (1976, chap. 4, "The Symbols of the Bird and Serpent"). Åke Hultkrantz also summarizes some parallel beliefs in reference to the Algonquians, noting both the South Asian and Nordic symbols of bird and serpent (1979,

50-51). To this list I would add not only other Native American but also the Greek, Near Eastern, Semitic, and Christian mythologies. Perhaps the most intriguing comparison does, however, lie between the Ojibwe and Nordic/Germanic complexes. Following the primordial deluge, Nanabush is said to have climbed up to the top of a tall pine, and it is at this level that he built the island of the present earth. It is conceivable that this "world tree" yet stands. As the Chippewa George Pine told Dorson at the end of his narration of the Flood Myth, "We're on four lengths of a big pine tree" (1952, 48). In Norse mythology, the sacred ash, *Yggdrasil*, acts as the *axis mundi*. At its top an eagle perches while his antagonist, a serpent, constantly gnaws at the tree's roots in an attempt to bring it down and reinstitute chaos. Likewise, Mishebeshu, who once succeeded in unbalancing the cosmos, undermines earth and water, his power now held in check, but not destroyed, by the Thunderers.

4. I must note here that when I speak of the *water* as a place of evil I mean just that and do not imply that the case exists, as it does in many mythologies, that *earth* or even the *underworld* is the residence of dark powers. Earth is a grandmother, a benevolent power who rests upon the waters of a primordial flood. These waters are, indeed, an earlier home and a creation of the water manitouk. See Chapter 6.

5. This would not be such a strange thing if one remembers that the actual flash of the lightning bolt does not occur when the electrical charge strikes the earth. The jagged flash of light which we see is, in fact, merely the "return of the flash, the electrical impulse retracing its path from earth to cloud . . . In other words, the lightning that we see presents no danger to us—its charge has already been spent" (Sanders 1985, 86). Since the downward thrust of the lightning is an invisible force that marks the path by which the visible bolt returns, in a sense lightning does travel upward.

6. The artist had very little to say about his painting. I knew Madahbee from my first visit to Manitoulin in 1986 when I had bought a painting from him and I commissioned this work because I had admired his portraits of Thunderbirds. While he was familiar

with Mishebeshu and his mythology, Madahbee had never before painted the monster. I asked him if he would be willing to paint a small picture of Thunderers doing battle with Mishebeshu and gave him absolutely no suggestions on color or composition. In spite of the fact that he does not like to do commissioned work, he said that he would try, perhaps because the subject intrigued him and presented something of a challenge. When I went to pick up the painting I found a canvas 3' 8" wide x 2' 2" high. The image of Mishebeshu is drawn from the Agawa rock painting, and Madahbee said that he owed the idea of merging clouds and thunder eggs to Carl Ray, whose work was a large influence on his own.

Further discussion of the work with the artist was fruitless, however. Madahbee is a very serious and private person and is well known for his reticence. When I asked him about the source of his inspiration he said, "I think of my talent as a gift from the Great Spirit. It just appeared. People say, 'Where do you get your ideas?' I don't know." He added that he knew of the myths through reading and through the work of other artists. "I never had the opportunity to listen to my grandfathers. I had no one to go to, plus I never talk anyway. When I was in high school nobody even knew I spoke English, I was so quiet." Madahbee is especially loath to speak about spiritual matters in any detail. When I mentioned that some people claimed to have seen Thunderbirds during a storm he replied, "Well I'd say that's their blessing, that they're allowed to see that. It was supposed to be their gift to keep secret. There's some things that's not supposed to be said."

7. For an extensive study of soul-beliefs in North America see Åke Hultkrantz (1953).

8. Jenness notes the extreme sensitivity of the baby's shadow soul (1935, 20). In order to protect the infant, mothers would hang charms on the *tikanogan* (cradleboard). A special protective charm was a spider web made of twine. "Two articles representing spider webs were usually hung on the hoop of a child's cradle board, and it was said that they catch everything evil as a spider's web catches and holds everything that comes in contact with it"

(Densmore 1929, 52). These charms were apparently earlier forms of today's dreamcatchers, made by many tribes and used to protect adults as well as children from nightmares.

We also recall Mishebeshu's habit of stealing infants and the belief that those whom he has drowned, be they infants or adults, do not travel to the afterworld. As the ego soul is said to go immediately to the land of spirits and the free soul may hang about the grave for an indefinite period before joining it, it is possible that the monster actually destroys the ego soul.

9. Relevant to the role of Thunderers as both purifiers and balancers is the scientific observation that thunderstorms perform this essential role in nature. They "result from an enormous amount of the sun's energy striking the earth and evaporating huge quantities of moisture, which is lifted thermally to higher levels of the atmosphere, where it condenses and releases its extraordinary powers in the form of the thunderstorm. Heavy rains drench the earth, but the latent heat of evaporation is returned to space; a thunderstorm is, on a much smaller and more temporary scale, a dispenser of the earth's excess heat and performs its duty (unlike a hurricane) on a daily basis. The sheer quantity of them over the earth's surface at any given time make them the *primary* (and most immediate) balancers of the earth's heat budget" (Sanders 1985, 82).

10. I would stress that this is not a marriage in the sexual sense and that any attempt to align these manitouk with genders or to characterize their relationship as a form of cosmic copulation is fruitless. While the Earth is understood as female, Mishebeshu is not of the Earth but of the waters, not a creative presence but a destructive one, and Mishebeshu as one or many is *invariably* understood as male. The Thunderers—at least those who travel, hunt and interact with humans—while predominantly male, include females among their ranks. One must resist the temptation to make assumptions based upon (largely Freudian) psychological interpretations here.

11. Jones translates *Kistigamig* here as sea. Literally, the word means great lake and usually denotes Lake Superior.

12. I am reminded here of a poem by Stephen Crane in which he extols the merits of grandfathers:

Once I saw mountains angry,
And ranged in battle-front.
Against them stood a little man;
Aye, he was no bigger than my finger.
I laughed, and spoke to one near me,
"Will he prevail?"
"Surely," replied this other;
"His grandfathers beat them many times."
Then did I see much virtue in grandfathers,—
At least, for the little man
Who stood against the mountains.
(from *The Black Riders and Other Lines*, XXII, 1895)

VI

THE ISLAND OF THE ANISHNAABEG

At this point the old woman suddenly ended her story,
but she added, "This earth that has been created by Menaboju
in this manner was the first world inhabited by Indians.
The earlier one that was drowned in the waters had only been
occupied by Menaboju and the wolves, and by the Snake King
and his monsters."
I asked her, "Does this mean that your story of Menaboju's
creation of the world comes to an end at this point?
And what happened to the snakes? Did they later give up their
war against Menaboju?" Here La Fleur interrupted,
"Did the story come to an end?! For heaven's sake, no!
The sagas of our storytellers do not end that quickly.
Even if you stayed with us for the whole winter my mother
would continue telling stories every night for three months."
—Johann Kohl,
Kitchi Gami, 1860

In this concluding chapter we turn to the beginnings of the world as
the traditional Ojibwe knew it by examining myths that tell about the
creation of this earth and the origins of humans and of their medicine
society. In this examination we will meet Nanabush, the culture hero
and trickster who, in conjunction with Mishebeshu and the Thunderers, first challenged and then instituted balance in the Anishnaabe life-
world. We will see how the alliances and conflicts which he began with
the other manitouk reflect and determine the human's position in the
cosmos. And having formulated a conclusion to the thesis with which I
began, I will return, finally, from the Ojibwe life-world to my own, a

post-critical Euro-American world view, in which, for better or worse, personhood tends to be synonymous with humanity. For here the natural world is neither en-souled nor continuous with our own structures of personhood but provides instead a physical context into which humanity has fallen or been thrown.[1]

personal transform'n

However, in returning to our own worlds we also return to ourselves, selves which should not be unaffected by the interpretive journey that we have taken. I promise no revolution in world view here, merely the potential deepening of experience and broadening of horizons, which is the aim of any hermeneutical project. There is no "answer" to human existence to be found in the Ojibwe experience of the world just as there are no "answers" to myths, but there is meaning and there is value. This conclusion will close neither the circle of hermeneutics nor the study of the dialectical existence which the Thunderers and Mishebeshu inscribe. It will, instead, *open* the circle, for not only do Anishnaabe stories not end quickly, they never really conclude. Nanabush may have retired from his career as founder and transformer, but we must remember that he has not died but gone to sleep. And there are contemporary Ojibwes who still feel his presence and are convinced that he can be awakened as a symbol of Anishnaabe identity and vitality.

This conviction is expressed most forcefully in the theatrical production, *Nanabush of the 80's*, written and performed by members of the Ojibwe De-ba-jeh-mu-jig theatre group, Wikwemikong First Nation, Manitoulin Island. In the group's press release of May 13, 1988, the meaning and purpose of their play is described.

> There is a legendary character in Indian lore who is known as Nanabush... Because he is half human and half spirit (he is the grandson of the Moon), the choices and challenges he brings force us to come to terms with the realities of the world we live in. Always present and ever active, Nanabush has been dormant as a character in our culture for many years, but is now acknowledged again, welcomed with open arms, and transformed into *Nanabush of the 80's*.

We begin, then, at the beginning, with the myth that relates the events surrounding the formation of the Anishnaabe island. While this tale is often called a myth of creation (Booth 1984; Dundes 1984; Vec-

Nanabush of the 80s
Blake Debassige
Poster
Used by permission of the artist
Photo by Fred Maize

'creation' story [handwritten margin note]

sey 1988) we should be careful to qualify such a description. First, the creation here is not *ex nihilo* but involves an act of world construction from existing material, specifically mud. More important, this foundational tale concerns a re-creation of the earth following a primordial deluge. Like the vast majority of Native American cosmogonic myths, the Ojibwe version does not begin with the absence of a world. In the Emergence myths of the Southwest, for instance, humans come up from the ground to the surface of a land which is already there. In the Earth Diver narratives, of which the Ojibwe is one, the movement is reversed: a creature dives to the bottom of the flood waters in order to recover the world. This original earth is still there in the Ojibwe cosmology and may actually be understood as that lower realm to which the souls of the dead eventually traveled or, alternatively, the land that is claimed and guarded by Mishebeshu.

Another area in need of clarification regarding what should properly be called the Re-creation myth has to do with its multiplicity of forms and its continuity with Nanabush's extensive mythology. First, as I have noted previously, transcriptions and oral performances of the myth differ both in form and content. There is no definitive version of the story, but among the many tellings there does exist, as Christopher Vecsey has demonstrated, a basic or core narrative (1983). In other words, there are certain events and actors that always appear, and the general movement of the narrative includes specific actions that produce unvarying results. The Underwater manitouk *always* kill Nanabush's companion, the wolf, who is often his brother or cousin, but sometimes his son or grandson (Chamberlain 1891, 198; Kohl 1860, 389; Vecsey 1988, 73). What matters here, of course, is that the two are closely related to one another and so the death profoundly affects Nanabush, who *always* seeks vengeance against the killers. Further, Nanabush *never* fails to kill the ogimaa Mishebeshu, and the surviving Underwater manitouk invariably flood the earth in retribution. And, finally, it is Nanabush who escapes the water by building a raft (Coleman, Frogner, and Eich 1962, 72; Jones 1919, 151) or climbing a tree (Barnouw 1977, 38; Chamberlain 1891, 202) and sends the earth divers (usually only the muskrat is successful here) to the bottom for mud. Nanabush takes the tiny bit of mud and forms the earth. Additionally, he is usually aided in his actions by birds and along the way almost always kills a toad medicine woman so that he can gain entrance, in her stead, to Mishebeshu's lodge.

characters of Nanabush stories [handwritten margin note]

Given the structural constancy of the narrative in its innumerable versions, we have a choice to make regarding our approach to this tale. We might take every transcription of the tale that we can find and attempt an exhaustive cross-referential treatment. Yet this would be a huge project and one yielding something more akin to a catalogue than a story. Alternatively, we could, through the comparison of common elements, select several of these versions and distill an "essential" myth from them. This is, indeed, what Vecsey has done: "[W]e chose to gather all the versions available from printed sources and manuscripts, breaking them down into component parts in order to see what elements stood out as the most logical (from an Ojibwa point of view) and interesting (from our point of view)" (1988, 68). This method provides a good guide for comparing the similarities and differences among forty-seven transcriptions; however, it also presupposes a struc- *caveats* turalist interpretation. Further, and more important, the method not only fractures the narrative movement, reducing it to a summary of episodes, but in fact creates its own myth, and one which is much less than the sum of its parts. For in choosing "elements" from this foreign source material one necessarily makes editorial judgments from the outside and, consciously or not, shapes the myth according to one's own projection. This editorializing adds another layer of interpretation upon the lived reality of the myth, limiting its immediacy and, in effect, artificializing its content. We should choose, as Gadamer (1985) has said, to "let the text speak" and not insist upon speaking for it.

For these reasons I have decided to include one version taken from William Jones' massive collection (1917, 89-101, and 145-59). I choose Jones' version recorded in Fort Bois and told (probably) by Wasagunackank not because it has any special claim to exhaustiveness or authenticity. It is, however, the only version given in Ojibwe as well as English and so the only translation that I was able to check with consultants. Raymond Armstrong indicated that he found the translation accurate and sensible. The use of this one version of the tale does not provide the false sense of mastery over the myth which constant reference to numerous versions might produce. By reading one story we come closest, I believe, to the traditional Anishnaabe experience of the myth; we hear the tale told not as an example of a narrative type but as a story at once complete and incomplete in itself. It is complete inasmuch as we hear how the world was first lost and then remade, and it is incomplete insofar as Ojibwe tales, especially the ones concerning

Nanabush, flow into one another as a stream of communal memory. So while others include Nanabush's birth and his early adventures as part of the Re-creation myth (Barnouw 1955 and Vecsey 1988), their inclusion of these events is no less arbitrary than my exclusion of them. We must, simply, choose to step into and out of the stream at some point just as Kohl's storyteller decided when to begin her tale and when to end it.

THE OJIBWE RE-CREATION NARRATIVE

from William Jones, *Ojibwa Texts*, Part I

Narrator: Wasagunackank(?)

THE DEATH OF NANABUSHU'S NEPHEW, THE WOLF

Thereupon they separated from one another. And when [he and the Wolf] went into camp, it was truly [the Wolf] that killed the game. Naturally not in one spot they remained, always from one place to another they went. And so truly was [the Wolf] ever killing the pick of game. Truly was he living well.

Now, once while they were moving about, in his sleep was [the Wolf's] uncle weeping. The Wolf indifferently signed to him with the hand, "I fancy that probably he may be having a bad dream about me," he said of him who was then taking his nap.

Thereupon when [Nanabushu] awoke, then truly was [the Wolf] informed by him, saying: "Verily, my nephew, have I had an exceedingly bad dream about you. I beg of you, please listen to what I shall say to you; please do what I tell you. If you have no desire to listen to what I have to tell you, truly then will you do yourself an injury. So please, even if it be when you are overtaking game, as you go along break off a little stick, no matter how small the dry bed of a brook may be, and there shall you fling the little stick. That is what you should always do."

Accordingly that truly was what he did whenever he was about to overtake [the game]. Now, once while he was in pursuit of some game,—for that was what he always was doing,—

truly, he grew tired [of throwing a stick into the dry bed of brooks]. For when once away from a certain place he was in pursuit of a moose,—since it was now getting well on towards the spring,—this was the feeling of the Wolf when in pursuit of the moose, truly a big cow was he following after. And then presently, when he came in sight of her,—indeed, when he was on the very point of seizing her,—he saw the dry bed of a small brook. They say [that thus] he thought: "Well, now, [without throwing the stick ahead of me,] I will leap right on across the dry bed of this brook." Then straightaway down into the middle of a great stream he fell, and all the while was there a ringing in his ears.   *error*

And now, while along was walking Nanabushu as he followed the trail of his nephew, he presently noticed by the sign of the tracks that [his nephew] was pressing close [upon the moose]; and once as he looked while going along, there, to his surprise, was a great river flowing across his path. Thereupon wept Nanabushu. Then repeatedly from place to place in vain he went [to get across], and all the while he wept as he wandered about. Truly sad he felt for his nephew. Now, [Nanabushu] knew that by somebody was he [thus] treated. Afterwards he started down the course of the river. Now, he wept as he went. And now, when he had followed the course of the river to where it opened out [into another body of water], then there he beheld the kingfisher looking down into the water. He made a grab for him, but he slipped hold of him at the head when he tried to seize him. And this was what he was told: "Confound Nanabushu! I meant to tell him something," he was told.

"Pray, do tell me," he said to him.

Thereupon truly hither came [the Kingfisher].

"Do please tell me, my little brother," he said to the Kingfisher. So this he was told: "Yes, I will tell you. But you must be Nanabushu," he was told.

"No," he said to him.

So this he was told: "Ay, without reason was Nanabushu's nephew taken away from him. It was the chief of the great lynxes, it was he who took away Nanabushu's nephew. Now, this was I thinking: 'Perhaps I too [shall have a share of] his gut when it is thrown out [from where he has been taken down]. I too wanted it, [that] was why I was perched up there, and watched for it while perched up there.'"

"Truly, then, all right! Pray, go ahead and tell me about it," he said to the Kingfisher. "In return I will make you so that you will be beautiful." Thereupon he truly was willing to do what he was asked.

Thereupon, when he painted the Kingfisher, it was his paint that he had used. And so he painted the Kingfisher. Now, this he was told: "Pray, take pains, Nanabushu; for I will help you in what you do," [thus] to him said the Kingfisher.

"All right," to him said Nanabushu.

"Listen! I will now tell you," he was told by the Kingfisher. "Yea, truly, there at the place where I stay, close to where [the river] flows out upon this lake," he was told; "and so out there upon the water is an island of sand. It is there they amuse themselves by day when the sky is clear; and there they all sleep. And so all day long they nap. And so there will you see the one that seized your nephew. Not till the last does he come forth out of the water to where have come all the manitous. And then there in the very centre lies the one that seized your nephew. He is white, and therefore by that sign will you know when he comes up to the surface. And there in the middle will he sleep. There, that is all I have to tell you. Now, therefore, there will I be present where you are. Ever so proud, truly, am I of what you have done for me. That you did so to me is why I shall not lack for what I shall eat."

Truly, always with ease will the Kingfisher obtain the little fishes; for with tiny spears was the Kingfisher provided. Accordingly very pleased was he with the gift.

Then truly Nanabushu followed the stream to where it opened out on the lake. Thereupon he willed that there should be a clear day. Whereupon truly there was a clear day. After he had found a place to stand very early in the morning before the sun was yet up, then into a dead pine stump he changed; there by the edge of the water he stood. But yet his penis did not change its form, whereupon he was at a loss to know what

penis problem!

to do, for as he stood he faced the water. "What shall I do?" He desired that his penis should not look that way. "Well, I will have a branch [there]." And when he was unable to produce it, he then had the Kingfisher mute upon it. And then, truly, after he had muted upon it, then continually lit he there upon the penis. Whereupon it truly could not be recognized from its appearance, by reason of [the Kingfisher] having muted upon it.

In time he truly beheld the water setting up a ripple. Presently he saw a creature come to the surface, then all kinds of beings began to rise upon the water; and then hither came they forth from out of the water upon the sandy island. Then in a multitude out of the water came the manitous, of every kind that were, and the way they looked. "But he is not there," he thought.

Now, up yonder was perched the Kingfisher. "It is nearly time," [Nanabushu] was told, "for him to come to the surface," he was told. "Of them all, he will be the last to appear," he was told.

And so they truly seemed to him like the manitous. And as they came, they went to sleep there upon the sandy island. It was a long while before the absent one came up to the surface. "Now, that is the only one, Nanabushu, yet to appear, [the one] that you have been wanting to see."

Now, at times the water moved in great ripples about over the lake.

"Now, then!" he was told by the Kingfisher.

Now, truly, as he looked out there upon the water from which the creature was coming forth, truly beautiful was the being. Presently the voice of him was heard saying: "It is Nanabushu that stands yonder," the voice of him was heard saying.

And this one of them was heard saying: "How could Nanabushu be changed to look like that?" one of them was heard saying.

And this was what another said: "He is without the power of being a manitou to that extent."

And this said the one yonder, who was yet in the water:

"He does not want to come. Go, Snake, [and] coil around him."

Truly [by the Snake] that came crawling was [Nanabushu] then coiled round about. Just as he was on the point of saying "Yo!" then [the Snake] uncoiled. "How is it possible for Nanabushu to take on such a form?" said [the Snake].

And this again was what the one yonder said: "I beg of you, Great Bear, do go [and] claw him," he said to him.

Whereupon truly out of the water came the Great Bear by whom [Nanabushu] was clawed. Just as he was about to say "Yo!" he was let alone by it. "How is it possible for Nanabushu to be changed to such a form?" said [the Bear].

"Nay, but into such a form has Nanabushu changed himself." Then cautiously over the water to where the others were, came the being; in their very midst was where he lay down.

"Would that he might go soundly to sleep!" thought Nanabushu. Whereupon he waited for him to go to sleep, but the other would not go to sleep till all [the rest] were asleep. Then this was he told by the Kingfisher: "I will tell you when he is asleep," he was told by the Kingfisher. "No doubt he is now asleep. Now, then, Nanabushu, come, go shoot him! Nanabushu, don't you shoot him in the body. It is impossible for you to kill him if you try to shoot him there in the body. Only there where he casts a shadow is where you will kill him when you shoot him," he was told by the Kingfisher.

Thereupon now on his way he started to go to him. In a while [Nanabushu] came to where [the manitou] was; as he went, he stepped over them that were lying there. Now, he was sure that they were all sound asleep. And when he got to where [the being] was, then truly he strung his bow, whereupon he then aimed to shoot [the being]. Now, in his side was where he shot him; he heard the sound of [his weapon] when it hit him. Another time in a slightly different place he tried to shoot with his arrow, and so again he heard the sound of his arrow when it struck. "Ah, this was the way my little brother told me: 'There where he casts a shadow is where you shall shoot him,' I was told." And so truly there into the side of his shadow was where he shot him.

"Confound Nanabushu! There, that it was Nanabushu I said, but to no purpose. And now perhaps he has slain me."

And now, as [Nanabushu] started in flight, then by the water was he pursued. With all his might he ran, seeking for a place where there might be a mountain; he was a long while finding it. And above his girdle was he wading in the water. "No doubt but that this earth is wholly under water," he thought. Now, while he was on his way up the mountain, still yet was it overflowing. When he had climbed [a tree], then nearly halfway up the trees was how far the water had risen; and then was when the water ceased rising. And then afterwards the water receded; and when the water receded, then down from the tree he descended.

NANABUSHU SLAYS
TOAD-WOMAN, THE HEALER
OF THE MANITOUS

And then on his way continued Nanabushu, on his way he continued walking. Now, this was what he thought: "Perchance he thinks he is free who robbed me of my nephew. The time has now come for me to look for him." Thereupon truly, while seeking for him, he suddenly heard some one singing:

From the ends of the earth do I come with the sound of my rattles, sha'."

And so when he went to where it was sounding, it seemed as if he heard the same sound as before:

"From the ends of the earth do I come with the sound of my rattles, sha."

Presently he saw the being; lo, it was a toad with her rattle hanging under one arm from the other shoulder. Then he addressed her, saying: "What, my grandmother, what are you working at?" he said to her.

"Why, I am seeking for some bast. Nanabushu has shot the chief of the big lynxes."

And so he said to her: "What are you going to do with the bast?"

"Why, an attempt will be made to ensnare Nanabushu. Perhaps he may be drowned, for almost flooded was this earth

166 of the Anishnaabeg

with water. And in what place can he now be alive? they said."

"Now, what was their purpose that they should deprive him of his nephew? He is really a manitou, so we claim Nanabushu to be."

"Ah, my grandson! you must be Nanabushu [himself]."

"Why, long since would you have been clubbed to death if I had been Nanabushu. How, my grandmother, is the one doing that was shot?"

"Oh, nearly now have we healed him, we ourselves are giving him treatment."

"My grandmother, how do you usually sing while you are giving him treatment?"

"Ay, this is the way I sing, this was how I sang while coming hitherward:

'From the ends of the earth do I come with the sound of my rattles, sha.' "

Now, quite everything he asked her, and quite everything he was told, even the place where she sat when she gave her treatment, likewise the place where she lived [in the wigwam]. "In one corner of the place do we live. Two are my grandchildren," he was told. Concerning everything was he taught, concerning all things was he instructed.

And so after he had clubbed her to death, he flayed her. And when he got into [the skin], he tore a small opening there at its head. And now, when he had lifted the bast upon his back, he then sang the way she sang when she went hopping along:

"From the ends of the earth do I come with the sound of my rattles, sha."

Now, such was the sound of his voice as he went hopping along in a newly changed form. Presently he came in sight of the place where [the manitous] lived. When on his way to the place, he lost the way [and] came to a different wigwam; while on his way to it, [he saw some children] coming racing out. "O my grandmother! why, here is where we live."

"Indeed."

"Pray, how, my grandmother, came you to lose the way?"

"Oh, by reason of too much weeping have my eyes become closed, and that is why I cannot clearly see where we live. Therefore, O my grandchildren! do you lead me thither by the hand." Whereupon truly, after he was seated, then there upon his lap played the children. Then was it discovered where he had ripped an opening in that toad-skin of his. "Why, my grandmother, like the skin of a human being is the look of your skin!"

"Ah, my grandchild! that was how I rubbed myself when working with the bast, as throughout the whole of every day I was making twine," she said to her grandchildren. And then he waited to be asked to where the smoking was being held. Already was the evening coming on. Then he truly heard the sound of footsteps approaching. Presently some one came and peeped inside. "My grandmother, come and smoke," [the person] came saying. Whereupon truly then away he went. Now, when he was come in sight of where they dwelt, he saw that his nephew was used as a cover over the entry-way. Even yet he could see it, and he almost wept. By reason solely of his power to control his feelings was why he did not cry when entering. Then, after he was seated, there was no one for him to see.

There was a hanging partition dividing the room, and there beyond was [the wounded]. Then, as they began ministering, he kept watch of them, and continuously round to the other side [of the partition they kept passing]. Presently he too began ministering to him. In advance had he made ready the way by which he meant to flee, some wood he had heaped in a pile. And so when presently he too went round to the other side, he then saw him who sat propped with a support at the back. Right in his side was the feather of the arrow barely to be seen. And with a careful grip he held it as he worked it vigorously back and forth.

"Confound Nanabushu! Now he is killing me!" he said.

Springing to his feet, Nanabushu seized the skin of his nephew as he went, [and] started in flight. Frightful was the roar of the water that came pursuing after, at top speed he ran. Then by degrees till up to the knee in water was he wading.

When truly, now, he thought he was nigh to his raft, then near by did he see his raft. When up to his waist he was wading in water, then he went aboard his raft.

When the water overflowed the trees, then at once he truly realized what a long way down in the water the earth was. He saw all kinds of game-folk swimming around. And when they wished to go aboard his raft, he kept them off. "Wait," he said to them. "Not till after a while do you come," he said to them. And so he then thought: "How shall I do [to select] what one is to fetch some earth?" he thought. Presently he spoke to the smaller animal-folk, and so the first was the Otter: "Would you not go after some earth?" he said to him.

Thereupon truly down into the water [the Otter] dived. And by and by the one that had gone down came up out of the water dead, he must have drowned. When [Nanabush] had breathed upon him, then he asked him: "Well?" he said to him.

"Just as I came in sight of the tree-tops, then was when I lost my wits."

"Pray, you O Beaver! go fetch some earth."

Truly then down into the water dived the Beaver. Presently he was another to come up out of the water dead. When [Nanabushu] breathed upon him, "Well?" he said to him. "Did you not approach anywhere at all to it?"

"Truly, as far as halfway down the trees I was, whereupon I lost my senses."

"Too bad", he said to him.

"Now, you, Muskrat."

Whereupon truly into the water dived the Muskrat. Presently he came up out of the water dead. As [Nanabushu] took him up, he was holding [the earth] in his clinched paws, in both paws he was holding the earth; also in his feet, in each foot was some earth.

"So therefore shall we now be able to create the earth," he said to them. So it was then that he breathed upon the earth, and by degrees it grew in size, larger he made it. Now, such was what he did. When he knew that it was grown larger, then this he said: "Pray, Wolf, do you see how big this earth is," he said to the Wolf that he had employed.

Thereupon truly away went [the Wolf] and then afterwards back home he came.

"[This,] indeed, shall not be the size of the earth," he thought. "Too small it will be." And so what he did next was to have it larger, whereat again he spoke to [the Wolf]: "Pray, do you see again how big it is," he said to him.

Thereupon truly off [the Wolf] started again. Lo, somewhat longer was he absent; then back was he come again.

Whereupon [Nanabushu] said to them: "Now, come, go you ashore," he said to all the various game-folk. And so it was true. So, then, now he had saved the lives of the game-folk. Now, back home came the one he had employed. "Ay, too small it will be," he said to him. "Though you have been gone two days, yet it will not be [big] enough to contain all that are to live in times to come," he said to him. And so when he had worked upon it again, "Now, once more," he said to him: "perhaps it is now big enough," he said to him.

Thereupon again off started [the Wolf]. And then he awaited his coming for the space of four days. When the four days were ended, then [the Wolf] arrived. "Truly far have I been."

"No," he said to him: "too short a time have you been gone. It will not be large enough," he said to him. And then he created some more of it; when four days were ended, "Pray, now, do you see again how large it is," he said to him.

Thereupon truly off started [the Wolf]. When again [the Wolf] had gone, then [Nanabushu] waited for his coming again. Oh, for a long while was he gone. Then he came back. "Truly far have I been," he said to [Nanabushu].

Thereupon, "Ay, too short a while have you been gone," he said to him. "Larger yet will we make this earth." Thereupon again he worked upon it, to the end that it might be larger he did his work.

Thereupon truly, after four days were ended, then again away started [the Wolf]. And so again [Nanabushu] waited for his coming; for a moon was [the Wolf] away. "Perhaps now he is gone forever," was his thought of him. But it was not time for him yet to be gone forever; so when he had been gone for a moon, then back he came. "Truly very far have I been," said the Wolf.

creation as process of trial + error

"Ay, but not for so short a time do I wish you to be absent," Nanabushu told him. "Not so very few will the number be of them who shall live here on earth," he said to him. "In time many will they be who shall live here on earth," he said to him. When they had created more of it, it was to the end that it might be larger that they worked.

Thereupon again away went [the Wolf].

And then [Nanabushu] waited for his coming again, as long as a full cycle of seasons was [the Wolf] gone. When for a full winter he had been gone, then back he came.

"Therefore it is now almost as large as it will be. It is not yet so large as it should be. Again will I make it larger." And when he had made some more of it, "Now again do you look," he said to him.

Then again off started [the Wolf].

And so when [Nanabushu] waited again for his coming, then for another cycle of seasons was [the Wolf] absent, and then it came to pass that for two full rounds of seasons was [the Wolf] gone. And then he waited for him, but he was not destined to come back. And this was what he thought: "He is gone," he thought. And so in vain he waited for him; but [the Wolf] was gone forever, at which he said: "Pray you, O Raven! do you fly round over [this earth] to find out how large it is," he said to him.

Thereupon truly then up [the Raven] rose on the wing. And so gone was he when he started flying away, and it was needless of [Nanabushu] to wait for him; for a long while he vainly watched for him, for one full round of seasons had he been gone when he came flying back home. "Rather large, O Nanabushu! is this earth," he was told.

"It is now almost big enough, but to the end that it yet may be larger will I make it," he said to him. Thereupon truly more of the earth did he make. After four days were ended, he then again spoke to the Raven.

Whereupon truly again up flew the Raven. And then again did he fly roundabout the earth.

Thereupon again for him did Nanabushu wait. For as long as two cycles of the seasons was [the Raven] gone; as time went on, there was no sign of him coming back, continuing so till he had been gone a long while; a long time afterwards he came back again. And this was what he said to him: "Well, let it be still larger." Thereupon truly, after he had been creating it for four days more, "Well, now, this time, again go you and see," he said to the Raven. Again he waited for him, but this time he was gone forever. In vain he waited for him. "That then, no doubt, will be the extent of this earth," he said to the [animal-folk]. And now, "[I] fear that this will float away," he said. "Therefore in order that it may be heavy will I make it so that it shall never be moved."

To begin the interpretation of this myth with reference to our study of the Thunderers and Mishebeshu we must start with its central figure, Nanabush. Culture hero and trickster, this person goes by many names, most of which are the result of differences in dialect and/or orthography. Thus he is *Nanabushu* (Jones 1917), *Nanapus* (Howard 1965), *Nanabozho* (Densmore 1929), *Menaboju* (Kohl 1860), *Wenebojou* (Barnouw 1977), and variations of the same among the Ojibwe. The Cree and some northerly Ojibwe know this character as *Weesakayjac* (Ray and Stevens 1984) or *Wisahkecahk* (Brown and Brightman 1988), and again we find a number of different spellings. Euro-Americans who live in Cree territory have been known to anglicize the name, calling him Whiskey Jack. I have chosen to use Nanabush because it is by this name that he is known on Manitoulin. The derivation of the name and its English translation are unclear. We do know that Nanabush is also referred to as the Great Rabbit or the Great White Hare (Coleman, Frogner, and Eich 1962, 56-57) and the "*abooz*" ending for his name may be derived from the Ojibwe word for rabbit, *wabooz*. Weesakayjac is also known as a Great Rabbit, and Elsie Stoney, an Ojibwe from the Severn River area, attempted to explain this name to me. She said that she had always heard that he was called a rabbit or appeared as a rabbit because he was so fast and tricky. Nanabush not only moved quickly but could disappear in an instant, like a rabbit going down a hole (Personal Communication, 1986). Blackbird says that the name *Nenawbozhoo* means clown in the Ojibwe language, but I have found nothing to support such a translation (1887,

73). It is possible that he refers, implicitly, to the fact that people who act like clowns or tricksters are said to be Nanabush or Nanabush-like. This was certainly the case on Manitoulin, and we recall Blake Debassige's remarks about some of his more amusing and problematic friends and his poster illustration of Nanabush as a sort of Rabbit-Man.

Whatever the original meaning of his name, the meaning of this person is integral to our understanding of the Re-creation myth. Nanabush is a completely ambiguous character. Like his Algonquian counterparts, *Messou* and *Glooskap*, he is a paradigmatic hero, "The master of life" (Densmore 1929, 97). As a "provider and deliverer" (Bierhorst 1985, 15), he fashioned the existing world, determined its landscape, transformed some features and animals, and battled malevolent manitouk. As a culture hero, he introduced the Anishnaabeg to fire, death, medicine, food sources, tobacco, hunting techniques, dances, and customs. Unlike his more dignified Eastern Algonquian counterparts, however, Nanabush is also a trickster, both a sly manipulator and a buffoon, who, even as he creates, destroys; as he gives, steals; and as he fools others, is himself fooled (Radin 1972, xxiii). He calls all humans animals, and manitouk, his relatives, but he constantly seeks ways to manipulate others. In part his schemes are born from the fact that he was, like traditional Ojibwes, always hungry and on the move, searching for food, rest, and shelter.

It is important to note that Nanabush is not understood to be a twin personality, or as Levi-Strauss put it, "incipient twins" (1979, 33). He does not have two distinct sides, a dark and a light, which are at war with one another. Rather, he is a whole self who sometimes responds to his instinct or appetites, sometimes to his intelligence, and very often uses the latter in the service of the former. Ron Messer has suggested that Nanabush "as a true representative of the 'self' . . . brings the [Jungian] shadow into harmony with the totality of his personality, integrating both positive (heroic) and negative (trickster-like) qualities into one mythological personage" (1982, 319). A clearer understanding of his totality can be found not through reference to Jungian typologies but within the Ojibwe categories of self.

In recalling the tripartite structure of Ojibwe personhood we see that, in Nanabush, the free traveling or shadow soul may be aligned with his instinctive/intuitive side, that part of the self responsible for the non-rational aspects of one's character and behavior. Likewise his cleverness and creativity are provided by his ego soul, the seat of intel-

Nanabush and the Sacred Pipe of Peace
Melvin Madahbee
Acrylic on canvas
Private collection
Used by permission of the artist
Reproduction courtesy of the collector
Photo by Paul Von Baich

ligence and judgment. In Nanabush's case, his bungling is caused not just by his blind desire to fulfill his appetites but by his failure to join instinct and intuition with reason. This is not to say that this aspect must be *controlled* by reason—in point of fact, it is the instinctual/intuitive side that reaches out to the spirit world, especially in dream. One must be willing to trust one's instincts but one must also understand that judgment may inform and organize pre- and even super-rational experience. When both souls function together, Nanabush is usually successful in his activity. However, the two souls must also act in harmony with one's physical form, and we find many instances where Nanabush, in mistreating or ignoring parts of his body, suffers indignity and pain as well as failure. A good example is found in a widely told tale frequently called "The Shut-Eye Dance" or "The Hoodwinked Ducks." Here Nanabush wants to eat a group of ducks or geese and convinces them to participate in a dance with their eyes closed, thus using his cleverness to satisfy his hunger. While the birds dance he slays them one by one until a particular dancer—usually a loon—opens his eyes and sounds the alarm. But Nanabush retains the birds he has killed and places them headfirst in a firepit to roast slowly while he sleeps. He tells his rectum to stand guard in case any people should come to steal his dinner. Thieves do come and Nanabush's rectum indeed sounds an alarm but the thieves hide before Nanabush can see them. This happens three times and Nanabush accuses his rectum of lying to him. Subsequently, either the rectum gives up its task or Nanabush ignores it and thieves make off with the birds. When Nanabush finds his dinner missing, he quite stupidly burns his rectum in order to punish it and only after the deed is done does he realize that he has caused himself a great injury. He suffers, then, not only because he has separated himself from his body but because he has failed to *trust* his body. In short, Nanabush shows us that failure to integrate the self—to act as a whole person—results in the concomitant failure to bimaadiziwin, or live well. During the course of the Re-creation tale we will see how Nanabush balances his acts both internally and externally. And through the myth we will have an opportunity to elaborate upon the essential structure of bimaadiziwin, delineating the content of appropriate Ojibwe behavior.

While the character of Nanabush, especially as he embodies the necessity for balance in the self, is worthy of more study, the point which I wish to make is that this person functions both as a reflection of and model for the Anishnaabeg. And he fulfills this role not in spite of his ambiguity but *because* of it. Further, his place as a mediator in the larger world of persons reflects his internal dynamic inasmuch as he appears to stand between humans and manitouk, the offspring of a woman (who may or may not have been a manitou-person) and a wind manitou. In his behavior, especially in his constant hunger and struggle for survival, Nanabush is more human than otherwise; however, his abilities, especially those of metamorphosis, are clearly greater than those enjoyed by even the most powerful human shaman. Perhaps the most telling clue to his mediating position lies in the fact that he seldom appeared to the traditional Ojibwe as a pawagan, or powerful dream visitor. For Nanabush, unlike the Thunderers and other pawaganak, is not a *grandfather* but, like the animals, an *older brother* to the Anishnaabeg. Rogers tells us that the Round Lake Ojibwe relationship between brothers and between sister and brother is characterized by great affection and mutual cooperation, with authority and responsibility being held by the older sibling. This is, of course, a common pattern among most cultures. But Rogers also adds that there is a great deal of joking among siblings including, but not confined to, sexual humor and the playing of practical jokes. We don't find this kind of joking behavior between grandparents and grandchildren or between pawaganak and Anishnaabeg. "There is a mild form of joking between grandparent and grandchild under certain conditions . . . Extreme joking, however, is frowned upon especially on the part of grandchildren" (1962, B15). We do, however, find it in the Ojibwe attitude toward and relationship with Nanabush. The implication is that while he is less distant from humans than the grandfathers, Nanabush also does not act as they do, that is, in a guardianship role. He committed his foundational acts long ago and gradually wandered away from the Anishnaabe world, intent on his own autonomous concerns. His official retirement into sleep is said to have occurred following the European invasion of North America, mirroring the dislocation and disillusionment of his siblings. He is at once a human and super-human person or, as one consultant put it, "Nanabozho is an ordinary Indian and an Indian extraordinary" (Coleman, Frogner, and Eich 1962, 36).

This rather detailed examination of Nanabush's ambiguity is directly relevant to our understanding of the Re-creation narrative. In

the narrative we see him acting as a tripartite person who uses in-
stinct/intuition, reason, and physical appearance to triumph over the
Underwater manitouk. He warns his nephew, the Wolf, to take care to
test riverbeds by throwing sticks into them before crossing. This practice recalls the function of the free, traveling shadow that was said to
move in advance of a hunter, alerting him to game and warning him of
danger (Jenness 1935, 19). His warning is born from a *dream* experience in which he sees the Wolf meeting his eventual fate. The Anishnaabeg, as we have seen, trust their dreams and the Wolf's death is, in
part, a result of his underestimation of the wisdom of the dream experience and of his own impatience and carelessness. Just because the
river bed *appeared* dry did not mean that it *was* dry. It may, for instance, have been covered by thin ice. This is a world, after all, in
which forms are mutable and nothing may be taken for granted. Caution is especially important when one is dealing with Mishebeshu's
realm, for he can whip the placid lakes into sudden frenzy or transform
a small brook into a great stream. And he does these things simply because it is in his power to do them. As the Kingfisher tells Nanabush,
"Ay, without reason was Nanabushu's nephew taken away from him. It
was the chief of the great lynxes, it was he who took away Nanabush's
nephew."

It is important that Nanabush asks the Kingfisher for help. One
shows good sense in calling upon the skills and knowledge of others,
especially those who stand with you both as relatives and as common
enemies of Mishebeshu. Even though the Thunderers make no appearance in this account, both the Kingfisher and the raven belong in
their sky realm, and one might read their assistance as a sign of the cooperation of the manitouk of the upper worlds (Vecsey 1988, 89). And
Nanabush is, of course, the traditional ally of the winds and the Thunderers. "Nanabozho . . . had formidable enemies in the gigantic underwater manidos (such monsters as the Great Horned Snake or the Great
Panther). On the side of Nanabozho in this long conflict were the good
thunderbirds (also powerful manidos). 'The thunderbirds helped
Nanabozho chase the big snakes,' was the explanation given by one of
the Ojibwa we interviewed" (Coleman, Frogner, and Eich 1962, 57).
Sometimes this alliance becomes almost an identification, and James
Simon Mishibinijima told me that Nanabush did not create the Thunderers (as the mide tales maintain) but was created by them: "The

Thunderbird, he's a creator. He created Nanabush and was a great big part of him" (Personal Communication, 1988). In a Menominee version of the tale, Nanabush seeks revenge on the Underwater manitouk by calling down the Thunderers and asking them to beat the water monsters in a ball game. In the confusion of the game Nanabush is able to attack the Underwater manitouk (Hoffman 1890, 249-54).[2] And in another Ojibwe version recorded by Dorson, the Thunderers are called upon to aid Nanabush, somewhat indirectly, by allowing him access to Mishebeshu: "Now he wanted revenge so he wished that the Thunders (the good gods) would send the summer warmth right away, to bring the Serpents (the bad gods) up from their cave. In four days the ice melted and the river began to flow" (1952, 44).

The point is that Nanabush, in battling the Underwater manitouk, acts not only as an extraordinary Indian but as one allied with the Thunderers. He is, in effect, a kind of proxy for them in this context. Later, in the human and medicine origin stories, the Thunderers will appear on their own in contrast and complement to Mishebeshu. And long after Nanabush has retired, they will continue to check the tendency of the Underwater manitouk to extend the boundaries of their rightful realm, to unbalance the precarious island of the earth.

To return to Nanabush's revenge, then, we see that, unlike the Wolf, he takes the advice which is offered to him. Not only does he take the advice but he also rewards his advisor for the help by giving the Kingfisher beautiful coloring and arrows (beak and claws) with which to hunt. Such reciprocity of favors and gifts is a hallmark of relations among Ojibwe persons. This person, who trusted his *instincts/intuition* and his *dreams*, shows that he can use his *intelligence* as well. He waits patiently and finally changes his *physical form* in order to hide from the Underwater manitouk. Of course the ogimaa Mishebeshu is suspicious of this Nanabush stump because, as a keen observer, he knows that it constitutes a new element in his familiar territory. And once again we see the ambiguity of Nanabush's position in the refusal of the lesser Mishebeshu persons to believe that he has the power to metamorphose: "How could Nanabush be changed to look like that? . . . He is without the power of being a manitou to that extent."

We should bear in mind that without the assistance of the Kingfisher Nanabush's disguise would have been less than complete. Like the Anishnaabe individual, he sought assistance from manitou persons, and like the power specialist, the shaman, his success was in large part dependent upon his ability to form lasting relationships with these powerful helpers. Throughout the tale he acts less like a manitou than a shaman, and so it is not surprising that he eventually takes on the form and role of the Toad Woman healer. Shamans act as liminal figures in the Ojibwe cosmos, moving somewhat routinely between layers of the world and changing their forms in order to heal or, in the case of bear-walkers, to attack. While it is true that all traditional Ojibwes "shamanized" inasmuch as they experienced dream, vision, and guardian relations, only the healing specialists approached the power beings over and over again.[3] Further, as we have seen, the conjuring shamans owed their abilities to the Thunderers and only the most powerful and/or daring among them turned to Mishebeshu for medicine and guidance.

This brings us to another important aspect of Nanabush's actions. We see, or rather hear, that any challenge to the Underwater manitouk is highly dangerous, and danger appears to increase according to the harm inflicted upon them. Nanabush's first attack, resulting as it did in a serious wound to Mishebeshu, caused a temporary flood. His failure to kill the monster was no doubt due to the fact that he did not heed the instruction of the Kingfisher to shoot Mishebeshu's shadow. The shadow and brain (and sometimes one's hair knot) were understood to be the seats of one's free soul, just as the ego soul resided in one's heart. Nanabush's second attempt, as Toad Woman, succeeds at the greatest cost imaginable—the world is lost. Again, we remember the terrible price that dreamers paid for the monster's medicines. You might buy a bit of his horn but only with the currency of your soul or the souls of your children. The Thunderers, in contrast, ask only for respect, and if that respect is not forthcoming, they appear satisfied to smite you with a thunderbolt, leaving both your soul and your family's souls intact.

That Thunderers can not only take the monsters from the waters with impunity but thrive on their flesh is a further indication of the power of the grandfathers. And by extension this fact signals the degree to which the traditional Ojibwe were dependent upon the protection of Thunderers. Even though the world is a tenuous place, the alliance between humans and Thunderers ensures that this island will not

sink again. In short, given the primordial acts of Mishebeshu, the respect of the traditional Anishnaabeg for the Thunderers and their
maintenance of relations with these manitouk through offerings and
prayers was an absolutely essential aspect of life. And, as we have seen,
this respectful relationship continues to thrive as a meaningful experience expressed not only in the articulation of contemporary attitudes
toward the Thunderers, but in the tangible forms of artistic and ritual
acts.

While Thunderers attack Mishebeshu with regularity and ease,
Nanabush must work very hard employing disguise and trickery just to
get the opportunity to kill the ogimaa manitou. He again shows his ambiguity, employing the techniques of a trickster in order to fulfill a
hero's task. When he has killed the Toad Woman, taken her skin, and
finally made his way to Mishebeshu's lodge, he finds that the Wolf's
hide is being used as a cover for the entryway. Since this use of his
nephew's skin is a sign of terrible disrespect, it moves Nanabush to
greater sorrow and anger. But he shows his resolve and strength of
character in masking these emotions. This ability to overcome emotional weakness was highly prized by traditional Ojibwes, who frequently faced starvation and hardship in the northern woods (Landes
1937). Their ability to press on or to hold out against great odds was essential to their survival, especially during the winter months. In fact,
even among contemporary Ojibwes Nanabush is judged most harshly
not when he manipulates other people but when he complains or
whines about his fate. Life was and still is hard for the Anishnaabeg,
and those who face it with equanimity and a minimum of talk and fuss
are judged to be most admirable.

Before we move to the final stages of the narrative, the death of
Mishebeshu and the flooding and reclamation of the earth, it is appropriate to recapitulate the behavior and characteristics we have observed to this point. First, Nanabush *balances* himself, depending
upon his body, his free soul (instinct/intuition), and his ego soul (reason) at appropriate times. He *seeks alliances* with others, exercises
caution and *emotional restraint,* and *reciprocates* for the help he has
received. In contrast, the Wolf *neglects the wisdom of dream,* and the
Underwater manitouk exhibit *unreasoning maliciousness* in their attack and *disrespect* in their treatment of their victim. All these behaviors indicate patterns either prescribed or proscribed in Anishnaabe

life. If one is to survive and prosper in this life-world, if one is to bimaadiziwin or live well, one must take the lessons contained herein to heart. It is not enough that Nanabush has made an island upon which humans may stand with other persons. Rather, humans must learn how to live here, how to dwell as balanced people in a layered cosmos wherein threats from below are mitigated by protection from above.

In his structuralist interpretation of the myth, Christopher Vecsey distills a central theme which has to do with the establishment, by Nanabush, of hunting rights for humans (1983, 84-100). Vecsey notes that "the idea of death permeated every aspect of [the myth]," and the myth instructed Ojibwes about the importance of death for the continuance of life, i.e., one must kill and eat game animals in order to survive. The Wolf, in this scheme, was punished for his great success at hunting and, by avenging his death, Nanabush thus ensured that the Underwater manitouk would relinquish their control over hunting territory. Even though success in hunting was of great concern to the traditional Ojibwe, I would argue that such an interpretation is not only narrow, as purely structuralist studies often tend to be, but strains credibility even as it flattens the rich symbolism inherent in Nanabush (and by extension the Thunderers), in Mishebeshu, and in the multi-leveled cosmos. The myth has much more to do with life than with death. Not only are the world and life reclaimed from out of the depths of the flood, but the content of the structures of bimaadiziwin is, as we have just seen, made explicit throughout the drama. And while the traditional dependence upon hunting is missing in contemporary Ojibwe culture, the values which the myth expresses concerning character and interpersonal relations continue to motivate behavior.

On Manitoulin I found that people admire sober, quiet, thoughtful, and respectful individuals above all others for they are said to possess wisdom. You do not become an elder there because you have reached a certain age but because people see that you are "living right." Thus not all elderly people are elders and some extraordinary middle-aged persons are, in fact, included in this honored group. In short, the immediacy of the myth as a meaningful narrative is not made concrete through reference to outdated hunting rights and practices. Rather it is experienced daily in continuing social values. This is not to say that traditional Ojibwe values have remained unquestioned as territorial and subsistence patterns changed over the years. But as I noted at the beginning of this study, elders have, in recent years, been actively turning people away from foreign value structures and back to traditional ways in an effort not only to preserve culture but to ensure the continuance of life itself.[4]

If we are indeed to look for a structural pattern in the Re-creation narrative, we find it not through aligning and opposing our own constructed categories but by looking at the eidetic pattern that is already there in experience. It is, of course, a pattern now familiar to us, a dialectical movement inscribed upon the cosmic structure of this lifeworld. For when Nanabush goes to kill Mishebeshu he takes the form of Toad Woman, an amphibian person who travels between land and water. And when he re-creates a world he must send earth divers: the otter, the beaver, and the muskrat, mammals who, like the toad, cross the boundaries of nature and power.[5] Like humans Nanabush cannot travel to the depths but must, as he has done before, and as the Anishnaabeg do after him, depend upon the assistance of other persons. By flooding the earth the Underwater manitouk not only exacted revenge but took the world for themselves. Thus it is up to these mediating characters to wrest it back again, to reinstitute balance. And in this act these relatively powerless beings become great just as Nanabush suddenly appears god-like, the master of life, one who may rejuvenate the dead and form a world. So, too, the small piece of mud redefines itself under his breath into the vast island of North America. The arena in which Thunderers and Mishebeshu will enact their eternal battles now has, at its center, a land on which the Anishnaabeg will soon stand.

While the island is formed it has yet to be measured, and this measurement will be performed by the Wolf (who may or may not be Nanabush's resurrected relative, later sent to rule over the land of the dead) and the Raven. Here, as in other creation mythologies, the earth is sufficiently charted when it becomes, in effect, *immeasurable*. Yet it remains for the earth to be *fixed* in space. Nanabush says, "I fear that this will float away . . . Therefore in order that it may be heavy I will make it so that it shall never be moved." We don't know exactly how Nanabush fixes the earth as the storyteller lets the thread of the narrative go here. Yet there is an interesting clue available to us in another tale wherein Nanabush creates human beings. This tale is taken from the stories of the midewiwin and it is to the sources of the medicine society teachings that we will now turn. We have seen how humans should bimaadiziwin or live on this hard-won island. Now it is time to understand how the Anishnaabeg came to be here in this middle place at all. In short, we turn from human morality and behavior to ontology, and looking at the roots of human existence we will find them embedded in the symbolism of the Thunderers and Mishebeshu.

In the tale which I mentioned, Nanabush creates a man from earth and places him upon the island. But he encounters a problem in that when he leaves his creation he finds, upon his return, that the human has vanished. This happens twice,[6] and Nanabush declares that someone—he never says who—is stealing them. Nanabush must, as he has done with the island, fix these creatures in some way so that they will remain and multiply. The solution which he hits upon indicates that it may well have been the Underwater manitouk who took the first humans, for Nanabush decides to create the Thunderers and charges them to watch over the people, telling them to strike first against the mountains.

> So then, speaking to them, he said: "Behold, against the mountains do you strike!"
>
> To be sure, the Thunderers struck against the mountains. Truly frightened were the evil manitous.
>
> "Therefore shall it be for you to watch over the people. By and by do I intend to create the people. Perforce, there shall be times when children are destined with unlucky dreams. If the people dream of the things whom you have caused to dodge underground for safety, then therefore shall they be unfortunate throughout life, in that they had been deceived by the evil manitous... So come, keep watch over these people!" thus were the Thunderers told. "If but once throughout a whole summer you fail to wander forth to observe them, then shall the people die; for too hot will the weather be. And it shall always be for you to render sustenance to the people. So, therefore, as long as the world lasts, there shall be people living. And so now do you depart, to all the directions from whence blow the winds do you go."
>
> Truly then did the birds depart. And so in time they found resting-places where to live at all the directions from

whence blow the winds. "In all things shall you harken to them, whensoever the people speak. Therefore this is all that I have to say to you" (Jones 1919, 551).

When Nanabush makes new people to replace the stolen ones, he finds that they do, indeed, now remain fixed. For with the protection of the Thunderers they may dwell on the earth as *living* creatures: "When the morrow came, Nanabush went over to the man, [he found] him still sitting there. Then he spoke to him, saying: 'Are you alive?' 'Yes, truly I am alive' " (553).

Life is, as we have seen, understood to be more than continuing physical existence for the Anishnaabeg. As bimaadiziwin it involves not only prescribed behaviors but a commitment to relations with the other persons of the cosmos, for only under their tutelage can one find the strength one needs to live well. Further, the guardianship of the grandfathers requires an active engagement of the Anishnaabe self; i.e., one must not only respect one's guardians but must demonstrate gratitude through offerings and prayer. This is why Nanabush prefaces his creation of the Thunderers with the following remark, an implicit instruction to human beings: "Behold, I will create them that shall be deserving of remembrance for some special thing" (Jones 1919, 551). In the course of this study we have learned how the Anishnaabeg depend upon the purificatory acts of the Thunderers. But only now do we understand the primordial nature of this dependence, the depth as well as the breadth of these symbolic realities.

It would be rather clean and simple to end the origin tales here on the clear and lofty note of Anishnaabe-Thunderbird relations, but origin tales are many in this complex world, and as we have seen, the symbol of Mishebeshu is not without his positive aspects. The relation between the persons of the upper and lower realms is, after all, not a duality but a dialectic. Therefore it is interesting but not entirely surprising to find that tales exist which indicate that humans originally came from out of the water. If this is the case, perhaps Mishebeshu was stealing Nanabush's creatures because he felt they belonged to him. And maybe this watery origin helps us to understand why, after his efforts to take the world by flood were frustrated, the monster continually tries to pull Anishnaabeg down.

The tales to which I refer also belong to the medicine society and describe humans as having been originally covered in enamel or scales (Barnouw 1977; Dewdney 1967; Landes 1968). In the account collected by Kohl we find a great deal of Christian influence for Kitche Manitou acts as Creator here, making a garden and strolling around in it like Yahweh (Kohl 1860, 195-99). Further, the first man and woman partake of a forbidden fruit and lose both their innocence and their garden. But a particularly telling element of traditional Ojibwe mythology remains, for when the humans ate the fruit, "the silver scales with which their bodies had been covered fell off; only twenty of these scales remained on, but lost their brilliancy, ten on the fingers and ten on the toes" (199). We should also note that these two were not the creations of Kitche Manitou but had, in fact, been found by him, "coming out of the water entirely covered with silver-glistening scales like a fish, but otherwise formed like a man" (195).

In other accounts these humans were made by the Underwater manitouk (Dewdney 1967, 40-41; Landes 1968, 95) or by the manitouk of the upper and lower regions working together (Barnouw 1977, 43-44). The scales with which they were covered are very much like the brassy scales of Mishebeshu himself and indicate that there may be a rather unsettling kinship between the monsters and the Anishnaabeg.[7] In shedding these scales humans not only lost the power and protection that their armor provided, but asserted themselves as land dwellers, as persons who stand *up* in this layered cosmos. By aligning themselves with the Thunderers, Anishnaabeg not only continually resist the imbalance of the primordial flood and remain *fixed* on this island, but signal their own decision to resist being pulled back down into the undifferentiated world of the waters. They may have been born in Mishebeshu's realm, but their relationship with the Thunderers ensures that they will live their lives as *human* people.

Throughout this study we have seen the way in which symbols connect with one another. We have witnessed the kaleidoscopic character and behavior of the Thunderers who move and change like the clouds in which they travel. We have searched for Mishebeshu in his labyrinthine network of lakes and rivers and underground passageways. And we have seen these persons meet in the lake storm, shrouded in the rain and fog which joins the worlds of air and water together. In this chapter the tripartite structure of Anishnaabe personhood came into focus in the character of Nanabush, whose foundational acts set the stage for human existence, forming not only the physical environment but modeling behavior patterns therein. Human existence is lived out upon an island that rests at the center of a multileveled cosmos, and Anishnaabeg find their roots here by reference to the worlds above and the worlds below. We know that Thunderers and Underwater manitouk meet here, at this level, when they battle one another. However, there remains one more connection to be made between these dialectically related persons, for not only do the manitouk stand over and under this island, not only do they protect and assault, but they came together following the deluge to make a tremendous gift to the Anishnaabeg.

This gift is the midewiwin or medicine society, the institutionalized shamanism to which I have often referred. In previous chapters I noted the roles that both the Thunderers and Mishebeshu play in the medicine society as patron manitouk and symbols inscribed on the mide scrolls. But inasmuch as this ending is a return to beginnings, I have held back the tales of the origins of midewiwin until now. While the tales are once again various, usually according to geographic area in this case, they all say that the midewiwin was a *gift* carried by the Bear manitou, the Otter manitou, by Shell, or by Nanabush himself to the Anishnaabeg (Dewdney 1967, 23-56). The Shell of which I speak is the great megis Shell which, as Warren tells us, first appeared in the Atlantic and moved westward, disappearing and resurfacing again and again until it reached Lake Superior (1885, 78-79). As the symbol of the midewiwin society, its journey reflected both the migration patterns of the Ojibwe people and the dissemination of the institution itself.

This Shell also appears in another form, as the small shells which mide members shoot at one another during initiation rituals. By "killing" a new member in this way and then reviving him, the initiate receives the power inherent in any death/rebirth ritual. The symbolism of the shell is not only rooted in the water but in Mishebeshu himself, for "these shells are thought by some to be the scales . . . of the Underwater panther, who taught the rites to Nanapus in the origin myth" (Howard 1965, 125).[8] This connection makes sense in that many sources tell us that the Underwater manitouk first created the midewiwin and gave it to Nanabush in order to appease him for having flooded the earth (Dewdney 1967, 42; James 1956, 185; Morriseau 1965, 55). And again, the gift is then frequently delivered to humans by Bear or Otter instead of Nanabush.

But the manitouk of the upper realms also have a role to play in the foundation and governance of the midewiwin. Sometimes, and especially among contemporary mide groups, Kitche Manitou is considered to be the patron manitou. And other sources tell us that the medicine itself came from above as well as below. Barnouw, for instance, includes a tale in which the knowledge of midewiwin was offered to Nanabush after he threatened the manitouk of the upper and lower realms:

> Then Wenebojo just sat down by the beach with his feet nearly in the water, and he hollered and cried. He sat there crying, remembering the *manidog* [manitouk] who made him angry, and thought of what he might like to do to those manidog. He spoke to the earth and said, "Whoever is underneath the earth down there, I will pull them out and bring them up on top here. I can play with them and do whatever I want with them, because I own this earth where I am now." . . .
>
> When Wenebojo spoke that time, the *manido* [manitou], the boss, heard him. Wenebojo spoke again. This time he spoke to the sky: "Whoever is up there, those manidog up there, I will get them and pull them down. I will play with them here and do just as I please with them. I will even knock down the sky." Then Wenebojo took a deep breath, and the earth shrank up. When he sniffed from crying, the sky made a loud noise like the cracking of ice (1977, 41).[9]

What follows is a council meeting of manitouk during the course of which Nanabush is taught the Medicine Dance. In the inception of this ritual the manitouk of the sky, led by Kitche Manitou, move down to the island of earth, just after the Underworld manitouk have broken through with the gift. One of Landes' consultants related this event.

> The Great Spirit advised him [Shell] [the deepest earth manitou—au.]: "Tell us when you are ready [to bring midewiwin from its birthplace in the bowels of earth]. You [and Bear] be the first ones to lift it out. We will come at the last." They commenced to move it. Earth made a great rumbling. As they came through successive layers to the top layer of Earth, the rumbling grew louder. Then they came out. At that time also he up above [Great Spirit], the mide manito, and other mani-

tos commenced to move it [the mide ceremony]. The noise
came down the layers of mide Sky. At the last layer of Sky they
paused, then met at the mid-point between Earth and Sky and
there was a terrible noise for a long time, indeed, a great
noise. Thus it was when midewiwin assembled from Earth and
Sky (1968, 103).

We see that the meeting takes place just above the earth, perhaps at the level of the clouds. And the foundational event is enacted
with a terrible noise, a noise which is, not surprisingly, like that of a
great Thunderstorm. The power of the mide medicine is derived from
the force of the meeting between the manitouk above and the manitouk below. It is an immeasurable gift for it holds within it a mysterious
and tremendous fulfillment, the synthesis of the dialectical relation between Thunderers and Mishebeshu. The midewiwin ceremony itself is
thus, as Grim says, "established as a unique event of cosmic centration
and participation by the assembled personalistic powers... [and
is]... ritually presented as the accumulated force of the multilayered
cosmos..." (1983, 79).

This peopled and layered cosmos is the context in which we
found ourselves at the beginning of our analysis. Along the way we isolated the symbols of Thunderbirds and Mishebeshu and rejoined them
in their dialectical relation. Now our circular journey has brought us
back to the world in which we first met these persons. In returning we
realize not only the richness of the religious landscape which we
glimpsed there, but the irrevocably incomplete character of our journey through it. The web of associations produced by just these two
symbols continues to grow as long as the memory of myth serves to inform the Anishnaabe experience of the natural world. Thus, the story
of the Anishnaabe island and of life on this island never ends. We end it
for ourselves only as we step away from it. As we return, finally, to a
world at once coexistent with and foreign to the island of the Anishnaabeg, we do so, as all travelers do, somewhat changed by our experiences. The nature and significance of the conversion of consciousness
inherent in this, as in all interpretive enterprises, is the subject of my
concluding remarks.

NOTES

1. The reference here is first to the Christian doctrine of the Fall of
    humankind (first articulated in the Creation narrative of Genesis
    2-4) from a primordial innocence and kinship with God to a state
    of sinfulness and estrangement. Secondly, I refer to the existen-
    tial notion (following Heidegger) that humans are metaphorically
    'thrown' into an existence which has no essential meaning and
    wherein humans must continually 'become' themselves through
    the responsible exercise of choice. In both world views there is a
    sense of alienation from the foci of the ultimate conditions of exis-
    tence, which in the first case we call God and in the second Be-
    ing. Even when it is not phrased in theological or philosophical
    terms, this sense of alienation pervades, to a large extent, the
    modern, and now post-modern, Western experience. And it is
    especially marked in the ways in which Western cultures relate,
    or fail to relate, to the natural world.

2. The "ball game" here is lacrosse, and the story bears an interest-
    ing resemblance to a historical tale told by Warren concerning
    the Ojibwe capture of the British fort at Mackinaw in 1763. The
    warriors pretended to organize for a game of lacrosse, and while
    the British watched they gradually moved the play closer to the
    open gates. "All at once, after having reached a proper distance,
    an athletic arm caught it [the ball] up in his bat, and as if by acci-
    dent threw it within the precincts of the fort. With one deafening
    yell and impulse, the players rushed forward in a body, as if to re-
    gain it, but as they reached their women [who had hidden weap-
    ons under their blankets] and entered the gateway, they threw
    down their wooden bats and grasping the shortened guns, toma-
    hawks, and knives, the massacre commenced . . ." (1885, 204).
    Alexander Henry, an eyewitness to the Ojibwe victory, also in-
    cludes a similar description in *Travels and Adventures in Canada
    and the Indian Territories* (1901).

3. Eliade makes the point that among Native Americans, generally,
    "the difference between shaman and layman is quantitative: the
    shaman commands a greater number of tutelary or guardian spir-
    its and a stronger magico-religious 'power' " (1974b, 315).

4. I am not being overly dramatic here regarding the importance of
    traditional values to the continuance of life. I would remind read-

ers of the incidence of suicide, especially among the young, on Manitoulin and the terrible problem of alcohol abuse. Many young people and elders with whom I spoke saw the reemergence of traditionalism as pivotal in their struggle against the alienation and despair that give birth to suicide and substance abuse. There is a strong feeling that if Native Americans can reestablish their cultural identities, they can gain the strength to act against these problems. This conviction is expressed in a prayer taken from a *Native Alcohol and Drug Abuse* pamphlet that Raymond Armstrong showed me. The prayer ends: "This has been our Prayer. The voice I have sent is very weak, for our Indian ways have almost been lost. Yet, I send this prayer with hope. Grandfather, please hear our call, and make our spirits one."

5. Other mediating creatures include the diving birds, especially the loon, who sometimes acts as an earth diver in the myth and a messenger in the physical world. "What the loon knows in our world he goes under to tell the water creatures—what's going on—because he stays under for a long time" (James Simon Mishibinijima, Personal Communication, 1988).

6. Sometimes Nanabush makes and loses a man and then a woman (Jones 1919, 531-33). In other versions the humans are two men (549-51).

7. We also cannot ignore the evolutionary echo of this tale wherein humans crawl out of a primordial soup. Like many myths of origin that seem to run very close to current scientific theories, this one leads us to speculate on the question of just how far back collective memory may go.

8. See also Densmore (1929, 88): "The rite of initiation is supposed to inject a certain 'spirit power' into the candidate who is expected to 'renew his spirit power' by attending the annual ceremony of the society . . . The 'spirit power' is conveyed by means of a small white shell, which is said to appear on the surface of a lake when the action of a manido causes the water to seethe."

9. It is not unreasonable to assume that the "loud noise like the cracking of ice" may have been the voice of the Thunderers, especially when we remember that thunderstorms were not thought to be the *result* of the advent of warm weather. Rather, the Thunderers *brought* the warmth with them, cracking the ice as well as the clouds with their arrival.

NEW HORIZONS

*"I believe that there is an energy—I prefer to call it a creative
energy; other people call it something else—which exists beyond the human's physical awareness... The energy exists
within the land—the North American continent. It exists
within human culture—the Anishnaabe's origins, history,
present and destiny. It exists within the Anishnaabe's spiritual
teachings which sustain him/her on the earth."*
—Leland Bell

In speaking about new horizons I do not refer to areas in need of further study vis-à-vis the Thunderers and Mishebeshu, or even Anishnaabe religion/lifeway in general. Given the nature of this particular
enterprise and the hermeneutical method which I have employed, the
opening of horizons denotes much more than the extension of this project into other areas of academic inquiry. When I speak of horizons being opened I am, of course, speaking of acts of conversion, of shifts in
consciousness brought about by the interpretive engagement of the
self in a foreign life-world. In simple terms, what we ask ourselves here
is, "How can the Anishnaabe experience of the world change Euro-
American ways of looking at the world?" In this case, the landscape of
the world is that of North America, a familiar ground made strange and
new by our understanding of the traditional Ojibwe symbols.

In the most basic terms, it is reasonable to assume that, having
once met the Thunderers and Mishebeshu, our apprehension of the

192 • New Horizons

natural phenomena which they at once cause and express is changed.
While I cannot say that I *believe* that the Thunderers cause storms I do
not, anymore, *experience* storms as impersonal explosions of sound,
energy, and moisture. Knowing that the animikeek speak from out of
the storm I find that my awareness of the unique character of each
thunderclap is heightened. I can now hear different voices in the
storm: the "approaching Thunders," the "searching Thunders," the
"Thunder that's going to hit." This is so because the Anishnaabe symbols and myths have become part of my memories. And when my self-
consciousness meets the phenomena of the natural world, these memories necessarily add not an artificial veneer to my perception of the
storm, but a *texture* to the very act of experiencing. I can no longer go
out on the water in a boat without the memory of Mishebeshu, a memory that at once clarifies and deepens my own worst fears, fears which
include not only the dread of drowning but a profound fear of experiencing the unfathomable depths of the world and of my own consciousness. Mishebeshu gives both meaning and form to these fears because,
as a symbol, he *articulates* them.

This interpretive journey has done more than create memories,
however. It has suggested alternative ways of being in the world. The
traditional Ojibwe rejected, as we have seen, the notion that humans
have fallen from a state of grace into our existence in this world. They
would also have rejected Heidegger's contention that we are 'thrown'
here, for humans in the Ojibwe cosmos knew not only from whence
they had come and where they were going but how to live—bimaadiziwin—right now and right here. Further, in the Anishnaabe life-world
humans do not '*ek-sist*' or stand out from other beings in the world.
Rather, as we have noted, they stand *in* the world as instantiations of a
transcendental personhood that at once meaningfully unites the life-
world and provides the values which motivate human behavior
therein. We are all persons here: humans, animals, plants, and
manitouk. Further, any object may hold within it a potential personhood, which it actualizes when it exercises volition through movement,
metamorphosis, and/or speech. Not all persons are identical, of
course, and we all have different needs and enjoy varying degrees of
power. But humans have no privileged or even unique status in this
world, for *all* beings necessarily exist as willful personalities who are
responsible for themselves. The Anishnaabeg do not look upon the

phenomena of the world as instruments and they do not *project* themselves into the world but *find* themselves in and through a relational interaction with other persons, human and otherwise.

The alternative which the Anishnaabe life-world presents is, in short, not one in which we anthropomorphize nature, but one in which we open our category of personhood to include non-human beings. When we expand our horizon in this way we do, indeed, experience the storm on the lake as something more than an event. It becomes an act. Further, the experience of the world as personal is not one which must necessarily be confined to the Anishnaabe context. Others have opened themselves to a similar world view, but the complexity and precision with which the traditional Ojibwes articulated this way of being in the world assists us in understanding just what Erazim Kohak is describing when he speaks of the 'moral sense of nature'.

> I do not believe that Whitehead's recognition of the "subjective aim" of all beings constitutes a pan-psychism, the attribution of a psyche to all material entities. Perhaps it is because, in the radical brackets of the forest clearing, nature does not present itself as "material," waiting to be endowed with a psyche to merit ontological dignity. Here the dignity of the world of nature, of the lichen-covered boulders no less than of the old badger and the young oak trees, is the primordial starting point. It is not contingent on the attribution of any set of traits. Nor is the overwhelming sense of the clearing as a "society of persons," as structured by personal relations, a function of any alleged personality traits of boulders and trees. It is, far more, an acknowledgement of the truth, goodness, and unity of all beings, simply because they are, as they are, each in his own way. That is the fundamental sense of speaking of reality as personal: recognizing it as Thou, and our relation to it as profoundly and fundamentally a moral relation, governed by the rule of respect (1987, 128).

The profound moral implications of this alternative way of being are not reducible to an ethical system, a codification of rights and wrongs, anymore than the complex dialectical dance of the manitouk was reducible to a dualism or two-step of good and evil. Rather, the balance of the cosmos is dependent upon moral relations which are, as

Kohak discovered in his world, "governed by the rule of respect." In all my dealings with consultants I found that they stressed this word above all others: *respect*, for one another, for animals, for plants, for grandparents, for all the various persons of the phenomenal world. This respect is not merely a veneration but a cautious and careful regard, born of the recognition that we exist in a web of interdependence. It is a simple but profound insight to say that humans go astray when they lose respect for themselves and for others and that the natural world is in jeopardy not only because we do not value it but because we do not experience it as meaningful.

In speaking of the revival of traditional ways, Kitty Bell articulated the interest that Anishnaabeg have in communicating their knowledge to others. She, like many other people with whom I spoke, sees Ojibwe tradition not as a culturally bound belief system but as a potential contributor to a new world philosophy.

> It's opening up more and more—I guess because more of us are going back to that way [the traditions] and pray that way. It's really coming. And we're not going to be the boss of this whole organization. It's got to be *all* of mankind coming together, just accepting it—that it is all one being, that we're all one being. We were just each given our jobs (Personal Communication, 1988).

In thinking about the island of the Anishnaabeg as it stands between protection and threat, I have often thought of it as a metaphor for the limits of ideality and obscurity that define the 'boundedness' of the project of interpretation and of human consciousness itself. But in reflecting on Mrs. Bell's words I also realize how this island upon which we stand may be experienced as something other than a prison of the mind or of the spirit. It is, after all, a peopled place and the continent which Native and Euro-Americans share rests upon a planet that is itself a kind of island in space. To understand this larger island and the way in which we should dwell here we have to remember our own myths and listen carefully to the memories of other peoples. But we might also, as Mrs. Bell indicated in my many conversations with her, need to assemble a new mythology, one that opens itself to broader categories and breaks down the cognitive boundaries that prevent us from understanding one another.

This is not to say that the Anishnaabe way of being in the world is the "best" way of being. For this life-world holds not only the beauty of relationships with grandparents, but contains as well the terror of the shadowy presence of Mishebeshu. Yet it is an alternative and it is a contribution to what Joseph Campbell has called " . . . the only myth that is going to be worth thinking about in the immediate future," the myth of the planet (1988, 32). Any planetary myth will require that we understand and act upon that which the Anishnaabe have always known—that the island upon which we dwell is at once immensely powerful and immensely fragile. It may also require that we open our horizons sufficiently to understand that this Earth is, herself, a person, a grandmother, who when treated with the respect rightfully accorded to all grandparents, will nurture and protect and who, when neglected, will act accordingly.

Guide to Pronunciation of Ojibwe Words

The sounds given as English equivalents here are not precise but approximate. Thus vowels and consonants are not sounded *as*, but *like* counterparts given in English.

I. VOWELS

There are *three short* vowels: a i o and *four long* vowels: aa ii oo e.

1. a is sounded like u in English *but*.
   1.a. a followed by *w* is sounded like English diphthong ou.
   1.b. a followed by y is sounded like English i.
2. i is sounded like i in English *bit*.
   2.a. i followed by w or y is sounded like English e.
3. o is sounded like oo in English *book*. In some orthographies it is indicated by /u/.
   3.a. o followed by w is sounded like English o.
4. aa is sounded like au in English *launch*. In some orthographies it is indicated by /a/ or /au/.
5. ii is sounded like e in English *reed*.
6. oo is sounded like o in English *hole*. In some orthographies it is indicated by /ou/.
7. e is sounded like e in English *beg*.
   7.a. e followed by w or y is sounded like English a.

II. CONSONANTS

There are fourteen consonants: b d g h j k m n p s t w y z.

These consonants are sounded in Ojibwe much like they are in English. We should note that in many dialects both **g** and **k**, and **b** and **p** are sounded essentially the same and many orthographies drop one letter from each pair. The true Ojibwe sounds for these consonants stand between the pairs. The sound indicated by **b** and **p**, for instance, is an unvoiced **b**; **g** and **k**, an unvoiced **g**.

The following combinations also appear: **ch nh zh**.

The consonants **f** and **r** appear only in loan words.

APPENDIX 2

Glossary of Ojibwe Words

1. animiki, animikeek (pl.): Most common name for the Thunder manitouk meaning Thunder, Thunderer, or Thunderbird.

2. Anishnaabe, Anishnaabeg (pl.): Name by which Ojibwe, Odawa, Pottawatomie, and Cree know themselves. Probably literally: "spontaneous people." In the Ojibwe life-world the term means "human person."

3. atisokan or aadsookaan (Manitoulin dialect), atisokanak or adsookaaneg (pl.): "Tales of the grandfathers, sacred tales." May be used as address, "grandfathers" to refer to beneficent manitouk, especially the Thunderers.

4. bearwalker: A malevolent shaman, one who misuses power to attack others physically and/or spiritually. Still prevalent on Manitoulin, bearwalkers are so named because of their powers of metamorphosis; i.e., they are said to travel frequently in the form of a bear but often appear as other animals, especially dogs, and as bright balls of light.

5. bimaadiziwin: Living, "living well." The goal of Anishnaabe existence, a life which includes longevity, good health, good fortune, and good relations with other persons (human and otherwise).

6. jessakid: Traditional "shaking tent" shamans or conjurers. Manitouk would visit these shamans in their tents, causing them to move and imparting powers of prophecy and the ability to find lost persons or things.

7. Kitche Manitou, always singular and capitalized: Great Manitou, Great Spirit. Traditional ruler of the heavens and Creator of the world prior to the deluge. Now often equated with the Christian God but almost certainly of pre-contact origin.

8. manitou, manitouk (pl.): Power beings of the Ojibwe cosmos understood to be other-than-human persons upon whom less powerful human persons (Anishnaabeg) depend.

9. Matchi-Manitou(k): Sometimes a shadowy underworld figure who, like the Christian devil, stands in contrast to Kitche Manitou. Properly and more commonly generic term for group of malevolent beings that includes Mishebeshu and the windigo.

10. megis, migis: Sacred shell of the Midewiwin Society. Term refers both to a manitou, the Great Shell, and to the small shells that mide shamans ritually shoot at members during initiation ceremonies.

11. mide, midewiwin: Great Medicine Society of the Ojibwe, an institutionalized healing group or the ceremony practiced by the group. Name is derived from mide (sound of the drum) and wiwin (doings).

12. Mishebeshu: literally, Great Lynx. This name for Underwater manitou(k) is used to denote both the singular and plural.

13. Nanabush: The culture hero and trickster of Ojibwe mythology. Also known as Nanabushu, Nanapus, Nanabozho, *Manabosho*, *Wenebojou*, and variations of the same. Nanabush is known as the Great White Hare and his name may be derived from wabooz (rabbit).

14. ogimaa: Boss or chief.

15. pauguck: Skeleton being who flies through the air and rattles through treetops on winter nights. Usually said to be the transformed remains of a victim of winter starvation and harbinger of sickness and death, but sometimes understood to be a Matchi-Manitou or even (especially among the Plains Cree) a potentially beneficent manitou.

16. pawagan, pawaganak (pl.): Dream visitor, a manitou who comes to Anishnaabeg in vision/dream and/or acts as a guardian. Thunderers are the manitouk most frequently called pawaganak.

17. pinesi, pinesiwak (pl.): Birds, especially Thunderbirds.

18. wabeno: literally, Man or men of the dawn, refers to a shamanic society or a member thereof. Traditionally wabeno manipulated fire in healing rituals and were one of four shamanic types who also included the mide, jessakid and *nanandawi* (sucking doctors).

19. Weesakayjac or Wisahkecahk: Name for Nanabush character among northernmost Ojibwe and Cree.

20. Wikwemikong: Largest unceded Reserve in Canada, located on eastern end of Manitoulin Island. Literally, bay of the beaver, known locally as Wiky.

21. Windigo, windigok (pl.): A Matchi-Manitou(k) who is one of the most feared, especially among the northern Ojibwe and Cree. Represented as a giant ice monster and/or cannibal and said to have once been a human who died from starvation or, alternately, who ate his family in order to survive. Windigok may attack Anishnaabeg and both starvation and gluttony can cause one to suffer windigo sickness (i.e., to become a windigo).

APPENDIX 3

List of Anishnaabe Consultants

Thunder Bay, Ontario
Larry Beardy
Elsie Stoney

Manitoulin Island, Ontario
Ojibwe Cultural Foundation
Celina Buzwah
Mary Lou Fox
Kate Roi

Sucker Creek First Nation
Melanie Madahbee
Melvin Madahbee

West Bay First Nation
Delores Armstrong
Raymond Armstrong
Abel Beboning
Shirley Cheechoo
Blake Debassige
David Migwans
Mamie Migwans

Wikwemikong First Nation
Kitty Bell
Leland Bell

Steve McGraw
James Simon Mishibinijima
Sam Oswamick
Angus Pontiac
William Trudeau

BIBLIOGRAPHY

Key to Abbreviations for Journals:

A.A.   American Anthropologist
JAFL   Journal of American Folklore
P.M.   Primitive Man
S.R.   Studies in Religion—Sciences Religieuses

Ahenakew, Rev. E.
    1929   "Cree Trickster Tales." *JAFL* 42: 309-53.
Baraga, Rev. Frederick
    1976   *Chippewa Indians as Recorded by Rev. Frederick Baraga in 1847*. New York and Washington: Studia Slovenica.
Baraga, R.R. Bishop.
    1966   *A Dictionary of the Otchipwe Language*. 1878. Reprint, Minneapolis: Ross & Haines Inc.
Barbeau, M.
    1952   "The Old World Dragon in America." In *Indian Tribes of Aboriginal America*, edited by Sol Tax, 115-22. Chicago: University of Chicago Press.
Barnouw, Victor
    1955   "A Psychological Interpretation of a Chippewa Origin Legend." *JAFL* 68: 73-85, 211-23, 341-55.
    1977   *Wisconsin Chippewa Myths and Tales and Their Relation to Chippewa Life*. Madison: University of Wisconsin Press.
Beck, Peggy, and Anna L. Walters
    1977   *The Sacred: Ways of Knowledge, Sources of Life*. Tsaile (Navajo Nation), Ariz.: Navajo Community College Press.

Bellah, Robert
1964 "Religious Evolution." *American Sociological Review* 29, no. 3: 358-74.
Benedict, Ruth
1938 "Religion." In *General Anthropology*, edited by Franz Boas. Boston: D.C. Heath.
Benton-Banai, Edward
n.d. *The Mishomis Book: The Voice of the Ojibway.* Indian Country Press.
Berger, Peter L.
1969 *The Sacred Canopy.* Garden City, N.Y.: Anchor Books.
1980 *The Heretical Imperative.* Garden City, N.Y.: Anchor Books.
Bierhorst, John
1985 *The Mythology of North America.* New York: Quill/William Morrow.
Black, Mary B.
1977 "Ojibwa Power Belief System." In *The Anthropology of Power*, edited by Raymond Fogelson and Richard Adams, 141-51. New York: Academic Press.
Blackbird, Andrew
1887 *History of the Ottawa and Chippewa Indians of Michigan.* Reprint, Petrosky, Mich.: The Little Traverse Regional Historical Society Inc., 1977.
Black Elk, and John G. Nierhardt
1932 *Black Elk Speaks.* New York: William Morrow and Company.
Blair, Emma, ed. and trans.
1911- *The Indian Tribes of the Upper Mississippi Valley and*
1912 Region of the Great Lakes. Cleveland: Arthur H. Clark Company. Reprint, 1969.
Bloomfield, Leonard
1930 *Sacred Stories of the Sweet Grass Cree.* Bulletin no. 60, Anthropology Series 11. Ottawa: Canada Department of Mines.
Boatman, John
1992 *My Elders Taught Me: Aspects of Great Lakes American Indian Philosophy.* Lanham, Md.: University Press of America.
Booth, Anna Brigitta
1984 "The Creation Myths of the North American Indians." In *Sacred Narrative: Readings in the Theory of Myth*, edited by

Alan Dundes. Berkeley and Los Angeles: University of
California Press.

Brinton, Daniel

1976   *Myths of the New World.* Blauvelt, N.Y.: Multimedia Pub.
Corp.

Brown, Charles E.

1941   *Sea Serpents: Wisconsin Occurrences of these Weird Water
Monsters in the Four Lakes, Rock, Red Cedar, Koshkonong,
Geneva, Elkhart, Michigan and Other Lakes.* Madison, Wisc.:
American Folklore Society.

Brown, Jennifer S. H., and Robert Brightman

1988   *The Orders of the Dreamed: George Nelson on Cree and
Northern Ojibwa Religion and Myth, 1823.* Winnepeg: The
University of Manitoba Press.

Brown, Joseph Epes

1985   *The Spiritual Legacy of the American Indian.* New York:
Crossroad.

Bunzel, Ruth

1929-   *Introduction to Zuni Ceremonialism.* Forty Seventh Annual
1930   Report of the Bureau of Ethnology. Washington, D. C.:
Government Printing Office.

Burden, H. N.

1895   *Manitoulin; or Five Years of Church Work among Ojibwe
Indians and Lumbermen, Resident upon that Island or in its
Vicinity.* London.

Burkholder, Mabel

1923   *Before the White Man Came: Indian Legends and Stories.*
Toronto: McClelland and Stewart.

Cahill, Joseph

1975   "An Amerindian Search: Propaedeutic to the Study of Religion
in Transition." *S.R.* 5, no 3: 286-99.

Campbell, Joseph

1960   *The Flight of the Wild Gander: Explorations in the Mythological
Dimension.* New York: Viking Press.

1976   *The Masks of God: Primitive Mythology.* New York: Viking
Press.

1988   *The Power of Myth.* New York: Doubleday.

Carson, William
  1917 "Ojibwa Tales." *JAFL* 30: 491-93.
Casagrande, Joseph B.
  1956 "The Ojibwa's Psychic Universe." *Tomorrow* 4: 33-40.
Cassirer, Ernst
  1953 *Language and Myth*. New York: Dover Publications Inc.
  1955 *The Philosophy of Symbolic Forms*. Vol. 2, *Mythical Thought*.
         New Haven: Yale University Press.
Chamberlain, A. F.
  1890 "The Thunderbird amongst the Algonkins." *A.A.* old series 3:
         51-54.
  1891 "Nanibozhu amongst the Otchipwe, Mississagas and other
         Algonkian Tribes." *JAFL* old series 4: 193-213.
Charlevoix, Pierre de
  1761 *Journal of a Voyage to North America*. 2 vols. Reprint, New
         York: Readex Microprint, 1966.
Cinader, Bernhard
  1978 "Manitoulin Island—Explorations of Past and Present and
         Future." In *Contemporary Native Art of Canada—Manitoulin
         Island*. Toronto: Royal Ontario Museum Ethnology Dept.
  1987 *Manitoulin Island—The Third Layer*. Thunder Bay, Ontario:
         Thunder Bay Art Gallery Exhibition Catalogue.
Clements, William M., ed.
  1986 *Native American Folklore in 19th Century Periodicals*. Athens,
         Ohio: Swallow Press/Ohio University Press.
Coleman, M. Bernard, Sr.
  1947 *Decorative Designs of the Ojibwa of Northern Minnesota*.
         Washington, D. C.: The Catholic University of American Press.
  1937 "The Religion of the Ojibwe of Northern Minnesota." *P.M.* 10:
         33-57.
——, Ellen Frogner, and Estelle Eich
  1962 *Ojibwa Myths and Legends*. Minneapolis: Ross and Haines.
Colombo, John Robert
  1982 *Windigo: An Anthology of Fact and Fantastic Fiction*.
         Saskatoon: Western Producer Prairie Books.
Conway, Thor, and Julie Conway
  1990 *Spirits on Stone: The Agawa Pictographs*. San Luis Obispo,
         Calif.: Heritage Discoveries Publications.

Cooper, Rev. John M.
  1933 "The Northern Algonquian Supreme Being." *P.M.* 6, nos. 3 and
        4: 41-111.
Copway, George
  1850 *The Traditional History and Characteristic Sketches of the
        Ojibway Nation*. Reprint, Toronto: Coles Publishing Company,
        1972.
  1860 *Indian Life and Indian History by an Indian Author*. Boston:
        Albert Colby and Co.
Corbiere, M., Margaret Fox, Mary Lou Fox, and Violet Pitawanakwat
  n.d. *Nishinabemda Pune*. West Bay Reserve, Manitoulin Island,
        Ontario: Ojibwe Cultural Foundation.
Costello, Peter
  1974 *In Search of Lake Monsters*. New York: Coward, McCann and
        Geoghan.
Covarrubias, Miguel
  1954 *The Eagle, the Jaguar and the Serpent: Indian Art of the
        Americas*. New York: Alfred A. Knopf.
Craik, Brian
  1982 "The Animate in Cree Language and Ideology." In *Papers of
        the 13th Algonquian Conference*, edited by William Cowan.
        Ottawa: Carelton University.
Danziger, Edmund J., Jr.
  1979 *The Chippewa of Lake Superior*. Norman, Oklahoma:
        University of Oklahoma Press.
Deloria, Vine, Jr.
  1973 *God Is Red*. New York: Dell Publishing.
Densmore, Frances
  1907 "An Ojibway Prayer Ceremony." A.A. 9: 443 ff.
  1929 *Chippewa Customs*. Smithsonian Institution, Bureau of
        American Ethnology, Bulletin 86. Reprint, Minneapolis: Ross
        & Haines, 1979.
Dewdney, Selwyn
  1967 *The Sacred Scrolls of the Southern Ojibway*. Toronto:
        University of Toronto Press.
——, and K. E. Kidd
  1967 *Indian Rock Paintings of the Great Lakes*. Toronto: University
        of Toronto Press.

Dinsdale, Tim
  1966   *The Leviathans.* London: Routledge and Kegan Paul.
Dixon, Roland
  1909   "Mythology of the Central and Eastern Algonkians." *JAFL* 22:
          1-9.
Dooling, D. M., ed.
  1984   *The Sons of the Wind: The Sacred Stories of Lakota.* New York:
          Parabola Books.
Dorson, Richard M.
  1952   *Bloodstoppers and Bearwalkers.* Cambridge, Mass.: Harvard
          University Press.
Douglas, Mary
  1969   "The Meaning of Myth, with Special Reference to 'La Geste
          d'Asdiwal.' " In *The Structural Study of Myth and Totemism*,
          edited by Edmund Leach. London: Tavistock Publishers Ltd.
  1982   *Natural Symbols: Explorations in Cosmology.* New York:
          Pantheon Paperbacks.
  1984   *Purity and Danger.* Boston: ARK Paperbacks.
Duerr, Hans Peter
  1987   *Dreamtime: Concerning the Boundary between Wilderness and
          Civilization.* New York: Basil Blackwell Inc.
Dundes, Alan, ed.
  1984   *Sacred Narrative: Readings in the Theory of Myth.* Berkeley and
          Los Angeles: University of California Press.
Durkheim, Emile
  1968   *The Elementary Forms of the Religious Life.* Translated by
          Joseph Ward Swain. London: George Allen & Unwin Ltd.
Eagleman, Joe R.
  1983   *Severe and Unusual Weather.* New York: Van Nostrand
          Reinhold Company Inc.
Eberhart, George M.
  n.d.   *A Geo-Bibliography of Anomalies.* Westport, Conn.:
          Greenwood Press.
Eliade, Mircea
  1961   *The Sacred and the Profane.* New York: Harper Torchbooks.
  1965   *Patterns in Comparative Religion.* New York: Meridian Books.
  1969   *Images and Symbols.* New York: Search Books, Sheed & Ward.

1974a   *The Myth of the Eternal Return or, Cosmos and History.*
         Princeton: Princeton University Press.

1974b   *Shamanism: Archaic Techniques of Ecstasy.* Bollingen Series.
         Princeton: Princeton University Press.

1975a   *Myth and Reality.* New York: Harper Colophon Books.

1975b   *Myths, Dreams and Mysteries.* New York: Harper Torchbooks.

Fire, John/Lame Deer, and Richard Erdoes

1972   *Lame Deer: Seeker of Visions.* New York: Simon and Schuster.

Ewers, John C.

1981   "Water Monsters in Plains Indian Art." *American Indian Art
         Magazine* 6, no. 4: 38-45.

Feldman, Burton, and Robert D. Richardson

1972   *The Rise of Modern Mythology: 1680-1860.* Bloomington:
         Indiana University Press.

Fiddler, Chief Thomas

1985   *Legends from the Forest.* Edited by James R. Stevens.
         Moonbeam, Ontario: Penumbra Press.

Fox, Mary Lou

1978   "Manitoulin Island." In *Contemporary Native Art of Canada—
         Manitoulin Island.* Toronto: Royal Ontario Museum Ethnology
         Dept.

1978   "Manitou—Minnissing(Island of the Spirits)." In *Contemporary
         Native Art of Canada—Manitoulin Island.* Toronto: Royal
         Ontario Museum Ethnology Dept.

Foucault, Michel

1972   *The Archaeology of Knowledge and the Discourse on Language.*
         Translated by A.M. Sheridan Smith. New York: Pantheon
         Books.

Freud, Sigmund

n.d.   *The Future of an Illusion.* Translated by W.D. Roberson Scott.
         Garden City, N.Y.: Doubleday and Company Inc.

Frost, Rev. F.

1904   *Sketches of Indian Life.* Toronto: William Briggs.

Gadamer, Hans-Georg

1985   *Truth and Method.* New York: Crossroad Pub. Co.

Gatschet, Albert

1899   "Water-Monsters of American Aborigines." *JAFL* 12: 255-60.

Geertz, Clifford
  1973   *The Interpretation of Cultures.* New York: Basic Books Inc.
George, Katherine
  1968   "The Civilized West Looks at Primitive Africa, 1400-1800: A
          Study in Ethnocentrism." In *The Concept of the Primitive*,
          edited by Ashley Montague. Toronto: Collier-Macmillian
          Canada Ltd.
Geyshick, Ron, with Judith Doyle
  1989   *Te Bwe Win (Truth): Stories by an Ojibway Healer.* Toronto:
          Summerhill Press.
Grim, John A.
  1983   *The Shaman: Patterns of Siberian and Ojibway Healing.*
          Norman: University of Oklahoma Press.
Hallowell, A. Irving
  1934   "Some Empirical Aspects of N. Saulteux Religion." *A.A.* 36:
          389-404.
  1942   *The Role of Conjuring in Saulteux Society.* Publications of the
          Philadelphia Anthropological Society, 2. Philadelphia.
  1946   "Concordance of Ojibwa Narratives in the Published Works of
          Henry A. Schoolcraft." *JAFL* 59: 136-53.
  1947   "Myth, Culture and Personality." *A.A.* 49: 544-56.
  1975   "Ojibwa Ontology, Behavior and World View." In *Teachings
          from the American Earth: Indian Religion and Philosophy*,
          edited by Dennis Tedlock and Barbara Tedlock. New York:
          Liveright Publishing Corporation. Originally published in
          Culture and History: Essays in Honor of Paul Radin, edited by
          S. Diamond, 19-52. New York: Columbia University Press,
          1960.
  1967   *Culture and Experience.* Philadelphia: University of
          Pennsylvania Press and Schocken Books.
Heidegger, Martin
  1975   *Poetry, Language, Thought.* Translated by Albert Hofstadter.
          New York: Harper Colophon Books.
  1977   *Basic Writings.* Edited by David. F. Krell. New York: Harper &
          Row Pub.
Henry, Alexander
  1901   *Travels and Adventures in Canada and the Indian Territories
          between the Years 1760 and 1776.* Boston: Little, Brown and
          Co.

Hewitt, J. N. B.
    1902   "Orenda and a Definition of Religion." *A.A.* 4, no. 1: 33-46.
Hickerson, Harold
    1960   "The Feast of the Dead among the 17th Century Algonkians of the Upper Great Lakes." *A.A.* 62: 81-107.
Higgins, Edward G., in collaboration with the Whitefish Lake Indian Reserve, no. 6
    1982   *Whitefish Lake Ojibway Memories*. Cobalt, Ontario: Highway Book Shop.
Hilger, Sister M. Inez
    1951   *Chippewa Child Life and Its Cultural Background*. Bureau of American Ethnology Bulletin no. 1946 Washington, D. C.: Government Printing Office.
Hill, T., M. L. Radulovich, B. Cinader, and E. McLuhan
    1978   *Contemporary Native Art of Canada—Manitoulin Island*. Toronto: Royal Ontario Museum.
Hodge, Fredrick Webb, ed.
    1974   *Handbook of the Indians of Canada*. Published as an appendix to the Tenth Report of the Geographic Board of Canada. 1913. Facsimile edition, Toronto: Coles Publishing Company.
Hoffman, W. J.
    1888   "Pictography and Shamanistic Rites of the Ojibwa." *A.A.* old series 1: 209-31.
    1890   "Mythology of the Menomoni Indians." *A.A.* old series 3: 243-58.
    1891   *Midewewin or Grand Medicine Society of the Ojibway*. 7th Report of the U.S. Bureau of Ethnology to the Smithsonian Institution. Washington, D.C.
Honigmann, John J.
    1975   Review of "Inkonze: Magico-Religious Beliefs of Contact-Traditional Chipewan Trading at Fort Resolution, NWT, Canada," by David Merrill Smith. *A.A.* 77, no. 2: 407-408.
Hooke, Hilda Mary
    n.d.   *Thunder in the Mountains*. New York and Toronto: Oxford University Press.
Howard, James H.
    1965   "The Plains Ojibwa or Bungi." Anthropological Paper no. 1, South Dakota Museum. Vermillion: University of South Dakota.

Hultkrantz, Åke

1953 *Conceptions of the Soul Among North American Indians.*
The Ethnological Museum of Sweden Monograph Series 1.
Stockholm.

1979 *The Religions of the American Indians.* Berkeley and Los
Angeles: University of California Press.

1980 "The Problem of Christian Influence on N. Algonkian
Eschatology." *S.R.* 9, no. 2: 161-83.

1983 "The Concept of the Supernatural in Primal Religion." *History
of Religions* 22, no. 3: 231-53.

Husserl, Edmund

1962 *Ideas: General Introduction to Pure Phenomenology.* Translated
by W. R. Boyce. London: Collier Books.

1965 *Phenomenology and the Crisis of Philosophy.* Translated by
Quentin Laver. New York: Harper Torchbooks.

1970 *The Crisis of European Sciences and Transcendental
Phenomenology.* Translated by David Carr. Evanston: Northwestern University Press.

Ihde, Don

1971 *Hermeneutic Phenomenology: The Philosophy of Paul Ricoeur.*
Evanston: Northwestern University Press.

Jacobs, Wilbur R.

1985 *Dispossessing the American Indian.* Norman, Oklahoma:
University of Oklahoma Press.

James, Edwin, ed.

1956 *A Narrative of the Captivity and Adventures of John Tanner.*
1830. Reprint, Minneapolis: Ross & Haines.

Jaspers, Karl, and Rudolf Bultmann

1958 *Myth and Christianity: An Inquiry into the Possibility of
Religion without Myth.* New York: The Noonday Press.

Jenness, Diamond

1935 *The Ojibwa Indians of Parry Island.* Bulletin 78, Anthropology
Series 17. Ottawa: Canada Department of Mines.

1977 *The Indians of Canada.* Toronto: University of Toronto Press.

Johnston, Basil

1976 *Ojibway Heritage.* New York: Columbia University Press.

1978 *Ojibway Language Lexicon.* Ottawa: Indian and Inuit Affairs
Program.

1982 *Ojibway Ceremonies.* Toronto: McClelland & Stewart Ltd.

Jones, Peter
   1861   *History of the Ojebway Indians*. Reprint, Freeport, N.Y.: Books for Libraries Press, 1970.
Jones, William
   1905   "The Algonkin Manitou." *JAFL* 18: 183-90.
   1911   "Notes on the Fox Indians." *JAFL* 24: 209-37.
   1916   "Ojibwa Tales from the N. Shore of Lake Superior." *JAFL* 39: 368-91.
   1917   *Ojibwa Texts, Part 1.* Edited by Truman Michelson. Publications of the American Ethnological Society 7. Leyden, N.Y.
   1919   *Ojibwa Texts, Part 2.* Edited by Truman Michelson. Publications of the American Ethnological Society 7, Leyden, N. Y.
Josselin de Jong, J. P. B.
   1913   *Original Odzibwe Texts.* Leipzig and Berlin: Bressler Archives.
Jung, C. G.
   1965   *Memories, Dreams and Reflections.* Edited by Amiela Jaffe. New York: Vintage Books.
   1980   *The Archetypes and the Collective Unconscious.* Vol. 9, pt. 1, *The Collected Works of C.G. Jung.* Bollingen Series. Princeton: Princeton University Press.
————, ed.
   1982   *Man and His Symbols.* New York: Dell Pub. Co.
Kellogg, Louise P., ed.
   1917   *Early Narratives of the Northwest 1634-1699.* New York: Charles Scribner's Sons. Reprint, 1967.
Kinietz, Vernon
   1965   *Indians of the Great Lakes (1615-1760).* Ann Arbor, Mich.: Ann Arbor Paperbacks.
Kitagawa, Joseph M., and Charles H. Long
   1982   *Myths and Symbols: Essays in Honor of Mircea Eliade.* Chicago: University of Chicago Press.
Knight, Julia
   1913   "Ojibwa Tales from Sault Ste. Marie, Michigan." *JAFL* 25: 91-96.
Kohak, Erazim
   1978   *Idea and Experience.* Chicago: University of Chicago Press.
   1987   *The Embers and the Stars: A Philosophical Enquiry into the Moral Sense of Nature.* Chicago: University of Chicago Press.

Kohl, Johann
  1860   *Kitchi-Gami: Life among the Lake Superior Ojibway.* Reprint,
         St. Paul: Minnesota Historical Society Press, 1985.
Kugel, Rebecca
  1983   "Utilizing Oral Traditions: Some Concerns Raised by Recent
         Ojibwe Studies: A Review Essay." *American Indian Culture
         and Research Journal* 7, no. 3.
La Barre, Weston
  1978   *The Ghost Dance: Origins of Religion.* New York: Delta Books,
         Dell Publishing Co. Inc.
Lahontan, Baron de
  1905   *New Voyages to North America.* 2 vols. Edited by Reuben
         Thwaites. 1703. Reprint, Chicago: A. C. McClurg and Co.
Laidlaw, George E.
  1915- "Ojibwa Myths and Tales". *Ontario Archeological Report*
  1918   27-30. Special 1918 reprint.
Landes, Ruth
  1937   "The Personality of the Ojibwa." *Character and Personality* 6:
         51-60.
  1938   "The Abnormal among the Ojibwa." *Journal of Abnormal and
         Social Psychology* 33: 14-33.
  1968   *Ojibwa Religion and the Midewiwin.* Madison: University of
         Wisconsin Press.
Langer, Suzanne
  1956   *Philosophy in a New Key.* Cambridge, Mass.: Harvard
         University Press.
Leach, Edmund, ed.
  1969   *The Structural Study of Myth and Totemism.* London: Tavistock
         Pub. Ltd.
Leach, Maria, ed.
  1984   *Funk and Wagnalls Standard Dictionary of Folklore, Mythology
         and Legends.* San Francisco: Harper & Row.
van der Leeuw, Gerardus
  1986   *Religion in Essence and Manifestation.* Princeton: Princeton
         University Press.
Leland, Charles G.
  1884   *The Algonquin Legends of New England.* Boston: Houghton,
         Mifflin and Company. Reprint, Detroit: Singing Tree Press,
         1968.

Lessa, William, and Evon Vogt

    1979   *Reader in Comparative Religion: An Anthropological Approach.*
            New York: Harper & Row.

Levi-Strauss, Claude

    1963   *Totemism.* Boston: Beacon Press.

    1979   *Myth and Meaning.* New York: Schocken Books.

Levy Bruhl, Lucien

    1985   *How Natives Think.* Princeton: Princeton University Press.

Lonergan, Bernard

    1979   *Method in Theology.* Minneapolis: The Seabury Press.

Long, Charles H.

    1963   *Alpha: The Myths of Creation.* New York: G. Braziller. Reprint,
            Atlanta, Georgia: Scholars Press, n.d.

Malinowski, Bronislaw

    1954   *Magic, Science and Religion and Other Essays.* Garden City,
            N.Y.: Doubleday Anchor Books.

Martin, Calvin

    1928   *Keepers of the Game: Indian-Animal Relationships and the Fur
            Trade.* Berkeley: University of California Press.

Mason, Herbert

    1980   "Myth as an 'Ambush of Reality.' " In *Myth, Symbol and
            Reality,* edited by Alan M. Olson. Boston University Studies in
            Philosophy and Religion, vol. 1. Notre Dame, Ind.: University
            of Notre Dame Press.

McLuhan, Elizabeth, and Tom Hill

    1984   *Norval Morriseau and the Emergence of the Image Makers.*
            Toronto: Art Gallery of Ontario.

Melville, Herman

    1851   *Moby Dick.* Reprint, New York: Bantam Books, 1986.

Messer, R.

    1982   "A Jungian Interpretation of the Relationship of Culture-Hero
            and Trickster Figure within Chippewa Mythology." *S.R.* 11, no.
            3: 309-20.

Michelson, Truman

    1911   "Ojibwa Tales." *JAFL* 24: 249-50.

Middleton, John, ed.

    1967   *Myth and Cosmos: Readings in Mythology and Symbolism.*
            Garden City, N.Y.: Natural History Press.

Miller, Christopher, and George R. Hamell
    1986 "A New Perspective on Indian-White Contact—Cultural
           Symbols and Colonial Trade." *Journal of American History* 73,
           no. 2: 311-28.
Mitchell, Mary L.
    1985 *Introductory Ojibwe (Severn Dialect)*. Draft Edition. Thunder
           Bay, Ontario: Lakehead University.
Moore, James T.
    1982 *Indian and Jesuit*. Loyola: Loyola University Press.
Morriseau, Norval
    1965 *Legends of My People, the Great Ojibway*. Edited by Selwyn
           Dewdney. Toronto: McGraw-Hill, Ryerson Ltd.
Muller, Werner
    1969 "North America." In *Pre-Columbian American Religions*,
           translated by Stanley Davis, 147-229. New York: Walter
           Krickiberg, et al.
Mundkur, B.
    1976 "The Cult of the Serpent." *Current Anthropology* 17, no. 3:
           429-55.
Murray, Henry A., ed.
    1960 *Myth and Mythmaking*. New York: George Braziller.
Neumann, Erich
    1973 *The Origins and History of Consciousness*. Bollingen Series.
           Princeton: Princeton University Press.
Nichols, John, and Earl Nyholm, eds.
    1979 *Ojibwewi-Ikodowinan: An Ojibwe Word Resource Book*. St.
           Paul: Minnesota Archeological Society.
Norman, Howard
    1982 *The Wishing Bone Cycle: Narrative Poems from the Swampy
           Cree*. Santa Barbara: Ross-Erikson Publishing.
    1982 *Where the Chill Came From: Cree Windigo Tales and Journeys*.
           San Francisco: North Point Press.
Olson, Alan M.
    1982 "Unfolding the Enfolding." In *The Seeing Eye: Hermeneutical
           Phenomenology in the Study of Religion*, by Walter J.
           Brenneman and Stanley O. Yarian in association with Alan M.
           Olson. University Park, Pennsylvania: The Pennsylvania State
           University Press.
——, ed.

1980   *Myth, Symbol and Reality.* Boston University Studies in
       Philosophy and Religion, vol. 1. Notre Dame, Ind.: University
       of Notre Dame Press.

O'Meara, Frederick A.
1848   *Report of a Mission to the Ottawas and Ojibwas on Lake Huron*
       and *Missions to the Heathen.* London: The Society for the
       Propagation of the Gospel nos. 6 and 13.

Overholt, Thomas, and J. Baird Callicott
1982   *Clothed-in-Fur and Other Tales: An Introduction to an Ojibwa*
       World View. Lanham, Md.: University Press of America.

Paper, Jordan
1980   "From Shaman to Mystic in Ojibwa Religion." *S.R.* 9, no. 2:
       185-99.

Parkman, Francis
1895   *The Jesuits in N. America.* Reprint, Boston: Little, Brown and
       Co., 1963.

Petrone, Penny, ed.
1983   *First People, First Voices.* Toronto: University of Toronto Press.

Pomedli, Michael
1987   "Beyond Unbelief: Early Jesuit Interpretations of Native
       Religions." *S.R.* 16, no. 3: 275-87.

Quaife, Milo Milton, ed.
1922   *John Long's Voyages and Travels in the Years 1768-1788.*
       Chicago: The Lake Side Press.

Radin, Paul
1914a *Some Myths and Tales of the Ojibwe of Southeastern Ontario.*
       Geological Survey, Memoir 48, Anthropological Series 2.
       Ottawa: Canada Department of Mines.
1914b "Some Aspects of Puberty Fasting among the Ojibwa."
       Geological Survey, Museum Bulletin 2, Anthropological Series
       2: 1-10. Ottawa: Canada Department of Mines.
1936   "Ojibwa and Ottawa Puberty Dreams." In *Essays in Anthropol-*
       ogy Presented to A. L. Kroeber, 233-64. Berkeley: Ayer Co.
       Pubs. Inc.
1957   *Primitive Religion.* New York: Dover Publications Inc.
1971   *The World of Primitive Man.* New York: E. P. Dutton & Co.
       Inc.
1972   *The Trickster: A Study in American Indian Mythology.* New
       York: Schocken Books.

———, and Albert Reagan

1928   "Ojibwa Myths and Tales." *JAFL* 41: 61-146.

Rands, Robert

1954   "Horned Serpent Stories." *JAFL* 67: 79-81.

Ray, Carl, and John Stevens

1984   *Sacred Legends of the Sandy Lake Cree.* Toronto: McClelland & Stewart Ltd.

Redsky, James

1972   *Great Leader of the Ojibwe: Mis-quona-queb.* Edited by James R. Stevens. Toronto: McClelland and Steward Ltd.

Rhodes, Richard A.

1985   *Eastern Ojibwa-Chippewa-Ottawa Dictionary.* Trends in Linguistics Series, ed. Werner Winter, Documentation no. 3. Berlin: Mouton Publishing.

Ricoeur, Paul

1967   *The Symbolism of Evil.* Boston: Beacon Press.

1970   *Freud and Philosophy: An Essay on Interpretation.* New Haven: Yale University Press.

1974   *The Conflict of Interpretations: Essays in Hermeneutics.* Evanston: Northwestern University Press.

1976   *Interpretation Theory: Discourse and the Surplus of Meaning.* Fort Worth: The Texas Christian University Press.

Ritzenthaler, Robert E.

1978   "Southwestern Chippewa." In *Handbook of North American Indians.* Edited by William C. Sturtevant. Vol. 15, *Northeast,* edited by Bruce G. Trigger. Washington, D. C.: Smithsonian Institution.

———, and Pat Ritzenthaler

1970   *The Woodland Indians of the Western Great Lakes.* Garden City, N.Y.: The Natural History Press American Museum Science Books.

Rogers, E. S.

1962   "The Round Lake Ojibwa." Royal Ontario Museum Occasional Paper, no. 5. Toronto: University of Toronto Press.

1978   "Southeastern Ojibwa." In *Handbook of North American Indians.* Edited by William C. Sturtevant. Vol. 15, *Northeast,* edited by Bruce G. Trigger. Washington, D. C.: Smithsonian Institution.

Sanders, Ti
> 1985 *Weather: A User's Guide to the Atmosphere.* Southbend,
> Indiana: Icarus Press.

Sapir, Edward
> 1985 *Selected Writings in Language, Culture, and Personality.*
> Edited by David Mandelbaum. Berkeley and Los Angeles:
> University of California Press.

Schoolcraft, Henry R.
> 1839 *Algic Researches.* 6 vols. New York: Harper & Brothers.

Schutz, Alfred
> 1970 *On Phenomenology and Social Relations: Selected Writings.*
> Edited by Helmut R. Wagner. Chicago: University of Chicago
> Press.

———, and Thomas Luckmann
> 1973 *The Structures of the Life-World.* Evanston: Northwestern
> University Press.

Sebeok, Thomas, ed.
> 1974 *Myth: A Symposium.* Bloomington: Indiana University Press.

Sharp, H. S.
> 1986 "Shared Experience and Magical Death—Chipewyan
> Explanations of a Prophet's Decline." *Ethnology* 25 no. 4:
> 257-70.

Skinner, Alanson
> 1911 "Notes on the Eastern Cree and Northern Saulteux."
> *Anthropological Papers of the American Museum of Natural
> History* 9, pt. 1: 119-77.
> 1914 "The Algonkin and the Thunderbird." *The American Museum
> Journal* 14: 71-72.
> 1919 "Plains Ojibwa Tales." *JAFL* 32: 280-305.

Smart, Ninian
> 1983 *Worldviews: Crosscultural Explorations of Human Beliefs.* New
> York: Charles Scribner's Sons.

Smith, Harlan
> 1906 "Some Ojibwa Myths and Traditions." *JAFL* 19: 215-30.

Smith, Theresa S.
> 1989 "Ojibwe Persons: Toward a Phenomenology of an American
> Indian Life-World." *The Journal of Phenomenological
> Psychology* 20, no. 2: 130-44.
> 1991a 'Manitou Minissing: Art from the Island of the Spirits." Indi-

ana, Penn.: The University Museum, Indiana University of
Pennsylvania.

1991b "Calling the Thunder Part One, Animikeek: The Thunderstorm
as Speech Event in the Anishnaabe Lifeworld." *American
Indian Culture and Research Journal* 15, no. 3: 19-28.

1992- "Outcast Women: Some Mythic Images of Female
1993 Empowerment in Native North America." *Scholars* 4, no. 1:
4-11.

1993 "From Grassy Narrows to Manitoulin Island: The Living Reality
of Traditional Anishnaabe Religion." In *Survival and Renewal:
Native American Values (Proceedings of the 1991 Native Studies
Conference)*. Sault Ste. Marie, Mich.: Lake Superior State
University Press.

Smith, Wilfred Cantwell
1963 *The Meaning and End of Religion: A New Approach to the
Religious Traditions of Mankind*. New York: The Macmillian
Company.

Southcott, Beth
1984 *The Sound of the Drum: The Sacred Art of the Anishnabec*.
Erin, Ontario: The Boston Mills Press.

Speck, Frank
1914 *Myths and Folklore of the Timiskaming Algonquin and
Timagami Ojibwa*. Geological Survey of Canada, Anthropologi-
cal Series 9. Ottawa: Canada Department of Mines.

1923 "Reptile Lore of the Northern Indians." *JAFL*: 273-80.

Sproul, Barbara, ed.
1979 *Primal Myths: Creating the World*. San Francisco: Harper &
Row.

Sturtevant, William C., ed.
1978 *Handbook of North American Indians*. Vol. 6, *Subartic*; Vol. 15,
Northeast. Washington, D.C.: Smithsonian Institution.

Tanner, Helen
1976 *The Ojibwas: A Critical Bibliography*. Newberry Library
Center for the History of the American Indian Bibliographic
Series. Bloomington: Indiana University Press.

Tedlock, Dennis
1983 *The Spoken Word and the Work of Interpretation*. Philadelphia:
University of Pennsylvania Press.

———, and Barbara Tedlock, eds.

1975   *Teachings from the American Earth: Indian Religion and Philosophy.* New York: Liveright Publishing Corporation.

Teicher, Morton I.

1960   *Windigo Psychosis: A Study of a Relationship Between Belief and Behavior Among the Indians of Northeastern Canada.* Seattle: American Ethnological Society.

Thompson, Stith

1976   *The Folktale.* Berkeley: University of California Press.

Thwaites, Reuben Gold, ed.

1896-   *The Jesuit Relations and Allied Documents.* 73 vols. Reprint,
1901   New York: Pageant, 1959.

Tillich, Paul

1958   *Dynamics of Faith.* New York: Harper Colophon Books.

Tooker, Elizabeth, ed.

1979   *Native North American Spirituality of the Eastern Woodlands.* New York: Paulist Press.

Vecsey, Christopher

1983   *Traditional Ojibwa Religion and Its Historical Changes.* Philadelphia: The American Philosophical Society.

1984   "The Ojibwa Creation Myth—An Analysis of Its Structure and Content." *Temenos* 20: 66-100.

1988   "The Ojibway Creation Myth." In *Imagine Ourselves Richly: Mythic Narratives of North American Indians.* New York: Crossroad Publishing Company.

Vennum, T.

1978   "Ojibwa Origin-Migration Songs of *mitewiwin.*" *JAFL* 91: 753-91.

Vizenor, Gerald

1965   *Anishnabe Adisokan.* Minneapolis: Nodin Press.

Vogelin, Eric

1978   *Amanesis.* Translated and edited by Gerhart Neimeyer. Notre Dame, Ind.: University of Notre Dame Press.

Waardenbury, Jacques

1980   "Symbolic Aspects of Myth." In *Myth, Symbol and Reality,* edited by Alan M. Olson. Boston University Studies in Philosophy and Religion, vol. 1. Notre Dame, Ind.: University of Notre Dame Press.

Wach, Joachim
  1961   *The Comparative Study of Religions.* New York: Columbia
         University Press.
Wagner, Helmut R.
  1983   *Phenomenology of Consciousness and Sociology of the Life-
         World: An Introductory Study.* Edmonton, Alberta: University
         of Alberta Press.
Walks, Job (performer), and Howard Normand (translator)
  1978   "The Killing of the Moss Falls Windigo." *Alcheringa* 4, no. 1:
         84-88.
Warren, William
  1885   *History of the Ojibway People.* Reprint, St. Paul: Minnesota
         Historical Society Press, 1984.
Watson, Lyall
  1984   *Heaven's Breath: A Natural History of the Wind.* New York:
         William Morrow and Company Inc.
Whorf, Benjamin Lee
  1964   *Language, Thought and Reality.* Edited by John B. Carroll.
         Cambridge, Mass.: MIT Press.
Williamson, Norman J.
  1981   "Adaptability—Getting the Best out of Two Metaphysical
         Worlds." *S.R.* 10, no. 3: 299-302.
Wilson, Edward F.
  1886   *Missionary Work among the Ojebway Indians.* London: Society
         for Promoting Christian Knowledge.
Young, Egerton
  1903   *Algonquin Indian Tales.* New York.

page numbers in *italic* type indicate illustrations

humor, 145, 146, 175
hunting power, 29, 35, 86, 180
Husserl, Edmund, 39n3, 94n3

Incas, 27–28, 40n7
Iroquois people, 53, 58

James, Edwin, 86–87, 102, 108,
 185
jays, 53
Jenness, Diamond: on free
 shadows, 176; on journeys with
 manitouk, 56; on midewiwin, 28;
 on souls, 133, 134, 151n8; on
 Thunderers, 74, 79, 83, 88; on
 underwater manitou, 111
jessakid (conjuring shamans), 199,
 201; converse with manitouk,
 49, 62n1, 70, 87; Jesuits and,
 104; Thunderers and, 178. *See
 also* shamans
Jesuit Relations, The, 40n4
Jesuits, 22, 40n4, 104, 105
Johnston, Basil, 48, 71, 80, 86,
 122n2
Jones, Peter, 80, 81, 83, 85, 104
Jones, William: Clothed-in-Fur
 tale, 52, 63n4; Floating-Net-
 Stick tale, 142–144, 152n11; He
 Who Over-Fasted tale, 105;
 Horned Sturgeon tale, 145;
 Mutcikiwis tale, 91; on myths,
 82; Nanabush tales, 158,
 159–171, 189n6; Now Great-
 Lynx tale, 147; Ojibwe/English
 texts, 39n1; Thunderers tales,
 70–71, 182–183
Jung, C. G., 22, 39n2

Kagige, Francis, 77
King, Jonas, 88
kingfishers, 55, 161–164, 176–178
Kinietz, Vernon, 97, 111, 122n1
Kitche Gami (Kohl), 155
Kitche Manitou, 200; Christian
 God and, 36, 184, 200; created
 Thunderbirds, 137; eagles and,
 23, 33; as Great Spirit, 44–46,
 200; midewiwin and, 186; to-
 bacco gifts to, 33
Kohak, Erazim, 39n3, 49, 94n3,
 193, 194
Kohl, Johann: on dog sacrifice, 120,
 125n9; *Kitche Gami* quoted,
 155, 160; on Kitche Manitou, 46,
 184; on Menaboju, 171;
 Mishebeshu tale, 109, 111; on
 Wolf, 158
Kugel, Rebecca, 39n1

La Cloche Mountains, Ont., 81
lacrosse, 188n2
Lahontan, Baron de, 45, 60,
 104–105
Lake Manitou, 60
Lake Nipigon, 115
lakes, 60, 112–116, 124n8
Landes, Ruth: on lightning, 69; on
 midewiwin, 28, 30, 38, 124n5,
 186; on Mishebeshu, 96, 179; on
 origin tales, 184; on patron
 manitouk, 61; on shamans, 105
language. *See* Ojibwe language
Leland, Charles G., 77, 79
Levi-Strauss, Claude, 172
lightning (wassmowin): electric
 power and, 60–61; strikes, 70,